Public/Private Finance and Development

Methodology

Deal Structuring

Developer Solicitation

Public/Private Finance and Development

Methodology

Deal Structuring

Developer Solicitation

JOHN STAINBACK

JOHN WILEY & SONS, INC.
New York • Chichester • Weinheim • Brisbane • Singapore • Toronto

This publication is designed to provide accurate and authoritative information in regard to the subject matter covered. It is sold with the understanding that the publisher is not engaged in rendering legal, accounting, or other professional services. If legal advice or other expert assistance is required, the services of a competent professional person should be sought.

ISBN 0-471-33367-0

Printed in the United States of America.

10 9 8 7 6 5 4 3 2

To my parents, Helen and John,
my wife, Barbara,
and to the future of
my daughter, Caroline,
and my special niece and nephew,
Madison and Lincoln Riley

Contents

Contents

Contents

Contents

About the Author

John Stainback has twenty-four years of experience in the real estate industry, including fifteen years in public/private finance and development, and has earned a reputation as one of the nation's leaders in the field. Since 1985, as a developer or consultant he has dedicated his career to assisting government, university, and school district officials to structure successful public/private real estate partnerships. He is currently a Senior Vice President and the National Director of Public/Private Development for LCOR, Inc., a national development and real estate asset management company. Prior to joining LCOR, he was a Principal and the National Director of Public/Private Development for E&Y Kenneth Leventhal Real Estate Group of Ernst & Young LLP. He serves on the Board of Directors of The National Council for Public-Private Partnerships, and is a full member of both the Urban Land Institute (ULI) and the ULI's Public-Private Partnership Council.

Mr. Stainback has authored over twenty published articles on public/private finance and development. He received a Bachelor of Architecture and a Bachelor of Arts in Urban Sociology from the University of Maryland, and a Master of City Planning and a Master of Architecture from the University of Pennsylvania.

Preface

This book was designed primarily for government, university, and school district officials, developers, and members of the finance and development team. The development team includes investment bankers, architects, planners, real estate consultants, financial analysts, civil engineers, and real estate attorneys. These are the professionals who will use the public/private partnership approach to structure, negotiate, and implement the finance, design, development, construction, and operation of needed public facilities and commercial developments sponsored by government, university, and school district officials.

This may be the first book dedicated to the emerging public/private real estate partnership industry. Therefore, it begins with a definition and describes the advantages and disadvantages of the public/private partnership approach from the perspective of the public and private partners. One of the more important features of the book is the detailed description of the public/private predevelopment process. This process provides future public and private project participants with a 14-step methodology, to go from project conceptualization to managing the developer solicitation process. An additional feature of the book is the continued reminder that one of the great qualities of the public/private development approach is the enormous amount of flexibility and creativity available to public and private partners to structure the finance and development of a building or complex of buildings. The book also provides government, university, and school district officials with an in-depth description of how to prepare a developer request for qualifications (RFQ) and a request for proposal (RFP), as well as offering six alternative methods to solicit interest from the development community.

All is not well in the emerging public/private partnership industry. A chapter has been devoted to identifying the looming problems, which could impede the accelerating growth of the public/private development industry.

This book represents an artful blend of highly technical information and methodologies with insights gained from having structured public/private finance and development plans for buildings and mixed-use centers with a construction value exceeding $11 billion. These projects include administrative office buildings for the public sector, major complex mixed-use developments, convention hotels, urban entertainment centers, hotel/conference centers, stadiums, arenas, university facilities, public school facilities, and golf courses.

Acknowledgments

I jumped into the public/private real estate partnership arena in the early 1980s. Quite frankly, at the time, I was one of a small handful of professionals primarily exploring the advantages and disadvantages of this approach to financing and developing needed facilities. I gave many speeches in the 1980s, but often I was talking to small audiences. There were many professionals and government officials interested in the privatization of services, but not many people were interested in the real estate side of the privatization industry.

In the late 1980s and early 1990s, I began to question my investment in the public/private partnership approach to real estate, because it was not being used by many governments and rarely used by university officials. Then in the mid-1990s, there was a substantial surge in growth. By 1997, the public/private finance and development approach experienced exponential growth. I frequently told people and the media that I had seen more public/private development projects from 1997 to 1999 than I had seen from 1985 to 1996. It was at this time I thought the most effective action I could take to accelerate the growth of the public/private development industry would be to write a book, so that I could share my 15 plus years of experience.

In previous attempts to share my lessons learned from 1985 to 1998, I wrote over 20 articles on public/private finance and development. During those years, I worked with some of the brightest people in this industry: Chuck Thomsen at 3DI, Dean Patrinely at Barker Interests, and Stan Ross at Ernst & Young Kenneth Leventhal Real Estate Group. Prior to my jumping into the public/private partnership arena, there were at least two people who stand out in my mind as my mentors—Joseph Passonneau, who was the Key Professor at the University of Maryland School of Architecture in 1972–1973; and Dr. David A. Wallace, a partner at Wallace, McHarg, Robertson & Todd, where I worked and he taught at the University of Pennsylvania, at which I attended graduate school.

Anne Brunell and Judy Howarth, my editors at John Wiley & Sons, diligently read and reread and corrected the entire manuscript. I want to also acknowledge my wife Barbara, who typed most of the manuscript and, equally important, put up with my long weekends and nights working on the book. Finally, the book was also improved by reviews of the manuscript by Eric Eichler, chairman of LCOR, Inc., and Peter DiLullo, president and chief executive officer at LCOR, Inc.

Thank you all.

Chapter 1

Public/Private Development Partnerships and Other Methods to Realize Projects

DEFINITION

Several features must be incorporated into an all-encompassing definition of public/private development partnerships, which is "The close collaboration of a public entity(s) and a private entity, or team, to structure, negotiate and implement the finance, design, development, construction and operation of building(s)." Many public/private developments are complex undertakings—often taking competing interests and accommodating both sides and still winding up with a successful deal structure or public/private partnership. It is not necessarily finding middle ground, but typically finding new ways to solve different problems.

RESPONSIBILITY AND RISK

Every public/private partnership is different and every deal structure must be customized to meet the objectives of the individual public and private partners. Of course, it is this ability to specifically tailor partnerships that make the public/private finance and development approach so attractive. The level of responsibility of each partner can be designed to meet their capacity to perform or to their desired level of involvement. The level of risk can be allocated to meet the level of risk with which the parties are comfortable. Clearly, the level of risk incurred by each party will be reflected in the economic return. If a public partner is risk averse, the risk can be placed with the party in a position to realize the greatest return on a capital and/or noncapital investment. This kind of logic can also be applied to equity and debt investment, ownership position, development cost, and other deal points.

1

An all-encompassing definition of public/private development partnerships should also address the following four features:

1. Different types of public and private entities are using the public/private partnership approach to realize needed facilities and/or commercial projects.
2. The public/private partnership approach applies to a wide variety of projects.
3. There is a wide range of building types for which the public/private partnership applies.
4. The public partner can often include several public entities, and in some instances private group(s), typically nonprofit organizations.

TYPES OF PUBLIC ENTITIES

The three basic types of public entities using the public/private development approach are governments, universities, and public school districts.

Governments

Government entities use the public/private development approach to finance and develop needed buildings and to optimize the value of underutilized real estate assets.

Federal government agencies. According to a recent General Accounting Office (GAO) report, the U.S. government is one of the world's largest property owners, with a real estate portfolio of almost 435,000 buildings and over half a billion acres of land. Most of the federal government's real estate assets are national parks, forests, other public lands, and military facilities. These assets are under the control of 30 agencies. Most of the assets are under the jurisdiction of only eight entities, which include: the Departments of Agriculture, Defense, Energy, the Interior, and Veterans Affairs; the General Services Administration (GSA); the Tennessee Valley Authority; and the U.S. Postal Service.

State government agencies. State governments are typically organized into agencies addressing governmental issues such as administration, public works, finance, real estate, public safety, economic development, and transportation.

County government. There are 3,043 counties in the United States.

City government. The 1992 Census of Governments reported that there were 19,279 municipal governments in the United States. Municipal government is defined by the Census Bureau as a "political subdivision within which a municipal corporation has been established to provide general local government." Nearly 154 million people in the United States live in areas with municipal governments. "Municipal governments" in this census corresponds to the "incorporated places" of the decennial Census of Population. Approximately 64 million of these municipal residents live in cities with a population of 100,000 or greater. The population groupings are as follows:

- 51 cities have a population of 300,000 or more
- 25 cities have a population of 200,000 to 299,999
- 119 cities have a population of 100,000 to 199,999
- 310 cities have a population of 50,000 to 99,999
- 566 cities have a population of 25,000 to 49,999
- 1,290 cities have a population of 10,000 to 24,999
- 1,566 cities have a population of 5,000 to 9,999
- 2,036 cities have a population of 2,500 to 4,999
- 3,670 cities have a population of 1,000 to 2,499
- 9,650 cities have a population of less than 1,000

Townships.   In addition to municipal governments, in 1992 there were 16,656 towns or townships.

Public authorities.   There are approximately 35,000 quasi-public governmental organizations in the nation.

Special purpose development corporations.   In many cities, the private and public sectors join forces to develop legislation as the basis to establish a quasi-public entity or a private entity to facilitate action on one or more projects. The sole or primary focus of this entity is on the development of a single project or district of the downtown area. This district has specific boundaries and is usually an area targeted for redevelopment. Unlike public authorities, this special district entity is primarily a coalition of private individuals, local business corporations, merchants, and/or landowners. There is a consensus among these "movers and shakers" to take action on a particular project or area in the city or town. Often the financing of the catalytic project for redevelopment of the area is provided by local banks and corporations. They provide debt and/or equity financing with a return on investment significantly less than the current returns required in the capital markets. The logic behind providing the private financing or credit enhancement is that it is far better than providing an outright contribution or grant that yields no return. In many instances the subject project(s), if implemented, will also affect the value or success of the businesses owned by the participating local corporations.

Business improvement districts.   A business improvement district (BID) is an organizing and financing entity used by landowners and merchants to direct the current and future state of their retail, commercial, and industrial areas. The BID is based on state and local law, which allows landowners and merchants to form a cohesive group to use the city's tax collection powers to assess themselves. The resulting funds are used for a variety of purposes, including capital improvements, additional security, special events, and maintenance. There are more than 32,000 special districts in the United States. BIDs with annual budgets of $40,000 to $250,000 are considered to be small assessment districts, while BIDs with annual budgets of $1 million to as high as $30 million are considered to be large districts.

Universities

There are approximately 2,000 four-year colleges and universities in the United States. In addition, there are nearly 1,400 two-year colleges. Public or state-funded universities and colleges across the country are using the public/private partnership approach to implement projects such as student and faculty housing, classroom and lab buildings, collegiate stadiums and arenas, bookstores, on- and off-campus hotel/conference centers, administrative office buildings, and garages. The total number of graduate and undergraduate students has grown, from under 4 million in 1900 to more than 14 million today.

Public School Districts

There are 14,422 school districts in the nation. Public school districts in some cities are using the public/private partnerships on two fronts: to finance and develop new schools and to leverage underutilized real estate assets. For example, the Oyster School/Henry Adams House building project is a national precedent for public schools. District of Columbia Public Schools, The 21st Century School Fund, and the author structured a public/private partnership whereby in exchange for developing an apartment building on an underutilized portion of the school property the private developer financed and developed a new public school on site.

APPLICATIONS OF THE APPROACH

The public/private development approach applies to a wide variety of projects, including:

- New building construction
- Rehabilitation of existing buildings
- Expansion of existing buildings

4

- Demolition of existing buildings
- Infrastructure improvements

Most public/private real estate projects include all, or some combination, of the above types of projects.

THE WIDE VARIETY OF BUILDING TYPES

The public/private development approach applies to a wide variety of building types, which can be categorized into three basic groups: civic facilities, commercial developments sponsored by public entities, and infrastructure facilities. Civic facilities include:

- Administrative office buildings
- Stadiums and arenas
- Convention centers
- Libraries
- Performing arts centers and opera houses
- Golf courses and ice rinks
- Municipal garages
- Fire and police stations

Often, civic facilities are developed in conjunction with commercial developments sponsored by government or institutions of learning. Commercial developments include:

- Office buildings
- Retail centers or retail support space
- Urban entertainment centers or urban entertainment districts
- Residential developments
- Mixed-use developments, which typically include housing, support retail space and office space, a hotel, and parking garage(s)
- Theaters
- Hotels
- Marinas
- Garages

Infrastructure facilities are the foundation blocks for cities, counties, and state entities. This third building type includes:

- Airports
- Waste water treatment plants
- Correctional facilities

PUBLIC PARTNERS

The public partner of a public/private partnership can often include more than one government or learning institution. In fact, different types of public partners can work together. For example, a university can work side by side with one or more government entities. When one government entity, in collaboration with another public entity, serves as the public partner, it is called a *public/public partnership* or intergovernmental agreement. For example, if a city agency or city authority wants to develop a mixed-use development to revitalize the downtown area, it may not only form a partnership with the private sector, but also with a county governmental entity with jurisdiction over the site, as well as the state government, both of which may realize tax revenue from the subject project.

THE THREE BASIC TYPES OF PUBLIC/PRIVATE PARTNERSHIPS

In the public/private real estate industry there are three basic types of partnerships between the public entity and the private developer. Exhibit 1.1 graphically summarizes the features of the three types of public/private partnerships.

1. Major Private Developer Participation with Minimal Public Partner Involvement

In this type of public/private partnership the private developer is primarily responsible for all aspects of the project. The project is typically a traditional commercial development and includes few if any public facilities or improvements. The private developer is responsible to design, finance, develop, construct, and operate the proposed project. Typically, the public partner provides little or no input on the design of the building(s) and would be considered a marginal investor. The public partner may or may not provide capital or noncapital investment, such as reduce the parking requirement or provide additional development rights.

Under this type of public/private partnership the public partner may or may not provide the land for the project.

2. The Traditional Public/Private Partnership

Under this type of public/private partnership, the public and private partners structure a fair and reasonable sharing of the costs, risks, responsibilities, and economic

Exhibit 1.1 The Three Basic Types of Public/Private Real Estate Partnerships

Type of Project and Participating Entities	Project Tasks and Ownership Position					
	Design	Finance	Develop	Construct	Operate	Ownership
1. Private Partner in conjunction with public entity(s)	Private with little or no Public Input	Private with Marginal Public Capital or Noncapital Investment	Private	Private	Private	Private
2. Traditional Public/ Private Partnership	Private with Public Input	Private and Public Entity(s)	Private	Private with Public Oversight	Private or Public	Private and/or Public
3. Public Partner in conjunction with private developer	Private contract or in-house Public	Public Entity(s)	Private Developer on a Fee Basis	Private with Public Oversight	Private or Public	Public

return. Sources of financing generally include bonds issued by the public partner(s) combined with private equity and conventional debt.

Under this scenario, the public partner provides the developer with a long-term lease of the project site. The private developer assembles the private team required to structure, implement, and operate the project.

Ownership of the project is usually divided into individual packages owned by either the private investors or the public entity(s).

3. Public Partner Is Primarily Responsible for the Project with Outsourcing Selected Tasks to the Private Sector

Under this type of public/private partnership, the public partner is primarily responsible for financing the project and therefore owns the project. The public partner has the option to outsource the design, development, construction, and/or facility management to the private sector. These responsibilities can be under the single-point of responsibility of a private developer or can be contracted out to separate private companies.

The risks and costs of ownership of the project is heavily weighted the public partner.

THE THREE BASIC PROJECT DELIVERY CONCEPTS

Design/Build

In the design/build type of partnership, a single contract is awarded to a private partner for the design and construction of a facility. Ownership of the facility remains with the public partner. The advantage of this type of partnership is that the private partner is the single point of responsibility for design and construction. In most instances, this approach to deliver a building substantially accelerates the delivery process. Under the traditional approach, the design contract is separate, sequential, and not necessarily in sync with construction.

Design/Build/Operate

In a DBO project, a single contract is issued to a private partner for the design, construction, and operation of a facility. On a traditional public project, the operation of a building is the responsibility of the public agency or a contract is awarded to the private sector under a separate operations and maintenance agreement. The driving force behind this concept is that combining all three responsibilities into a DBO program maintains the continuity of the private partner involvement and can facilitate private-sector financing of public projects supported by user fees.

Design/Build/Finance

This type of project delivery is the same as design/build, but the private sector is also responsible for structuring and obtaining the required financing.

Ownership of the project lies with the equity investor(s), although it is possible that ownership of the completed building may be transferred to the public sector after the equity returns are met and the debt is satisfied.

THE SIX BASIC OWNERSHIP AND INVESTMENT SCENARIOS

One of the great qualities of the public/private partnership approach is the wide variety of ownership and investment options available for each party. For most projects, the public partner can select from a large number of alternative ownership and investment positions, ranging from full ownership and being responsible for 100 percent of the required investment to a scenario whereby they simply provide the private partner a long-term lease of the subject site. For a typical public/private partnership, there are six different ownership and investment scenarios. For example, the public partner has the option to elect one of the following.

Public Partner as Sole Owner

The public partner is the sole owner of the subject building. A private developer completes the development of the facility on a fee basis. Under this scenario, the public partner is totally responsible for financing and operating the facility. A private developer manages the construction process for a fee. Under this scenario, the public partner incurs all of the risk of ownership, but controls most aspects of the predevelopment and development processes.

The typical sources of financing for this scenario include bonds issued by the public partner and secured by project revenues or bonds secured by the public partner's balance sheet and credit rating.

Public Partner as Sole Owner, but Outsources Design, Development, and Operation

The public partner is the sole owner of the building, but outsources the design, development, and operation of the facility. The public partner secures all of the financing. Again, the private developer is providing development management services for a fee. A private firm operates and maintains the facility according to the standards described in the operations agreement. A private architect and an engineer(s) execute the design of the building. In some instances, a private broker or tenant specialist secures tenant commitments, if the subject project is a commercial building. With the exception of facility operations, this scenario is often referred to as a "design/build" method of delivery.

Public Partner as Controlling Interest in Partnership

The public partner is the controlling owner in partnership with a private partner. Under this scenario, the public and private partners share the burden of structuring and obtaining financing for the building. The public partner maintains a controlling ownership position by providing over 51 percent of the financing. As the private partner, the developer takes on most of the traditional responsibilities of a developer. These responsibilities include assembling and managing the private-sector team to finance, design, develop, construct, and operate the subject project.

Nonprofit as Owner

A nonprofit entity is formed by the partnership to serve as the owner. The nonprofit entity is formed to reduce the cost of financing and to incur the risks and responsibilities of ownership and operation of the facility. Often, the nonprofit entity is directly or indirectly tied to the primary public partner in order to capture the perceived financial stability, which reduces the cost of financing. The nonprofit entity also serves as the operator of the facility.

Private Partner Bears Risk Burden

The private partner is the primary owner and incurs most of the risk, responsibilities, and costs required to structure and implement the project. The public partner provides some combination of capital and noncapital investments and/or credit enhancements. Typically, the public partner also assembles the land and provides the site to the private developer with an expected return on that investment. The deal structure of this scenario represents the traditional public/private partnership, whereby the public and private partners share the risks, responsibilities, costs, and economic return on a fair and reasonable basis. The ultimate ownership of the building could be with the public or private partner, depending on negotiations.

The private partner obtains private equity and debt that may or may not be secured by credit enhancements, guarantees, or a long-term lease commitment for the development. A prime example of a lease commitment by a public partner is the lease purchase agreement. Under this scenario, which is typically used for new construction, the private partner structures the private equity and debt to develop a facility and then leases the facility to the public partner. The public partner accrues equity in the facility with each lease payment. At the end of the lease term, the public partner owns the facility or purchases it at the cost of any remaining unpaid balance in the lease arrangement. Under this scenario, either the public partner or the private sector may operate the facility. The lease/purchase arrangement is often referred to as an installment-purchase contract.

Private Developer as All-Encompassing Partner

The private partner is the owner, developer, and operator. The public partner is a passive investor with little or no risks and responsibilities. Because public partners incur little or no risk and may provide only the land required to develop the project, they receive a corresponding smaller share of any economic return. This scenario is particularly attractive to risk adverse government entities and learning institutions. Under this scenario, the cost of finance may be the highest of all the scenarios, but the schedule required to structure and implement the project may be the least of all scenarios. This scenario is also attractive to a public partner that does not have the financial or human resources, or is totally risk adverse to structure and implement the proposed project.

There is a seventh concept that is available to public partners, but which is rarely used. This concept uses the value of a long-term facilities management contract as the basis to wholly or partially privately finance a needed facility.

Finance and Develop a Facility in Exchange for an Operation Contract

Government, university, and school district officials should realize that for certain large projects or systems of facilities, there may be the potential to structure a public/private partnership with an operator or facility manager to facilitate action on a project. The private operator is responsible to form a team to finance, develop and operate a new facility, and/or rehabilitate an existing facility in exchange for a long-term operations contract. Depending on the scope of the project and market conditions, this approach may still require public participation in some manner.

Clearly, these are only the basic ownership, investment, development, and operation scenarios to realize a needed building or complex of buildings. As described earlier, one of the most significant qualities of the public/private partnership approach is the ability to customize the deal structure to meet the constraints and opportunities available to the public and private partners.

Chapter 2

Emergence of Public/Private Development Partnerships

CORE REASONS BEHIND THE GROWTH OF PUBLIC/PRIVATE PARTNERSHIPS

Over the last 25 years or so, government, university, and school district officials have begun to realize that the traditional methods of financing and delivering needed facilities and catalytic commercial projects may not always be the most effective methods. Previously, there was increasing pressure to reduce the amount of public funds required to finance the desired buildings and redevelopment areas. The time required by many government entities to complete the predevelopment and development processes averaged four to seven years, far longer than the three to four years required by the private sector. These factors were compounded by the taxpayer revolt of the 1980s and 1990s.

Privatization

When government officials needed additional funds in the decades prior to the 1980s, they simply increased taxes or introduced new taxes. However, by the 1980s, that approach was no longer working. It was about this time that government officials earnestly began exploring alternative ways to finance and deliver services and needed facilities. Privatization began to emerge as the most effective way to deliver services. In addition, governments around the world began to sell state-owned companies to the private sector. Organizations such as the Reason Foundation began tracking the annual volume of state-owned companies being privatized around the world. In 1985, the first year they began tracking the privatization of state-owned companies, the annual sales totaled $10 billion in U.S. dollars. In 1998, the annual total value of transactions had reached $140 billion. The focus of the mid-1980s was clearly on the privatization of services and government-owned companies.

Real Estate Growth

There had been incremental growth of public/private real estate transactions from the early 1970s to the mid-1980s, but it was not until the mid-1990s that this segment of the privatization market began to experience substantial growth. In fact, from 1994 to 1999, the estimated annual cost of buildings financed and developed on the basis of public/private partnerships may be equal to the total cumulative cost of public/private development transaction completed from the early 1970s to the mid-1990s.

BENEFITS OF PRIVATE/PUBLIC PARTNERSHIPS

Real estate projects required that the public sector work hand-in-hand with the private sector. That was different from basically transferring the delivery of services from the public sector to the private sector. For many services, it was clear that the private sector could deliver services faster and cheaper than the public sector. For most real estate projects, neither party could independently structure and implement the finance, design, development, and operation of a facility. The word *privatization* simply did not apply to real estate. Many public/private real estate projects will not proceed beyond conceptualization if left to one or other of the parties. These projects require a collaborative effort: a fair and reasonable sharing of the risks, responsibilities, and costs.

Among other benefits, these public/private partnerships help to reduce development costs, enhance cash flows, and provide access to new sources of capital. Furthermore, public partners have the power to streamline the design and development approval process, thereby saving developers substantial time, cost, and effort.

After approximately 10 to 15 years of the increasing use of the public/private finance and development approach, both the public and private partners have concluded that by working together they can structure and implement most projects quicker and at less cost for each party. Over the years, both parties have become more creative. Public/private finance and development techniques fully utilize the assets of both parties. Problem solving has become more sophisticated. New legislation has been introduced at the federal, state, and local government levels, which is more entrepreneurial. Government officials have more flexibility to structure innovative deal structures. If all parties work hard, there truly can be win–win deal structures.

BRIEF OVERVIEW OF THE HISTORY OF PUBLIC/PRIVATE PARTNERSHIPS

One of the most significant early examples of projects based solely on the use of the public/private partnership approach occurred in 1973, when the U.S. Congress passed legislation to establish the Pennsylvania Avenue Development Corporation (PADC). It was clear to almost everyone that the nation had to take action to redevelop Pennsylvania Avenue from the White House to the U.S. Capitol. It was the "main street" of America, and it was in deplorable shape. This was particularly noticeable during President Kennedy's inauguration, and although there were attempts to facilitate action in the 1960s, nothing seemed to work.

The legislation behind the formation of the PADC was revolutionary at the time. The dual objectives of the legislation required PADC officials to structure partnerships with the private sector to realize the redevelopment of the 22 blocks along Pennsylvania Avenue and ultimately not cost the U.S. government a dime. In other words, when the redevelopment was completed, the land lease payments to the PADC and the PADC's share of the nontax economic return from the various projects would cover the cost of operating the PADC. The approximate cost, to redevelop the designated PADC district from 1974 to 1996, was nearly $2.5 billion. Exhibit 2.1 is a list of some of the more significant projects, completed in the past 25 years. (The author participated in a number of these ventures.)

Exhibit 2.1   The Most Significant Public/Private Projects of the Past 25 Years

- Inner Harbor, Baltimore, MD (1960s–1980s)
- Foley Square Office Building, New York, NY (1991–1994) (an LCOR project)
- Fairfax County Office Complex, Fairfax, VA (1985–1987)
- 42nd Street Redevelopment, New York, NY (1990s)
- U.S. Judiciary Office Building, Washington, DC (1987–1992) (author participated)
- Department of Defense (DOD) Housing Revitalization Support Office (HRSO), a $20 billion national housing program (1996–present) (author participated)
- City of Cleveland downtown area (1980s–1990s)
- Oyster School/Apartment project in Washington, DC (1995–present) (an LCOR project—author participated)
- University of Pennsylvania's "Sansom Commons" (1997–1999) (author participated)
- Veterans Administration enhanced-use lease program
- Amtrak's renovation of 30th Street Station, Philadelphia, PA
- Selected projects completed by the U.S. Postal Service
- Selected projects completed by the Centre City Development Corporation (CCDC), San Diego, CA
- Selected projects completed by the Empire State Development Corporation (ESDC), New York, NY
- Selected projects completed by the New York/New Jersey Port Authority (LCOR is the owner/developer for the new $1.2 billion Terminal 4 at the JFK International Airport. This project is under construction and scheduled to be completed in 2002.)
- City University of New York (CUNY), a series of student housing and campus facility projects (1985–present)
- State of New York's Master Lease Financing Program, the most comprehensive governmental certificate of participation (COP) program in the nation
- Copley Place, a 3.7 million-square-foot mixed-use center in Boston completed in 1985
- Numerous stadiums and arena projects
- Hundreds more, but many have not yet been constructed

CONFLUENCE OF TRENDS LEADING TO THE INCREASING USE OF THE PUBLIC/PRIVATE PARTNERSHIP APPROACH

Over the last 15 to 25 years, there have been a growing number of activities, needs, and trends, which have led to the increasing use of the public/private partnership approach. The cumulative effect of these trends has recently generated exponential growth in the public/private partnership industry. The estimated annual volume of construction in the United States, which is the result of utilization of the public/private finance and development approach, now exceeds $50 billion. As recently as three years ago, the annual construction value of public/private projects was estimated to be in the range of $25 billion. The confluence of trends, activities, and needs leading to that enormous growth include the following:

- The U.S. population has experienced significant growth over the last several decades. This increasing population requires new, expanded, and/or rehabilitated facilities, infrastructure, and services.
- The "echo boom" has created a substantial demand for additional school facilities. The baby boom generation has produced another explosion of smaller, but still numerous families, which has created enormous demand to expand existing school facilities, as well as build new facilities.
- The cost of social programs has dramatically increased, which has caused public officials to divert funds from capital improvements.
- With the increasing number of successful public/private developments, public officials, private investors, and developers have become comfortable with the process of forming public/private partnerships, confident that such partnerships can meet their performance expectations.
- The capital markets are increasingly comfortable working with public entities.
- Deal structuring is experiencing an increasing level of sophistication. There are a larger number of techniques and instruments to use to successfully structure a public/private partnership. The partnership can fully utilize government-owned real estate; alternative sources of public and private financing; an increasing number of creative finance and credit enhancement techniques; a multitude of techniques to reduce development costs and enhance cash flow; and a wide variety of development, investment, and operational incentives available from state and local governments.
- Voters are highly resistant to any increase in taxes; therefore, government officials are less likely to attempt to gain voter approval for tax increases and the funds needed to publicly finance needed facilities. Voters often will not approve funding of projects that are financed solely by the public sector.
- Government, university, and school district officials are beginning to realize the value of their underutilized and surplus real estate assets. According to the National Realty Committee, the 1998 value of U.S. government–owned real esta

estimated to be $4.5 trillion. Many of these assets are vacant, well located, already assembled, and therefore well suited to be developed. The commercial development of these assets is generating both nontax income and tax revenue from properties that have been off the tax rolls for decades.

- The cost of credit-enhanced private financing is becoming competitive with the cost of public finance. In many instances, the difference in cost between government-issued debt and conventional debt, which has been enhanced by a commitment by the public partner, is only 50 to 100 basis points.

- The sharing of costs, risks, responsibilities, and economic return between the public and private partners is attractive to the capital markets and also accelerates the finance and development process. The equitable sharing of costs and risks facilitates action, because these deal points are reduced for both parties. By sharing the risks and costs, the public partner is illustrating political and economic will to implement the project.

- The U.S. Congress and some state and local governments often require government agencies to explore public/private finance and development prior to the release of traditional funding.

- Many public entities lack the resources and real estate expertise to complete major public facilities and/or economically driven commercial developments in dysfunctional markets.

- Public entities can provide incentives and some form of investments, whereas private developers add essential ingredients such as invaluable knowledge and insight on national and local markets, entrepreneurial orientation, vision and creativity, development and management skills, prospective tenants or buyers, and risk capital.

These trends and factors are interrelated and are cumulatively the driving force behind the enormous growth of the public/private partnership approach. With these reasons behind the emergence of using the public/private finance and development approach to realize needed facilities and commercial development, growth of the industry in the future may not have a cap. Once the majority of government, university, and school district officials have successfully used this approach, there will be an increasing use of this approach. That success will start a "snowball effect," which will further accelerate the growth of this emerging industry.

Chapter 3

Advantages and Disadvantages of Public/ Private Development Partnerships

For most public/private real estate partnerships, the advantages of working together for the public and private partners far outweigh the disadvantages. Public/private partnerships are not perfect. In fact, the core of Chapter 9 is devoted to identifying the problems of the public/private partnership approach and how these problems are inhibiting the use of this approach to realize needed facilities and commercial development.

It is important to understand these advantages and disadvantages from the often conflicting viewpoints of the public and private partners. Therefore, the advantages and disadvantages of the public/private partnership approach to building development have been organized into the following four sections:

1. Advantages from the Perspective of the Public Partner
2. Disadvantages from the Perspective of the Public Partner
3. Advantages from the Perspective of the Private Partner
4. Disadvantages from the Perspective of the Private Partner

ADVANTAGES FROM THE PERSPECTIVE OF THE PUBLIC PARTNER

There are a multitude of reasons why government, university, and school district officials should work with the private sector to finance, design, develop, construct, and operate selected public facilities and commercial developments.

Facilitated Action by Both the Public and Private Partners to Proceed with a Project

Many needed public facilities and commercial building developments would not proceed beyond the project conceptualization stage if these projects were totally dependent on the traditional sources of finance and delivery methods. In many instances, by combining the resources and expertise of the public and private partners, projects become financially feasible or politically acceptable or meet a schedule requirement, or all three and more.

If the public and private partners have the will, energy, and determination to creatively structure and implement a project, a project can be transformed from infeasible to acceptable in the capital market.

Reduced Ownership, Development, and Operational Risks

One of the most powerful aspects of a genuine public/private partnership is the fair and reasonable sharing of risks, costs, responsibilities, and economic return. Both partners must enter the partnership arena determined to assist each other, not wondering how they can unload the burdens of ownership, development, and operation on the other party. If either party attempts to use the public/private partnership approach to completely shift all project costs, risks, and responsibilities, the project will more than likely never be implemented.

Generating Nontax Income or Private Financing of a Needed Public Facility

Most public/private partnerships can be designed so that the public partner can realize some level of economic return on capital or noncapital investments. This nontax income can be in a wide variety of forms, such as land lease payments if the public partner provided the project site, profit participation if that is financially feasible, or a percentage of the proceeds from any refinancing or sale of the development. In some instances, the private partner finances and develops a needed public facility in exchange for the long-term lease of the project site, or other forms of public capital and/or noncapital investment.

The amount of the nontax income for the public partner is clearly dependent on factors such as the level of capital and noncapital investment provided by the public partner, the level of risk incurred by the public partner, and the responsibilities taken on by the public partner. Again, one of the great qualities of the public/private partnership approach is the ability to customize the deal structure and financing to meet the objectives of each partner. For example, if the public partner is risk averse, the deal structure can be designed to reduce risk in exchange for a corresponding reduction in deal points such as nontax return or level of responsibilities and so on.

Public partners often have the option of structuring the return on their investment(s) to be in a form other than nontax income. For example, in exchange for their investment (1) public partners can receive a needed public facility privately financed and developed; (2) a public amenity traditionally financed with public funds is incorporated into the project, and privately financed; or (3) the cost of rehabilitating an existing public facility is covered by the private partner.

Monetizing Excess or Under-Performing Government-Owned Real Estate Assets

Governments in the United States control over $4.5 trillion of land. A significant portion of those real estate assets is underutilized. Governments can invest those assets in partnership with the private sector to realize needed public facilities and/or catalytic commercial projects to begin the rejuvenation of a downtown or selected redevelopment area. Many properties owned by the government, university, or school district are very valuable; consequently, the economic return to the public partner can be substantial.

Optimizing Private Equity and Debt Financing, Reducing the Investment Required from the Public Partner

Public partners have a wide array of techniques and methods to reduce development costs and enhance cash flow for a project. Depending on the level of capital and noncapital investments, guarantees, and/or incentives provided to the partnership, the public partner can shift all or a major portion of project financing to the private partner.

Eliminating or Reducing Government-Issued Debt, Thereby Saving Debt Capacity for Essential Services or Facilities

If public partners need to conserve their debt capacity or if their ability to issue debt for purposes other than a capital improvement or facility is important, they have the ability to structure a public/private finance plan whereby project financing is the primary responsibility of the private partner.

Fully Utilizing Private Partner Expertise and Creativity in Finance, Design, Development, and Facility Management

Many government, university, and school district entities do not have the resources or real estate expertise needed to structure and implement a project. Nearly every city in the nation has direct access to private developers, contractors, and investors, who specialize in real estate and/or financing and developing buildings. Developers often have in-house finance experts or direct access to investment specialists who are actively participating in the capital markets on a daily basis. These professionals can develop state-of-the-art public/private finance plans to solve problems that initially appear to be insurmountable by government and learning institution officials. One of the strengths of the typical private developer is managing the predevelopment and development phases of a project. For large development projects, the predevelopment phase entails literally thousands of highly interrelated tasks, which must be completed at specific times during the process. Most developers have extensive experience managing the complex problems with multiple tasks included in the predevelopment process. Facility operators, or managers should be brought into the predevelopment phase, so that their insights from managing buildings on a daily basis can be incorporated into design decisions and development strategies.

In summary, the predevelopment and development phases of a project are enormous and complex undertakings. Public partners should rely on the expertise of the private team of a developer, architect, construction company, and operator if they want to minimize their problems.

Generating Long-Term Commitment by the Investor(s) and/or Operator through Private Investment

Most public/private deal structures include some form of private investment. Types of investment include cash equity and conventional debt secured by an asset owned by the private partner. The private partner is vested with his or her own cash or valuable asset. This represents a substantial commitment of the public partner to complete the project on time and on budget, as well as a commitment to maintain the property to the highest standards over the life of the building.

Generating Tax Revenue from Land and/or a Project That Would Not Proceed without a Public/Private Partnership

Land owned by governments, public universities, and school districts is exempt from property tax. Once these assets are commercially developed, the leasehold interest is subject to property tax as well as other taxes, such as hotel occupancy tax, sales tax, utility tax, and other applicable taxes. Depending on the scope of the public/private development, the annual tax revenue represents a substantial new income stream. The cumulative tax generated over the life of the building can total tens of millions of dollars. This new stream of tax revenue would not have been generated if the subject project did not go forward, so in some instances public partners should consider providing rebates of one or more of these taxes for a term to be negotiated. The logic is that the public partner would not have realized any tax revenue if the subject project was not implemented. For many projects, the tax abatement is allowed only during the "ramp-up" years, or until the project begins to generate the return on investment required by private investors.

Completing the Public/Private Partnership Process and Forcing the Project to Be Market Driven and Financially Feasible to Build

In some instances, a government, learning institution official, or community group believes a project is the keystone, for example, to rejuvenating the downtown area, but the backers of the subject project have not determined the market demand for the proposed land use(s). The urban design plan for the downtown is developed with this vision of "project X" anyway. In several months, it is decided to issue a request for qualifications/request for proposal (RFQ/RFP) to the private development community to form a public/private partnership to structure and implement the project. One of the first questions most developers ask is "What is the market demand for the proposed land use? Does the project pencil?" In other words, has anyone prepared a cash flow analysis to determine the financial feasibility of the project? It is this type of reality check that can be very valuable to the public sponsor during the predevelopment process.

DISADVANTAGES FROM THE PERSPECTIVE OF THE PUBLIC PARTNER

Reducing the Level of Control over the Design, Delivery, and Building Quality, As Well As the Use of the Facility in Some Instances

One of the trade-offs for a public partner when entering into a public/private development partnership is the reduction of control. This is especially true when compared to the traditional project delivery methods used by public partners in the past. Depending on the negotiated deal structure between the public and private partners, the level of control over issues such as master plan, architecture, building materials and equipment, and facility management can be customized to meet the desired level of control. If government or learning institution officials want control over those issues that can be negotiated, the danger is the potential delays to obtain the approvals requested. Public partners and their consultants have the option to develop standards by which the building should be managed. In fact, the public partner has the option to structure performance-based contracting incentives. Performance-based contracting employs specifications and a statement of work, which focus on the purpose of the work to be performed and allow the vendor latitude in the manner of performing it. Performance-based incentives are contract provisions calling for the imposition of positive consequences for excellent performance and negative consequences for unsatisfactory performance by the vendor or operator. The quality of building materials can be dictated by the agreed-upon building standards.

Reliance on the Competitively Selected Developer to Obtain All or a Portion of the Financing, Manage the Construction, and Successfully Operate the Facility

In many instances, the public partner does not know the developer selected through a competitive selection process. To a certain extent, the public partner has to take a leap of faith and assume the private development team selected will deliver the building envisioned. A sense of trust must be established between the public and private partners or the project is not likely to succeed. This is another example of how important the developer selection process is. The RFQ, RFP, and interviews of the candidate developers are important for the public partner to be comfortable working with the virtually unknown private parties.

All of the above factors introduce the need for:

- A competitive developer RFQ process and optimal RFP process
- Exclusive right to negotiate for the developer
- Memorandum of understanding
- Development agreement
- Operations agreement

All of these documents could have legal ramifications. It will be necessary to complete most if not all of the documents described during the predevelopment phase of a project. It is one of the trade-offs of using the public/private partnership approach. These are tools for each partner to use to help ensure that each party delivers what they promised.

Possibility of Structuring a Partnership That Is Not a Fair Sharing of Costs, Risks, Responsibilities, and Economic Return

If the public and private partners are not careful in structuring and negotiating the deal structure and financing, or completing tasks, such as the total development budget, financial analysis, development schedule, financial sensitivity analysis, ownership and investment structure, and other deal points, problems for one or both parties could occur. Because many public/private developments are high-profile projects, the media may be tracking every aspect of the partnership and therefore uncover unresolved issues and potential problems. For example, if the public partner does not review the finance model prepared for the project and the potential return on investment is in excess of industry standards, this could make for bad headlines in the local media, which could be potentially harmful and embarrassing.

Private Ownership Entity Often Has the Right to Sell the Project to a Third Party Unknown to the Public Partner

One of the most effective ways for a developer to leverage the value created in the public/private development project is to sell it at the right time. If selling the project to an unknown third party is a concern of the public partner, the terms of selling the project can be negotiated.

Economic Return to the Public Partner for Capital and Noncapital Investment(s) Is Often Highly Dependent on the Performance of the Private Partner Ownership and Facility Management Entities

In a genuine public/private partnership, there is a fair and reasonable sharing of costs, risks, responsibilities, and economic return. In some instances, in order for the project to be financially feasible and/or attractive to the capital markets, the economic return to the public partner is contingent on the project achieving specified financial hurdles. The public and private partners should make every effort to combine contingent non-tax income with noncontingent income. Achieving noncontingent income for the public partner may require both parties to be very creative, but every effort should be made to provide the public partner with at least a minimum payment not tied to the performance of the project and provide contingent nontax income, which provides the public partner income if the project performs well.

Predevelopment Process Can Be Placed under a Microscope by the Media, Administration, and Others

Another trade-off of using the public/private partnership approach is that most of the hundreds of activities and events completed during the predevelopment process occur in a fishbowl atmosphere. Most if not all of the public partner participants will want to know the results of studies, presentations, and negotiations between the public and private partners. This is particularly true if the project is perceived as being pivotal to the future of the local community. The more important the project is to the community, the more involved the media will be. Most projects are subject to the Freedom of Information Act, so the media and community groups have access to any of the documents generated during the predevelopment phase of the project. Working in the public arena requires concentration and stamina, as well as patience, and can be disruptive.

Any Private Partner Has the Right to Protest the Developer Selection Process

This factor could not only extend the predevelopment schedule, but also require that extensive legal fees be paid. Before government, university, and school district officials enter into any public/private partnership, they should recognize that any private developer could file a protest if he or she believes the developer selection process was not open, fair, and objective. This is another reason for public partners to engage a consultant with experience in managing the developer solicitation process. The consultant is the objective third party. Good consultants will complete their analysis of developer proposals logically and systematically. Consequently, if the public partner does not interfere with the consultant's evaluation of developer proposals, developers will have little or no grounds to file a protest.

Selection of a Private Developer Based in a City or State Other Than the Public Partner Can Be Contentious

Most developers who are based in cities where the proposed public/private development project is to be located believe they are the most appropriate developer for the opportunity. These developers believe they have paid their dues in their town. In addition, they know the local marketplace. They know most if not all of the key public partner participants and they may have been involved in conceptualizing the proposed project. Consequently, they believe they have more to offer than an outside developer. Therefore, if a public partner distributes a developer solicitation beyond the local community and an outside developer is selected, potential disappointment, or worse, could be created by one or more members of the local development community.

ADVANTAGES FROM THE PERSPECTIVE OF THE PRIVATE PARTNER

Most Major Public/Private Developments Are High-profile Civic-oriented Projects That Can Enhance the Image of the Selected Developer If the Project Is Successful

Many public/private developments are catalytic projects for redevelopment of downtown areas or special districts. These projects are perceived to be the linchpin to the future of the city. These developments also tend to be large and pivotal.

Consequently, these projects become major targets for local, regional, and national development companies. In some instances, the recognition of the selected developer can be nearly as valuable as the economic return.

Government-Owned Real Estate Assets That Have Never Been Available In the Commercial Market Are Available For Development For the First Time

Governments, universities, and school districts have often controlled strategically located properties for 50 to 100 years. Over time, these properties have been engulfed by commercial development. The current use of these sites is tremendously underutilized. These assets are perceived by the development community as being premier sites for commercial development.

Many Public/Private Development Partnerships Include the Long-Term Lease of a Development Site That Eliminates the Initial Cost of Land Acquisition

One of the most popular types of public partner investments into a public/private partnership is the lease of real estate assets owned by governments, universities, or school districts. Often avoiding the outright purchase of these assets can make or break the financial feasibility of a public/private development opportunity. Public partners should recognize that land costs are typically equal to only 10 to 15 percent of the total development budget for a project. For more difficult projects, public partners may need to provide other capital or noncapital investments to facilitate action by a private developer.

Government and University Entities Often Share Project Costs With the Developer, Thereby Reducing the Private Partner Investment

There are numerous ways public partners can reduce project costs, if the financial feasibility of the project is in question. For example, the public partner can cover the costs of related capital improvements, infrastructure, all or a portion of the required parking, and public amenities. Sharing project costs can require creativity. In one instance, the public spaces within a convention hotel were financed and owned by the public partner in order to enhance cash flow of the overall hotel project.

Government and University Entities Have the Capability of Enhancing Cash Flow If the *Pro Forma* Indicates a Shortfall

One of the most powerful reasons to use the public/private partnership approach to develop buildings is that there are a multitude of ways a public partner can facilitate action by the private partner. Chapter 7 contains a detailed description of the methods available to public and private partners to enhance financial feasibility. Generally, these methods can be organized into five categories:

1. Use of government-owned land
2. Multiple sources of public and private finance
3. Creative public/private finance and credit enhancement techniques
4. Techniques to reduce development costs and enhance cash flow
5. Incentives available from various levels of government

A Good Public Partner Will Develop a Consensus among the Government Participants and Voters for the Project That Facilitates Action by the Private Partner

One of the key steps during the predevelopment process is to gain a consensus among key public and private project participants on various project issues. If key project participants are not in agreement on issues such as site location, land use, and project scope, it is highly unlikely that the project will proceed beyond the initial steps of the predevelopment process. Key public and private project participants can include participating government entities, special districts, community groups, merchants, and landowners. Having the public partner assist in gaining a consensus among the key public and private participants is very important to a developer, especially if he or she is not based in the city.

Government Entities Have the Power to Streamline the Design, Construction, and Operations Approval Processes

Public partners have the power to facilitate action by the participating government entities when it comes to project approvals such as master plan, architecture, public right-of-ways, construction methods, and operational features such as hours of operation and the like. Reducing the time required to obtain these approvals is very valuable to private developers.

Government and University Entities Often Share the Risks and Responsibilities of Public/Private Developments, Thereby Reducing the Risks and Responsibilities of the Developer

Many public partners have the ability to provide their private partners with credit enhancements, thereby reducing the cost of finance and level of risk. Public partners have the option of taking on many of the responsibilities for predevelopment activities such as structuring and obtaining finance, securing required entitlements and/or zoning changes, making sure adequate utilities are available for the project, financing and implementing needed capital improvements, and so on. The results of completing these tasks can generate substantial cost savings for the private partner and, therefore, the public/private partnership.

Public/Public Partnerships Also Reduce Investment Risks

For some public/private development partnerships, not only does the primary government participant invest in the project, but the primary public partner structures intergovernmental agreements with other governments that will benefit from the project, thereby further reducing private partner investment. With large and complex public/private development projects, the primary public partner may need to form intergovernmental agreements, sometimes called *public/public partnerships,* with other government entities to share the public partner's risks, costs, and responsibilities. The logic behind forming public/public partnerships is that if a project generates tax revenue for government entities other than the primary public partner, those government entities should provide capital or noncapital investments in the project.

DISADVANTAGES FROM THE PERSPECTIVE OF THE PRIVATE PARTNER

The Private Partner Must Abide by the Requirements of the RFQ/RFP Process and the Negotiation Process

Chapter 9 is devoted to one of the largest problems with using the public/private partnership approach: the extensive amount of time required to complete the developer RFQ, RFP, and negotiation process. One of the other more significant problems looming over the public/private development approach is the trend by government and learning institutional officials of continuing to tighten the requirements of developer solicitations to the point of turning off developers and closing off any creativity. RFQs and RFPs should allow developers the opportunity to generate and share creative solutions with their public partner.

The Traditional Process Used by a Private Developer to Finance, Design, and Develop a Typical Project is Significantly Different Than the Process Required to Structure and Implement a Public/Private Partnership

The traditional development process is fairly straightforward. Developers are not asking governments, universities, or school districts to share the risks, costs, and responsibilities of implementing a project. The government's primary role is to approve the design, development scope, and quality of building materials.

    The predevelopment process of a public/private partnership can require far more time, effort, and expense than the traditional development process. The developer is often not directing the process. He or she is following the steps outlined by the sponsoring government. In addition, it is very difficult for the private partner to accelerate the public/private development process. Chapter 4 describes the highly integrated and complex predevelopment process. In some instances, even the implementation of the project must meet government requirements.

The Public/Private Development Process Can Require Significantly More Time

In many instances, government and university entities do not have extensive real estate expertise and therefore, without a consultant, they often are skeptical, overly concerned, and hesitant to make decisions, thereby slowing down the predevelopment process or, in some instances, stopping the process altogether. Many government and university officials still view developers as their adversary instead of their partner. In these instances, no trust has been established between the public and private partners. If government and university officials do not have the proper expertise to structure the public/private finance, design, development, construction, and operation of the project, they should seek consultants who have experience structuring public/private partnerships. This is important not only to structure a successful partnership but to also accelerate the completion of the predevelopment process. Again, one of the biggest problems with using the public/private partnership approach is the amount of time and cost required to complete the process prior to construction.

A Consensus to Proceed with the Project Is Essential

If the public partner has not developed a consensus in favor of the project, the private developer must take on this responsibility, which can be costly, require enormous patience, and further extend the time required to complete the predevelopment process. One of the key responsibilities of the public partner prior to involving a private developer is to at least begin to obtain a consensus to proceed with the implementation of the project. The job of a developer is tough enough without adding this sometimes monumental task. For many projects, the selected developer does not have a local presence or insights into the local political scene or the community environment. Therefore, requiring the outside developer to resolve conflicting positions about a project is not efficient and is highly likely to significantly extend the time required to complete the predevelopment process.

Political Stability Is Another Important Ingredient

The elected government official(s) advocating the project can be unseated in elections during the predevelopment process, which could potentially delay or, in some instances, stop the project. Developers with extensive public/private development experience will determine the stability of key members of the primary public partner before they invest a significant amount of time on a public/private development opportunity. They know if a key member of the public partner is unseated, he or she could be replaced by a government official who is not a strong advocate of the project. One of the nightmares of a developer is to invest a tremendous amount of time and money pursuing a public/private development opportunity only to have the project terminated by a new administration.

Public Partner Expectations Must Be in Sync with the Local Market

In some instances, the expectations of the public partner can be too high when compared to market demand or other project-related problems. If the public partner has not completed a market demand analysis of the subject land uses, their expectations regarding their share of risks, costs, responsibilities, and economic return may not be in balance with the marketplace. In other words, for projects facing a multitude of problems, the developer may need to demonstrate the basis for additional government investment and/or reduced economic return.

To Achieve Some Projects, New Legislation Must Be Prepared and Approved

The public/private partnership industry in the United States is still evolving. Therefore, governments, universities, and school districts may be required to introduce new legislation to successfully structure public/private development partnerships. This can substantially increase the time required to complete the predevelopment process, as well as cause additional scrutiny of the public/private partnership or the predevelopment process completed to date.

SUMMARY

The advantages of the public/private partnership approach to finance, design, develop, construct, and operate public facilities and commercial developments far outweigh the disadvantages. The key to minimizing the disadvantages is for public partners to complete most if not all of the 12 steps (prior to issuing a developer solicitation) included in the public/private finance and development process described in Chapter 4. If public partners complete the 12 steps, they can dramatically reduce the scope and number of potential problems. Many government, university, and school district officials make the big mistake of jumping from project conceptualization (Step 1) to issuing an RFQ or RFP to the development community (Step 13). When public partners leap frog from Step 1 to Step 13, they are potentially creating an opportunity that may be riddled with obstacles. If that is the case, they may lose their credibility with the development community, and, equally important, the project will most likely not proceed to implementation.

Chapter 4

A Highly Integrated Process Is Required to Achieve Successful Public/Private Development Partnerships

When government and university officials want to facilitate a public/private partnership to finance, design, develop, construct, and operate a civic facility or commercial development, they often make the mistake of issuing a developer request for qualifications (RFQ) or request for proposal (RFP) without knowing enough about the project to negotiate a fair and reasonable sharing of the risks, responsibilities, costs, and economic return. The logic used is that public sector officials do not know the land and building development business. Therefore, they complete the project conceptualization phase and issue a solicitation to the private sector requesting that the developer be responsible for structuring and implementing the public/private finance, development, and operation of the project. Although this may substantially reduce the responsibilities and cost incurred by the public partner in the predevelopment process, this position may ultimately cost the public partner far more than the studies and analyses required to be completely knowledgeable about the proposed project. In other words, if public-sector officials issue a developer RFP without knowing important project characteristics, such as the market demand for the proposed space, the cost required to complete the project, or the potential return on investment, then public sector officials are entering into a public/private partnership blindly—susceptible to not realizing an appropriate return on the public sector investment or having less control of design and quality of development and so forth.

PUBLIC OFFICIALS SHOULD CONTROL THE PREDEVELOPMENT PROCESS

One of the most important driving forces behind this book is for government and university officials to take control of the predevelopment process. Do not allow the developer to control the process. Knowledge is king. By controlling the predevelopment process and knowing more about the needed civic facility or commercial development, public officials have the ability to negotiate with developers from strength. If public officials issue an RFP to developers without being sufficiently knowledgeable about the proposed project, they will not be able to evaluate developer proposals well and may be vulnerable when negotiating a public/private development partnership.

In addition to missing the opportunity to realize the appropriate return on public investment, public officials will not know the most advantageous ownership and investment position for the government or university. A prime example was the University of Pennsylvania's "Sansom Commons" mixed-use development. University officials were clear on the importance of a market demand analysis. They hired a consultant to determine the demand for hotel rooms and the appropriate average daily rate, but they were not clear on what ownership, investment, and development position to take. After working with this consultant on the cash flow analysis, university officials realized that the potential return on investment was substantial because the demand for hotel rooms in the local marketplace was very strong. Working with their consultant, they explored six alternative ownership and investment scenarios ranging from a scenario for which the university was the full owner (providing 100 percent of the required financing and served as the developer) to a scenario at the other end of the spectrum, in which the university did not have an ownership position (provided the land as their only form of investment and hired a private developer to take full responsibility for structuring and implementing the development). After carefully weighing the university's level of risk, responsibilities, control, and other aspects of the alternative scenarios, university officials opted to own the development, provide financing, and went to the private sector only for development management services for a fee and a hotel operator. Under a traditional scenario, the university would have given away the substantial return on investment and only invested, possibly even contributing the project site to the developer/operator.

The public/private finance and development process to be discussed next provides public sector officials with a systematic and methodical process to follow for all projects to be financed, designed, developed, and operated on the basis of a public/private partnership. If public officials work with consultants to complete each step of the process, they will place themselves in a much stronger position to form a partnership with a developer.

Using this process also allows public officials to be proactive in realizing a needed civic facility and, with commercial developments, to optimize the value of their underutilized real estate assets. Upon completing the public/private finance and development process, public officials will know:

- The most advantageous ownership position, if any
- The type and amount of capital and/or noncapital investment, if applicable
- The most effective position for the private sector to take regarding financing, design, development, construction, and facility management

- The projected return on equity investment
- The general level of risk for any investment
- The level of responsibility to finance, design, develop, construct, and operate the development
- Whether the development should be developed in phases
- The approximate schedule required to finance, design, and construct the facility

This knowledge will place public partners in a position to make rational and financially sound decisions rather than be wholly dependent on a developer and/or operator.

THE HIGHLY INTEGRATED AND MULTIDISCIPLINARY PUBLIC/PRIVATE FINANCE AND DEVELOPMENT PROCESS

The recommended public/private finance and development predeveloper RFP process includes fourteen steps. To complete many of the steps requires a particular expertise and each step is vital to the next. These fourteen steps should be viewed as the basic process. Public officials should assume that the process to structure a public/private partnership will never be the same. Some projects will require more public participation. Some projects will require more emphasis on "selling" the project and/or the basis for public investment than other projects. Larger and/or more complex projects will require a greater level of detail to minimize risk. These more complex and more costly projects often require more sources of public and private investment. Exhibit 4.1 is a diagram that notes the importance of adhering to the fourteen steps.

The public/private finance and development process has been organized into six categories of steps:

- Programming, design, and development phasing
- Budget and schedule
- Financial analysis and deal structuring
- Developer RFQ/RFP process
- Negotiation of the required partnership agreements
- Obtaining the required financing and project management oversight (PMO)

In an attempt to simplify the process and better understand the interrelationship among the steps:

- The building program is market-driven, the result of a market demand analysis.
- The total development budget is derived from the building program and design.

Exhibit 4.1 Public/Private Finance and Development Process

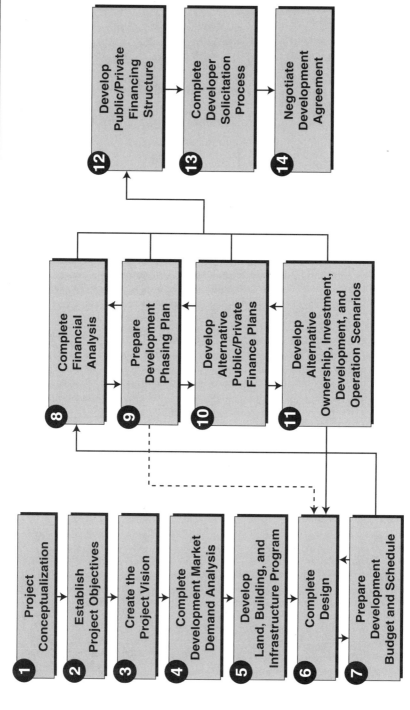

- The financial analysis and budgets can cause changes in the design and/or development phasing.
- The financing structure can cause changes in the financial returns and development phasing.

In summary, public officials do not want to skip any steps. This process should be seen as a "house of cards." For example, if the return on investment does not meet the current requirements of the capital markets, public officials have five alternative ways to solve the problem and proceed or the project is halted, or the public partner provides a capital investment with less than desirable return on that investment.

Basic alternative ways to solve insufficient returns on private investment include:

- Reducing development cost
- Reducing the building program
- Incrementally developing the project over time
- Finding investor(s) who require less of a return on their investment
- Restructuring the public/private finance plan

These alternative methods do not include the multitude of techniques included in the author's five-part approach, which will be described in Chapter 7. One of the great advantages for public officials in using the public/private partnership approach is the creativity and multitude of methods that exist to solve a problem.

THE STEPS OF THE PUBLIC/PRIVATE FINANCE AND DEVELOPMENT PROCESS

Step 1: Project Conceptualization

The project conceptualization step includes several tasks to be completed. The primary task in Step 1 is to formulate a concept of the proposed public/private development project. The public partner(s) should attempt to describe or graphically illustrate the project and its importance to the community. They should concurrently identify the project site or alternative project sites to be evaluated. At the same time, they should estimate the scope of the project by documenting and quantifying the proposed land and building uses.

During the conceptualization period, the public partner(s) should also address the following issues.

Begin to establish a consensus among project participants to structure and implement the project.   It is extremely important for the primary public partner to begin to establish a consensus among the major public and private project participants and the parties that may be affected by the proposed project. These project participants and affected parties may include local merchants, major landowners, and public entities that own and operate public facilities or infrastructure in the immediate context of the project area. Any participant in a successful public/private partnership can confirm that without a consensus among the major project participants, most projects will never be implemented.

Determine what specific public entity will serve as the primary public partner in the public/private partnership. For many major public/private development projects, there will be several government entities participating. Consequently, it is important to determine which of these entities will be the single point of responsibility to the competitively selected developer and to manage the predevelopment and development processes. There will be instances in which governments at the city, county, state, and federal levels participate, as well as one or more private entities and a university.

Determine the most advantageous project delivery method. At this early stage in the predevelopment process, the primary public partner should also begin to think about which project delivery method is most advantageous. The public partner can choose from the following types of delivery methods:

- Traditional competitive bid
- Design/Build
- Design/Build/Finance
- Some form of a public/private partnership
- Build-Operate-Transfer or Build-Transfer-Operate

Identify the project leader—the single point of responsibility for the public partner. During Step 1, the public partner should also begin to identify an individual who will serve as the manager for the proposed project. It is highly recommended that this person be identified as soon as possible to coordinate activities among all of the public and private project participants. This project manager will also serve as a conduit for communication among all of the public and private participants.

Some of the tasks included in Step 1 can be completed in later steps, but the longer officials wait, the more detrimental it is to the successful completion of the public/private finance and development process.

Step 2: Establish Project Objectives

The objective(s) of the project can be established by the public partner, owners of the land and buildings, or a district, such as a business improvement district (BID). Whatever entity is leading the process at this early stage must establish, prioritize, and document the primary objectives of the project. Objectives could include:

- Developing a "catalytic" project to stimulate adjacent or nearby development
- Commercially developing the site to generate nontax income and/or tax revenue
- Developing the project to demonstrate to potential private partners that the public partner is serious about redeveloping the area or district
- Reinforcing other recently completed projects in the immediate area or district
- Leveraging recently completed capital improvements

The objectives of the project will have a significant effect on project features such as:

- Method of project delivery
- The schedule to structure and implement
- The finance plan, especially the balance of public and private investment
- The willingness of the public partners to incur risk

Public-partner officials should not underestimate the importance of establishing project objectives as soon as possible in the predevelopment process. Project objectives become the guiding principles of the project, thereby influencing many if not all project decisions.

Step 3: Create a Basic "Vision" of the Project

In order to communicate the objectives of the project and/or the intended purpose of the project, some member of the public partnership—in conjunction with a consultant, or without a consultant—needs to develop a "vision" of the project. The vision for the project should be some combination of the following:

- A preliminary building program
- A perspective sketch of the project
- An urban design concept plan illustrating how the catalytic project will begin the redevelopment of the area or district
- Preliminary elevations of the building to demonstrate how the project will "fit" the building context or set the desired standard of redevelopment
- Preliminary phasing plan

This visioning process will vary, depending on the scale of the overall project area or district. The visioning process can be completed by the sponsoring public or private entity and may include other participants, such as:

- Public and private land owners
- Public and private building owners

- Business merchants
- Retail tenants
- City council
- Redevelopment agency
- Citizen committee(s)

The results of the visioning process should provide a sufficient amount of information on the project to provide project participants a target to achieve. The vision should be inspiring. It serves as the initial flag to rally project participants.

Step 4: Determine the Market Demand for the Proposed Building Uses

The market demand analysis may be the single most important step in the predevelopment process. The results of this step "ripple" throughout the process beginning most directly with Step 5, but affecting Steps 5 through 12. The primary objective of the market analysis is to assess the demand or need for the proposed space and the appetite of the local marketplace to pay the cost of renting the space or, in the case of a hotel, determine the average daily rate (ADR) or acceptability of the admission cost to a stadium, arena, or performance arts center. The analysis will also analyze the existing supply of rooms or space, as well as any proposed development in the near future.

One of the first tasks included in a market analysis is to analyze the economic and demographic information pertaining to the market area. The market analyst will use this analysis to evaluate the present and near future economic climate and to estimate future growth potential, particularly as it relates to the demand for the subject development, for example, a hotel.

For a hotel, the market analyst would interview key representatives of the local convention and visitor bureau, the planning department, commerce, and industry with respect to:

- The area economic base
- Population
- Employment trends
- Retail and office space trends
- Tourism
- Visitation count
- Convention activity
- Proposed additions to lodging supply
- Recent hotel dispositions or acquisitions

The analysts would also obtain information on any current or proposed major developments for the local area and other competitive areas to determine the potential impact on the area's lodging market performance. The analyst will also evaluate existing and proposed transportation and public improvements to determine the degree to which accessibility may affect the marketability of the proposed hotel development.

Next, the market analysis consultant will interview the management of competitive properties in the immediate area to assess operational issues. The consultant will also analyze the competitive lodging market in the local area and quantify the current overall demand for rooms, as well as the share of market demand that is generated by individual travelers; wholesale, group, convention, and commercial travelers; and any other identifiable sources of demand. Each type of traveler is defined as a market segment. The consultant would also analyze and quantify the historic competitive lodging market data, including a penetration analysis of fair share by each market segment.

At this point in the process, the consultant will prepare estimates of future demand for and supply of hotel accommodations in the market area, including the estimate occupancy level of the competitive room supply.

A good market analysis consultant will develop a detailed survey of meeting planners and key representatives of area businesses in order to evaluate their perception and potential demand for an additional hotel, like the proposed subject hotel. After completing these interviews, the consultant should summarize and analyze the findings. These findings and the other analyses completed will be the foundation for the following types of recommendations:

- Market positioning for the hotel, including number of guest rooms, overall level of quality price, and annual occupancy level
- The building area, quality, and amenities of support facilities, such as meeting rooms, restaurants, banquet facilities, health facilities, room amenities, and capacity

The last step for most consultants is to complete a five-year cash flow analysis and compare this analysis with the Smith Travel Research Host Report ("Host Report").

The results of the market demand analysis feeds directly into Step 5: the building program. Without the results of a market demand analysis, the building program will not be soundly based on in-depth research and analysis and therefore subject to uncertainty and second guessing.

Every government and university official should realize that they might as well complete the market analysis during the early stages of the public/private finance and development process, so that Steps 5 through 12 are built on a solid foundation. The equity and/or debt investors will eventually require that a market analysis be completed by a reputable consultant *before* firm commitments are made to issue debt or provide an equity investment.

Step 5: Develop a Land, Building, and Infrastructure Program for the Proposed Project

One of the most important aspects of the public/private finance and development process is that the proposed building program be market driven. If the building program is simply the building area the project site can accommodate, the entire process is weakened. Before the equity and debt investors will provide capital, they will require a current market demand and supply analysis. If the public partner is controlling the public/private finance and development process, they should take the initiative early in the process to contract a consultant who has credibility in the development industry and capital markets to complete a market analysis. By taking this initiative, the public partner will be assured that the proposed building program and development phasing plan is based on a credible analysis of the marketplace, and not simply a building program conjured up during Steps 1 through 4—not a program desired by the public partner—not a program perceived to be "what is needed for the revitalization of the downtown."

The building program should be comprehensive. It should provide project participants a complete description of the proposed project, including:

- Building uses
- Gross building area
- Gross leasable area
- Parking requirements based on local zoning and regulations
- Infrastructure improvements required to implement the project

The market-driven building program provides the public partner a realistic foundation for project design (Step 6) and the total development budget (Step 7).

Step 6: Complete Urban Design, Architectural Concepts, and Design Guidelines

Many public partners make the mistake of jumping from Step 3 (Creating the Project Vision) to Step 6. This mistake is compounded when public officials do not limit the scope of services of the architect or planner. Remember, the public/private finance and development process is leading to a developer RFP and negotiation of a development agreement, thereby turning the project over to a developer to implement. It is not the responsibility of the public partner to complete the design process. In fact, at this point in the process, the public partner only needs to illustrate the concept plan and a perspective sketch of the desired scale, massing, and character of the proposed project. In the developer RFP, the public partner purposely does not want to be too specific, in order to provide flexibility for developers to be creative in their proposals.

The objectives of Step 6 should be to develop the site plan and building architecture to a sufficient level of detail to convey the "vision" and be specific enough to develop a preliminary estimate of the construction cost to implement the project. For most projects, this translates to the level of design architects refer to as *schematic design* (SD). For most buildings, architects require six to eight weeks to complete the SD phase of the design process. The only qualifier to going beyond SD is that at some point in the process the public or private partner may want to proceed to the design development (DD) stage in order to obtain a guaranteed maximum price (GMP) from the construction contractor. This is yet another way that the public/private partnership can reduce their risk. Most construction companies do not feel sufficiently comfortable with the level of detail included in SD drawings to provide a GMP.

If the subject project is larger than a single building or a single block in a downtown area, the public partner may want to consider having the architect/urban designer develop an urban design plan (1:100 or 1:50 scale) supplemented by design guidelines. Again, the intent is to provide private developers a clear illustration of the desired development but not a design plan that is rigid and inflexible. Design guidelines are an excellent technique to guide private developers and not dictate project design.

For larger projects, such as the redevelopment of a downtown area, public partners will also want to work closely with their consultants to package development opportunities with the anticipation of preparing solicitations for each opportunity. Clearly, each development opportunity will be brought to the marketplace based on market demand. Otherwise, the solicitations to the private development community will not be responsive.

Public partners should also analyze potential problems and assets beyond the subject project site or project area. There are many contextual factors that will have a significant impact on the success of the subject project. These factors include:

- Vehicular access to the subject site from major vehicular corridors and from nearby freeways. For example, if the exit for the area does not provide visitors direct access to the project this could reduce the number of potential buyers.
- Visual access to the site from major arterials is important.
- Access from the project site to alternative forms of transportation can play an important role in the success of the project.
- Availability of parking in the area surrounding the project site.
- For a retail/entertainment development the number of occupied residential units will help to determine the demand for space after office employees complete their day of work.

In other words, it is important for both the public and private partners to look at the immediate and regional context of the project site.

At this point in the public/private finance and development process, the public partner has a building program, design plan, and development phasing plan that is based on current market research.

The next step is to prepare a budget to implement the acquisition of land, the building program, and the required capital improvement projects.

Step 7: Prepare Total Development Budget and Project Schedule

Many public partners of public/private partnerships make the mistake of assuming that the estimated construction cost for the project—the "hard cost"—is the only cost required to finance, design, develop, and construct a project. Many of these public officials are surprised later in the process when the "soft costs" are added to the hard costs. Soft costs can add 25 to 40 percent to the hard cost. Primary soft costs include:

1. A wide variety of professional fees (architects; civil engineers; mechanical, electric, and plumbing engineers (MEP); attorneys; accountants; appraisers; real estate consultants; and possibly environmental engineers, traffic, and economic impact specialists)

2. Transaction fees for raising equity capital and structuring and issuing debt by the public partner and/or obtaining conventional debt for the private partner(s)

3. Development management fees, which cover the project costs incurred and the management personnel required by the private developer to complete the predevelopment and construction phases of a project. The amount of the fee is based on the complexity of the project. The fee for a typical midsize project is 3 to 4 percent of the total development budget less the development management fee. For projects with a budget of $10 million or less, the developer fee is based on level of effort and no longer directly tied to the project budget.

4. Interest during construction (IDC), which represents a fairly large part of the soft costs. It is the interest payments on the amount of debt during the construction period. For example, for a building that requires 18 months to construct, the interest during construction is 1.5 (one year and six months) multiplied by the stated interest rate, multiplied by the amount of debt. So, in the case of a project with $50 million in debt, at an interest rate of 8 percent, the IDC would total $6 million for a project requiring 18 months to construct. The IDC can be somewhat offset by the interest income generated on the unused portion of the debt during the construction period.

The hard cost portion of the total development budget should also include:

- Land cost, if not provided by the government or university partner
- Site preparation
- Building demolition, if any
- Infrastructure improvements, if not provided by the public partner
- Site remediation, if applicable

- Landscaping
- Furniture, fixtures, and equipment (FF&E), which can be a significant portion of the budget for buildings requiring special equipment or furnishings. For a hotel, this cost can be $15,000 to $20,000 per room, or in the range of 10 percent of the total budget.

By completing this step, public partners avoid any major surprises later in the predevelopment process. For example, the total cost of a project with a hard cost of $50 million could actually be in the range of $60 to $70 million.

Predevelopment and Development Schedule

This step could occur before or after Step 7, or it could be completed by the private developer during the negotiation of the development agreement. The public partner should require the competitively selected developer to complete an estimate of the time to deliver the proposed building. The public partner wants to do this because they want to incorporate into the development agreement an agreed-upon time frame to complete construction, which, if not met, the developer has to either explain why he or she did not meet the deadline or be penalized in some fashion. Otherwise, the developer can tie up the public partner's project site for an unacceptable amount of time.

Another reason to complete a predevelopment/development schedule is so that all project participants understand the time frame required to complete the predevelopment and construction phases of the project. This is particularly important for projects burdened with an excessive project approval process.

A predevelopment/development schedule would be extremely important for a project that includes participants not familiar with the extensive amount of time required to complete schematic design, design development and construction drawings, and the time required to structure the final financing, obtain equity investments, and to issue debt, especially if that debt is issued by the government.

Step 8: Complete a Cash Flow Analysis of the Project

Public officials may wonder why they cannot proceed from Step 7 to issuing a developer RFP. Those government officials should realize that while they now know the scope of the project, how much it actually will cost, and how long it will take to realize the project, they still do not know whether it is financially feasible and whether their ownership and investment position is most advantageous. Equally important, if the project is not financially feasible using the traditional approach, is there a creative public/private finance and development plan that could transform the project to one that is acceptable to the current capital markets?

Now that project participants know the estimated total cost of the project, they, with their consultants, can assume an equity/debt split. This is critically important to the cash flow analysis, because two of the most important line items in the cash flow analysis is the annual debt service on the assumed amount of debt and the return on cost (ROC) and internal rate of return (IRR), which are essential to determine whether the net cash flow provides a sufficient return on the assumed amount of equity. The ROC is based on the equity and debt invested divided by the total cost of the project.

The cash flow analysis is one of the most important steps in the public/private finance and development process. If the net cash flow (NCF), which is basically the income less operating expenses, is insufficient to provide an adequate ROC and IRR, then the public partner and their consultants must develop creative solutions to solve the cash flow shortfall, or they need to increase their investment in the project. If the NCF shortfall cannot be solved by either of these two methods, the project will not proceed. It has been the author's experience that 90 to 95 percent of the public/private development partnership projects, which initially appear to be financially infeasible, can be, using the five-part approach described in Chapter 7, converted to projects that optimize private equity and debt financing and minimize public capital investment.

In addition to a traditional cash flow analysis, it is usually insightful to complete a financial sensitivity analysis. The results of a financial sensitivity analysis will provide public partners with a sense of the level of risk faced by private and public investors.

Basically, a financial sensitivity analysis is a financial analysis technique that demonstrates the effect on NCF of increasing and decreasing selected assumptions. The assumptions identified in this analysis are assumptions that can easily experience change in the capital markets and/or operation once the development begins. Prime examples of such variables include:

- Interest rate
- Attendance for a public assembly or sports facility
- Occupancy for a hotel
- ADR for a hotel
- Amount of equity

Using the benchmark cash flow analysis and decreasing and increasing one or some combination of these variables by increments of 5 percent up to 10 or 15 percent can provide public officials and consultants with valuable information to assess the volatility of the financial feasibility of the project. For example, if decreasing the occupancy and/or ADR for a hotel project by 10 or 15 percent significantly affects the NCF, the project is susceptible to problems in the future and therefore higher risk. The finance structure should be restructured, or at least modified, to strengthen the financial condition of the project.

The financial sensitivity analysis can also be used by the public partner and their consultants to determine the impact of selected variables on the private partner's return on investment.

If the public partner believes that certain developer assumptions are overly conservative, in a sense downplaying substantial net cash flow for the private equity investor, this may be grounds to reduce the public partner's capital and/or noncapital investment.

Step 9: Prepare Development Phasing Plan

This step is only applicable for public/private development projects that include more than one building. If the proposed project includes more than one building, or a large building that is constructed incrementally over time, then a development-phasing plan should be prepared. This phasing plan should be prepared after Step 4 (Market Analysis) is completed and refined after Step 8 (Cash Flow Analysis) is completed. The primary basis for determining how implementation of the project is phased is the condition of the local market. If there is sufficient demand to construct 100 percent of the proposed building program, and it is financially feasible, then clearly a phasing plan is not needed. If the market demand analysis indicates the marketplace can only absorb a portion of the desired building program then the project must be incrementally constructed in accordance with the projected absorption rate. Equally important, if the financial analysis in Step 8 indicates that developing 100 percent of the building program creates significantly higher risk for investors, the project should be constructed in phases to reduce investment risk.

The results of the financial sensitivity analysis could demonstrate that the project is not feasible with a 5 or 10 percent decrease of one or two variables. This could be the basis to modify the phasing plan, which in turn could affect the proposed design plan completed in Step 6. This explains why in Exhibit 4.1 there is a dashed line connecting Steps 9 and 6.

The importance of the development-phasing plan should not be underestimated. Phasing could impact one or all of the following:

- Land acquisition
- Total development budget
- The master plan
- The public/private finance plan
- Ownership and investment by the public and/or private partners

This step amply illustrates how the 14 steps of the predevelopment process are highly integrated. The predevelopment process is very fluid and must be highly managed by the public/private partnership.

Step 10: Develop Alternative Public/Private Finance Plans

Typically, the overriding objective of Step 10 is to structure the financing so that the project is financially feasible. For many public/private development projects, either the project is not financially and/or politically feasible for the government sponsor or public partner to be solely responsible for financing the project, or it is not feasible for the private sector to solely finance the project. Therein lies the primary reason to form a public/private partnership. In order to facilitate action by the public/private partnership, there must be a public/private finance plan that is acceptable to both parties. The public/private finance plan must provide a strong basis for the public partner to provide capital and noncapital investments and, concurrently, meet the current requirements of the capital markets for private equity and conventional debt.

Many public/private development projects can not be implemented if either the public or private sector is solely responsible for financing, designing, developing, constructing, and operating a project. There must be a fair and reasonable sharing of the following project features between the public and private partners.

- Risks of ownership
- Risks of operation
- Risks of development
- Financing responsibilities
- Ownership position
- Return on investment
- Design and construction responsibilities

If the results of Step 8, the cash flow and financial sensitivity analyses, reveal an insufficient return on a traditional private equity and conventional debt financing, the public partner must provide either a capital investment or additional noncapital investment(s), or generate creative public/private finance plans to reduce development costs and/or enhance cash flow. It is the latter that is the primary purpose of Step 10.

For many public/private projects, this sharing of project responsibilities, cost, risks, and return on investment may be required to go beyond the government sponsor and the competitively selected private developer. In order to reduce the responsibilities, cost, and risks of a project, the two primary public and private partners may need to extend the partnership to other government entities, which will also benefit from implementing the proposed project. The sponsoring or primary government entity may want to structure what is called *public/public partnerships* or intergovernmental agreements with other government entities that will realize tax revenue and/or an economic impact, as well as new employment opportunities.

In summary, the driving forces behind developing alternative public/private finance plans at this point in the public/private finance and development process:

- Demonstrate specific financings whereby the public and private partners can invest in the project and have a high probability of obtaining approvals from the issuers of debt and from equity investor(s)
- Reduce the investment risk of both the public and private partners

- Structure the non-tax return on investment so that each party believes their investment is warranted
- Demonstrate that the tax revenue is a sufficient basis for public partner investments

Chapter 7 discusses the enormous flexibility and creativity available to structure project financing that is acceptable to both the public and private partners.

Step 11: Develop Alternative Ownership, Investment, Development, and Facility Management Scenarios for the Public and Private Partners

Most of the activities included in Steps 10 and 11 should be completed concurrently. The wide variety of investment positions are highly related to the ownership position taken by the public and private partners. For example, if a public or private partner is burdened by 51 percent or more of the required investment to realize the project, that party takes on a controlling ownership position of the project.

The overriding objective of Step 11 is to develop five to seven alternative scenarios for the public and private partners to finance, design, develop, construct, and operate the proposed project. Each scenario is feasible both financially and politically. The objective is for the public partner to better understand the advantages and disadvantages of each scenario. In Step 11, public or private partners will use the evaluation matrix methodology to organize and evaluate each of the alternative scenarios. The criteria used to evaluate each scenario includes:

- Level of responsibilities for each partner as:
  - Owner
  - Investor
  - Developer
  - Facility manager
- Level of risk as:
  - Owner
  - Investor
  - Developer
  - Facility manager
- Ability to obtain financing
- Cost of financing
- Level of control over:
  - Design
  - Development quality
  - Operations

- Return on investment
- Implications on the predevelopment and development schedule
- Implications on obtaining investment and project approvals

The most effective approach to present and develop the alternative scenarios is to organize the scenarios along a spectrum ranging from an alternative whereby the public partner is the 100 percent owner, investor, developer, and facility manager to an alternative scenario whereby the private partner is primarily responsible for ownership, financing, developing, and operating the facility. This approach allows the public partner to analyze the full range of project positions available to them. This analysis of each scenario is highly interrelated to Steps 2, 8, and 10. In fact, all 14 steps are highly interrelated; Steps 2, 9, 10, and 11 are particularly intertwined.

For example, if we assume in Step 2 it was established that a high priority for the public partner was to minimize investment and/or risk, and in Step 8 the cash flow analysis revealed that the return on investment was not sufficient to meet the requirements of the current capital markets, and in Step 10 the public partner and their consultant have a difficult time enhancing cash flow or reducing development costs, then the public partner should shy away from any scenarios whereby the public partner is the primary owner.

The completion of Steps 8, 10, and 11 is pivotal to the public/private finance and development process. By closely interweaving the results of Steps 1 through 11, but especially these three steps, the public partner determines the most effective deal structure and is ensured that the project can be implemented prior to issuing or responding to the developer RFQ/RFP completed in Step 13. The public partner is confident the project should be successful because the following issues have been adequately addressed.

The most advantageous ownership and investment position for the public and private partners has been developed. After completing Step 11, the public partner has selected an ownership and investment position that best "fits" their project objectives, specifically, their capacity to provide cash and/or issue debt, an acceptable level of risk, and their desired level of project responsibilities and project control.

The level of investment and risk is acceptable to other participating government entities. After completing Steps 8, 10, and 11, the primary public partner has determined that the level of investment and risk for the participating government entities is justified. In other words, the amount of nontax income and tax revenue is appropriate for the proposed level of risk and investment required by the government entities participating in the project other than the primary public partner.

A general schedule for the project has been established. The time frame required to complete the balance of the predevelopment process and the development process has been determined. In order to accurately estimate the time required to structure and implement the finance, design, and construction of the project, the public partner will need to obtain input from a consultant, an investment banker, and a construction company.

The project appears to be financially feasible. The results of the financial analysis completed in Step 8 should give the public partner a strong indication that the projected returns will satisfy the current requirements of debt and equity investors. Clearly, if the return on equity is not competitive, most projects will not be implemented. Public partners should be reminded that the key to Step 8 is the assumptions regarding a multitude of factors, such as cost of finance, project scope, construction cost, and operating expenses and income.

The selected developer will have a high probability of obtaining project approvals. After completing Steps 1 through 11, the public partner has a good sense of whether the design, investment, and construction approvals will be granted by the participating public partners. This component of the public/private partnership is very important in that in the RFQ and/or RFP it allows the project sponsor to give candidate developers some assurance that they can obtain the approvals necessary to complete the predevelopment and development processes.

The proposed building program and development phasing plan is market driven. By completing the market demand analysis in Step 4 and the building program in Step 5, the public partner should have confidence that the proposed building program and development phasing plan are in sync with the local market conditions. This is another critically important component of a successful public/private development project. If the proposed scope of the project is arbitrary and capricious and not based on a market demand analysis, the public partner will lose credibility with the private development community. Equally important, public partners should realize that few projects are ever privately financed without a market demand analysis completed by an objective third-party consultant.

Step 12: Prepare the Public/Private Financing Structure

One of the more significant responsibilities of government and university officials during the predevelopment process is to explain the proposed public/private development partnership between the public and private partners. Members of the primary public partner can be certain that they will be repeatedly asked by the following groups to explain how the public participants will interact with key members of the private partner participants:

- Government officials in a position to approve or disapprove proceeding with the project
- Key community groups
- Major merchants affected by the project

- Legislators responsible to prepare new legislation or modify existing legislation to allow the public partner to provide capital or noncapital investments
- The media

When Steps 1 through 11 have been completed, government and university officials are ready to prepare the public/private financing structure. The public/private financing structure is an excellent devise to describe the proposed deal structure among the major public and private participants. The public/private financing structure is basically a sophisticated diagram illustrating the cash flow and basic legal interrelationships of the major public and private project participants. The project participants in a public/private financing structure for a government-sponsored project include:

- The government entity entering into a contractual arrangement with the private partner for the development of the project. A public/private partnership can also include facility management or operation of the project on completion of construction.
- The private developer as development manager and investor
- The construction contractor
- The operator or facility manager
- The issuer(s) of public and/or private debt
- The equity investor(s)
- Trustees for bond financing
- The major tenant(s)

This public/private financing structure reflects the proposed function(s) of the project participants at this point in the predevelopment process. The public/private partnership could significantly change after completing the developer RFQ/RFP process (see Chapter 8) and subsequent negotiations. But at this point in time for each project, this diagram explains the proposed public/private partnership that is presented to the capital market and other key project approval entities.

Step 13: Complete the Developer Solicitation Process

This step in the public/private finance and development process is so important that an entire chapter has been devoted to this subject (see Chapter 8).

Step 14: Negotiate Development and Operation Agreement(s)

Upon completion of Step 13 the public partner should have confidence that they are well positioned to proceed with the project and that the selected private partner is the most appropriate team to complete the proposed project.

During Step 14 public and private partners can expect to work closely together to refine the results of the 14-step predevelopment process. During the negotiation process the public and especially the private project participants will learn much more about the project, related projects, and proposed capital improvements. At this point in the process the primary public partner will join forces with the private developer's team to resolve remaining issues and problems. The relationship between the public partner and private developer is no longer an arm's length relationship. They should be a cohesive team to:

- Refine the building program
- Proceed with more detailed design work
- Refine the total development budget
- Incorporate these refinements into the cash flow analysis
- Refine the public/private finance plan based on the collaborative effort to uncover public/private finance techniques and additional sources of financing to reduce investment risk
- Modify the development-phasing plan to reflect more market research, the additional financial analysis, and design changes
- Jointly continue to build consensus to implement the project
- Better understand the project approvals required to start construction
- Determine the specific responsibilities of each partner
- Finalize the specific capital and noncapital investment provided by the public and private partners
- Finalize the ownership position of each partner

Also, during the negotiation process, the public/private partnership will jointly develop the agreements required to formalize the partnership and obtain the required financing from the public and private project participants. The legal documents may include development and operation agreements.

SUMMARY

The primary purpose of the public/private finance and development process is to provide public and private partners with a "road map" to follow for most if not all building development projects financed, designed, developed, and operated using the public/private partnership approach.

By completing each step of this process, few mistakes should be made, and there should be few if any surprises at the start of construction.

Chapter 5

The Role and Responsibilities of the Public Partners

The public/private partnership approach to realize projects is based on the premise that the public and private sectors will work collaboratively to structure the appropriate finance, most effectively implement the project, and then determine the most effective way to operate the facility or commercial development once constructed.

A successful public/private partnership requires that all project participants collaboratively work together to complete the predevelopment and development processes. A public/private partnership will include the basic government entity sponsoring the project and the private developer. Many projects also require the partnership to be expanded beyond the basic partnership to include one or more other government entities and other private participants such as a codeveloper and/or operator. All of the project participants must work as a cohesive team during the predevelopment process in order to realize the project.

Before public officials begin the public/private partnership process, they should realize that to successfully complete the process will require tremendous effort and determination on their part. While public officials can expect a developer to take on a more than fair share of the responsibilities, they cannot shed all of the required responsibilities.

THE PUBLIC PARTNER

The ultimate implementation role and responsibilities of the public partner(s) will be determined during the latter steps of the public/private finance and development process and after negotiations with the selected developer are completed. However, the government entity that serves as the catalyst and leader for the proposed public/private development has a major role and a multitude of tangible and nontangible responsibilities during the predevelopment process.

The responsibilities of the controlling government entity have been organized into five categories:

1. Governmental Issues
2. Project Team
3. Project Process
4. Developer Solicitation Process
5. Deal Structuring and Negotiations

For most projects the government entity sponsoring the project or needing the facility has a role and responsibility before any other public and private sector members of the team are even identified.

1. Governmental Issues

Determine the need for the public facility and/or the commercial development(s).   The project could be the result of a needs assessment, the conclusion of a planning process, or a general consensus that the city, county, or state needs a facility or needs to facilitate action on a commercial development perceived to revitalize the downtown, for example.

Develop a consensus among government officials and/or residents or key merchants that the project is needed.   A proposed project without the backing of key public and private members of the town is not likely to survive the predevelopment process.

Conceptualize the project.   One of the most important first steps is to conceptualize the project. Define the project concept. Identify the project site or the alternative site(s) for the project. Develop the purpose of the project—its role in the context of the project site.

Establish guiding principles.   The primary government entity should form a small project committee (no more than six or eight members to be effective) to develop the guiding principles to structure and negotiate a public/private finance, development, and operational plan for the project. This is an important part of Step 2, Establishing Project Objectives. The purpose of the public partner's guiding principles is to provide public partner consultants, other government participants, and the private partner insights into the public partner's position regarding issues, such as:

* The general level of risk the public partner is willing to incur to realize the project
* The general level of control required by the public partner over design, schedule, quality of building materials and facility management
* A sense of how important economic return is compared to other issues
* A sense of how important design and aesthetics are
* A sense of the desired social and economic impact on the community

Identify potential sources of funding. The public partner must identify one or more sources of funding for the project based on the assumption that there may be a cash flow shortfall if wholly financed by the private partner and/or a need for funds to operate and maintain the project.

Identify basic techniques to realize the project. The primary or sponsoring government entity should identify basic finance, development, and operational techniques to realize the project using the public/private partnership approach—to facilitate action by the private sector.

Begin to identify the regulatory constraints and opportunities. There may be a multitude of policies or regulations that are applicable to forming a public/private partnership with the private sector to own, finance, develop, and/or operate the project. These regulatory constraints and opportunities should be identified as early as possible in the predevelopment process.

2. Project Team

Identify and assign a project manager. One of the most important tasks of the primary government entity is to assign a government official or staff member to serve as the public partner's leader of the project. Ideally, the controlling government entity should, at a minimum, create a project leader or small committee that serves as the single point of responsibility for the public partner of the public/private partnership. The purpose of the single point of contact for the public partner is to facilitate action by the public partner's consultants, private participants, the primary government entity, and any other government entities participating.

The public project leader is the project manager for the public partner. This project manager is the "go-to person" on a day-to-day basis. The project manager keeps the predevelopment process on schedule. The project manager is the liaison between the private partner and the final decision maker of the public partner. The public partner project manager is also the point person for all of the participating government entities. This alone represents substantial work because the more complex public/private proposals can involve one or more cities, counties, and the state, as well as the federal government and/or a local university. The project manager for the primary or sponsoring public partner will also be responsible for completing the evaluation and selection process for any consultants and the private developer partner, as well as manage the public partner's consultant team.

The government's project manager should be generally more technical than political, yet be fully apprised as to the political context of the proposed project. This project manager should know the public/private finance and development process (see Chapter 4) inside out and should also be familiar with the basic requirements of operating the business once construction is completed. Knowledge of the requirements of facility management is also important.

In summary, the project manager for the public partner must be knowledgeable of finance, budgeting, design, development, construction, and operations. Ideally, the project manager will be a leader as well as a manager, a professional who can inspire people and have the stamina to complete the predevelopment and development processes. He or she must be determined to implement the project.

Hire the right consultants at the right time.   Public partners can complete many of the tasks included in the public/private finance and development process (see chapter 4). However, many times the public partner may want to have a consultant to serve as the objective third party, or equally important, hire specialist(s) to complete specific tasks that require professionals with extensive experience in a certain niche, such as financial analysis, market studies, etc.

In fact, there are a growing number of consultants specializing in assisting government and university officials throughout the public/private finance and development process. The sole purpose of these professionals is to place public partners in a position of strength to structure and negotiate successful public/private partnerships. One major advantage of working with one team throughout the predevelopment process is that the team is a thread of continuity for a lengthy and complex undertaking. Many developers like to see a credible consultant working with the public partner for reasons such as:

- The consultant will help to depoliticize the developer selection process.
- The consultant knows the real estate business; many government and university officials do not have extensive experience in the industry.
- The consultant's expectations in structuring public/private finance and development plans are soundly based because they are participating in the marketplace on a daily basis.
- These consultants bring a methodology to the predevelopment process. This often facilitates action and accelerates completion of the process.
- Because of their extensive experience, public/private partnership consultants have garnered significant lessons learned, thereby helping their government and university clients to avoid the ever-present pitfalls.

The consultant team.   Whether the sponsoring government or university hires one or several consultants to assist them to complete the public/private finance and development process, the consultants should include expertise in the following areas:

- Market-demand analysis
- Land and building programming
- Planning and design
- Financial analysis
- Deal structuring
- Developing alternative public/private finance plans
- Identifying and analyzing alternative ownership, investment, development, project delivery, and operation scenarios

- Managing the developer and/or operator solicitation process (whether the public partner uses the two-step request for qualifications/request for proposal [RFQ/RFP] process, the RFP process, or the RFQ/negotiate process)
- Negotiating development and/or operating agreements
- Determining the most appropriate project delivery method

3. Project Process

While the public/private finance and development process described in Chapter 4 is a proven process, there are a multitude of spin-offs of that process. Government and university officials can simply conceptualize the proposed project and issue an RFP to the development community to submit proposals to finance, design, develop, and operate the project. Although this approach forces the public partner to be totally dependent on a developer, the project will more than likely be implemented. One of the problems with this approach is that developers are unlikely to incur the cost of completing much of the predevelopment process without having some form of a commitment from the public partner. For example, the developer will require an exclusive right to negotiate (ERN) for 180 days prior to hiring a consultant to complete a market demand analysis.

4. The Developer Solicitation Process

Like the public/private finance and development process, there are numerous techniques available to government and university officials to solicit interest from the private sector to finance, design, develop, construct, and operate a facility (see Chapter 8). The alternative techniques to solicit the private sector to assist in implementing the project include:

- The two-step RFQ/RFP process
- The traditional RFP process
- The prequalified RFP process
- The sole-source method
- The RFQ/negotiate method

There are various types of private-sector companies specializing in implementation of a building development project:

- Developer as owner/investor/development manager
- Developer as a development manager compensated on a fee basis
- A finance/design/build company or team

- Design/Build companies
- The traditional architect–contractor team

Whichever solicitation technique is used and whichever project delivery method is selected, the official representing the primary public partner is responsible for arranging the solicitation process. Specifically, it is the responsibility of the project manager of the public partner to:

- Select the consultants that appear to be the most appropriate companies to structure the project
- Develop the solicitation
- Issue the solicitation
- Respond to questions prior to the proposal due date
- Evaluate developer proposals
- Interview selected developers
- Rank and select the developer proposal that is most likely to be implemented

During the solicitation process, the public partner is also responsible for keeping the process on schedule—to avoid inordinate delays. One of the most significant problems with the public/private partnership approach is the length of time required to complete the RFP process and negotiate a development agreement.

Another looming problem with the public/private partnership process is the ever-tightening requirements and constricted formats demanded in developer solicitations. Government and university officials should guard against the tendency to be too regimented in their solicitations to the private sector. There is a fine balance of structuring RFPs that will allow an "apples-to-apples" evaluation of developer proposals and not limiting the ability of the developer to structure creative public/private finance plans and/or partnerships, or for the architect to develop a design that the public partner has not developed. Government and university officials want to facilitate "out-of-the-box" thinking by the proposing private partner teams.

5. Deal Structuring and Negotiations

By completing Steps 1 through 13 of the public/private finance and development process—especially Steps 8, 10, and 11—government, university, and school district officials should be confident that when they enter Step 14 (the negotiation phase of the predevelopment process), they are on solid ground. They should be in a position of strength. They know, using their assumptions, that the project is financially feasible, and they have determined the most advantageous ownership, investment, and operation position for them and their public partner participants, if any. If this process is not utilized, government and university officials will be required to structure deals and negotiate only after the developer is selected. This phase of the predevelopment process should require only 90 to 120 days. If negotiations require more time than that, one or both of the public and private partners may not be doing everything possible to keep negotiations focused and within some reasonable time schedule.

The project manager for the public partner should begin the negotiation phase of the process by outlining the desired deal points. In addition, a term sheet should be prepared by one of the negotiating parties. The term sheet is similar to a fact sheet in that it describes the critically important components of the proposed development and a bullet-formatted summary of the desired terms of the deal structure between the primary public and private partners. The preferred public/private financing structure (Step 12) may include several public and private project participants. The primary parties of the public/private partnership are typically the sponsoring government entity and the developer, or the primary equity investor, which has a controlling ownership position.

In addition to the primary public and private partners, the preferred public/private financing structure may include secondary project participants, such as the developer (if not the controlling owner), the contractor, and the operator (especially if the operator provides equity and/or credit enhancement). On the public side, the secondary partner may include one or more government entities, which will realize some form of benefit from the development and operation of the proposed development. These benefits are wide-ranging and include one or more types of tax revenue and new temporary and permanent jobs.

A large part of the task required to negotiate a development agreement is to complete a variety of financial analyses in order to determine the capital and noncapital investments required by the primary and secondary public and private project participants. The negotiation process is described in detail in Chapter 4, but the purpose of the in-depth financial analyses is to determine returns on investment, levels of risk for all project participants, and level of responsibility for all public and private partners.

Both the public and private partners need to enter the negotiation phase with their eyes wide open. More than likely, most of the negotiation phase will be completed in a fishbowl atmosphere. There will be substantial public scrutiny, and many of the people scrutinizing the process will believe they could do a better job of structuring a deal. Both primary partners will need stamina and determination to successfully negotiate a public/private partnership in an open forum.

SUMMARY

Both the primary public and private partners should make every effort to stay focused and structure a development agreement that will be acceptable to the critically important project participants. Equally important, this must be completed on a timely basis. In order to be timely, both parties need to start negotiations with a strong sense of direction, maintain reasonable expectations, and remain flexible.

Chapter 6

Partnerships Can Be Customized to Meet the Objectives of Both Partners

One of the great qualities of using the public/private development partnership approach is the enormous flexibility and creativity available to both the public and private partners to structure an agreement that meets the objectives of both parties. In planning a project, the partners can manage a number of variables or deal points to suit their objectives. These variables generally can be categorized as follows:

- Level of participation in structuring, implementing, and managing the project
- Financing sources
- Financing techniques
- Financing, design, construction, and operational responsibilities
- Finance structure
- Nontax income and tax revenue for the public partner(s) and return on investment for the private partner(s)
- Distribution of cash flow among the public and private entities
- Ownership position
- Design, construction, and operational risks
- Level of control
- Implementation schedule
- Legal interrelationships among the project entities

By carefully structuring these deal points, government, university, and school district officials and their private partners can effectively customize a deal structure to meet the public/private partnership's particular needs and requirements.

Exhibit 6.1 The Flexibility and Creativity of Public/Private Partnerships

	Private (with public participation)	Public/Private Partnership	Public (Traditional Process)	Public/Public/Private Partnership (Intergovernmental Agreement)
Source of Finance	Private Equity and Taxable Debt	Private Equity, Taxable Debt, Gov't Incentives, Land and Infrastructure Investments	General obligation Bonds or Revenue Bonds	General Obligation Bonds or Revenue Bonds
Financing Structure	Equity investor, lender, Gov't, and Developer	Equity Investor, Lender, Special Gov't Equity, Local Development Corporation	Government and Bond Underwriter	Government and Bond Underwriter
Ownership	Private	Public and/or Private	Public	Public
Risk	Private (High) Public (Low)	Fair and Reasonable Split	Public (High) Private (Low)	Public (High)
Responsibility				
Finance	Private	Private and/or Public	Public	Public
Design	Private	Private and/or Public	Public	Public
Development	Private	Private or Public	Public or Private	Public or Private
Operation	Private	Private or Public	Public or Private	Public or Private

Economic Return				
Project Income for Gov't	None	Depends on Ownership Structure	All, but at Risk for Deficit Operations	All, but at Risk for Deficit Operations
Profit Participation for Gov't	Low to Moderate	Moderate to High	NA	NA
Property Tax Revenues for Gov't	High	Depends on Ownership Structure	None	None
Level of Control				
Government	Low to Moderate	Moderate	High	High
Private	High	Moderate	Low	Low
Implementation Schedule	Private Financing and Procurement Accelerates Process	Creative Financing and Enhancing Operating Performance Accelerates Process	Limited by Traditional Funding and Procurement Methods	Limited by Traditional Funding and Procurement Methods
Voter Approval or Referendum Required	No	Depends on Deal Structure	Yes	Yes

For example, assume that a city has decided that development of a facility or commercial project is a necessary catalyst to the redevelopment of its downtown area. City officials have also agreed that they have no interest in owning, developing, or operating this cornerstone project, but they do want to control the project's design and ensure its quality. The city and its private partner can structure a public/private partnership to achieve the city's objectives, assuming that the parties agree on a fair and reasonable sharing of the risks and responsibilities as well as the economic return. Thus, city officials could choose to put most of the financial and development responsibility for the project on the developer, with the understanding that it would receive little or no economic return.

Following is a more detailed examination of some of the most important variables.

PROJECT PARTICIPATION

As shown in the partnership creativity and flexibility matrix (Exhibit 6.1), there are four basic types of public and private involvement in a project.

In the traditional process, the public entity owns and controls the project, bears most of the risk, and is primarily responsible for project financing and design. It receives all of the returns from the project. A private developer may develop and manage the project for a fee but does not share any of the return.

In a private project, a private entity such as a developer owns and controls the project, incurs most of the risk, and is responsible for project financing, design, development, and operation. The public entity has comparatively little responsibility or risk, but it does not receive any of the project's economic return (although it may collect substantial tax revenue from the project).

The public/public partnership is a partnership in fact as well as in name. The public and private partners may share project ownership, control, risk, and responsibilities and finance the project from a variety of public and private sources. How the economic returns are shared depends on the ownership structure.

The public/public partnership, another form of partnership, involves more than one government entity and includes intergovernmental agreements. In this structure, the sponsoring public partner may solicit investments (both capital and noncapital) from other government entities that would benefit from the project's successful completion. Under this structure, the public entities own and control the project, bear most of the responsibilities and risks, and receive all of the return, or the public partners could structure a partnership with a private partner. This arrangement would be called a public/public/private partnership.

Public and private involvement is not limited to these four types. With imagination and creativity, participants can structure many other combinations to satisfy their requirements.

OWNERSHIP OF THE PROJECT

Ownership can range from 100 percent public to 100 percent private and anywhere in between. Again, this is where creativity plays a critical role in the deal structuring process. For example, assume that private investors will not provide all of the required equity for a project because the projected returns do not meet their expectations. In this case, the parties may agree to reduce the equity required of the private partners and increase the equity contributions (ownership positions) of the participating government entities. For example, if a cash flow analysis of a convention hotel shows that the internal rate of return (IRR) is less than that required by a private equity investor, the ownership of the hotel may be structured so that the private areas are owned by the equity investors and the public, or common, areas are owned by the sponsoring government. This, in effect, reduces the development cost for each partner and allows the use of public funds and government-backed finance techniques.

OWNERSHIP, INVESTMENT, DEVELOPMENT, AND OPERATIONAL RISKS

Depending on market demand, the required return on investment by the public and private partners, and the desired level of control, risk-averse public partners can structure the ownership of a project, their investment, and the development and operational responsibilities to minimize risk. For example, if the local demand for the proposed building use(s) is strong; the return on cost (ROC) required by the developer is reasonable; and the public partner's control over design and building quality is within reason, the public partner should be in a good position to negotiate a development agreement whereby the public partner has little exposure to quantifiable risk. Public and private partners need to realize that the multitude of deal points are highly interrelated and therefore many of the deal points need to be addressed concurrently.

RESPONSIBILITIES

Both the public and private partners have the flexibility to structure a partnership whereby each partner can tailor the level of responsibility for design, finance, development, construction, and operation to adapt to the capabilities and resources of each partner. For example, if the public partner wants to be responsible for design, they can complete design and construction drawings, as well as building specifications, and require the developer to abide by those drawings. What the public partner has to realize is that if they want that level of control, they may pay a price by not having the day-to-day opportunity to incorporate the expertise and lessons learned from the developer and operator. This may in turn cause the cost of the building to increase—possibly to the point that it becomes financially infeasible to develop.

ECONOMIC RETURN

Another advantage of the public/private partnership is that the financing, design, development, and operation of a project can be structured to maximize nontax income, yet generate substantial tax revenue from private ownership and operation. In many projects, the city can reduce or even eliminate its capital investment by fully utilizing city-owned real estate assets, as well as its legislative powers and any available investment, development, and operational incentives. At the same time, it can share in the cash flow from successful management of the project. Of course, if the city takes on a substantial part of the project risk and responsibilities and makes a substantial investment in cash or in kind, it should expect an appropriate share of the upside.

LEVEL OF CONTROL

If a city, for example, wants to control the design and quality of building materials of a facility and operate it as well, a public/private partnership can be structured to achieve these goals. But this level of control must be balanced with the requirements of private financing. Moreover, under this structure, the private partner may be blocked from fully utilizing their ability to reduce predevelopment and development costs, as well as expedite the design and construction schedules.

Bottom-line, control of a project depends on a partner's ownership position, amount of investment, risk exposure, and responsibilities. The partnership can be structured to include control features important to the city. Nevertheless, if the balance of risk, responsibility, and funding is tilted toward the private participant, the city will have less control over the development process and operation of the facility.

IMPLEMENTATION SCHEDULE

For many large public projects, the time required to obtain government funding approvals and complete the traditional design and construction process is typically four to seven years. But by optimizing private equity and debt financing of public facilities, and fully utilizing the expertise and experience of the private sector in design and construction management, city or university officials can substantially reduce the time required for the long, arduous, frustrating, and often costly government funding and procurement process. A well-executed public/private partnership should reduce the time required to structure and implement a project to four years, which shaves two to three years off of the traditional public process.

ADVANTAGES

Major city or university facilities, commercial real estate projects, and infrastructure improvements usually cannot be carried out by the public or private sectors separately. Instead, both sectors need to work together to finance, design, develop, and manage facilities, infrastructure, or commercial projects in a cost-effective and timely manner. These projects increasingly require multiple financing sources, a substantial investment of time and energy, and close cooperation among the public and private participants. Moreover, they must meet the requirements of the capital markets and respond to the condition of the local development market.

The ability of public and private partners to work together is enhanced by the flexibility and creativity inherent in structuring public/private partnerships. Because of the many variables in such partnerships, the participants have the flexibility to customize projects to meet their particular needs. The ability of governments and universities to work with the private sector to realize common dreams is limited only by the innovation and creativity of the participants.

Chapter 7

Structuring Public/Private Finance Plans

The primary reason the public/private partnership approach is rapidly emerging as the preferred methodology to finance and develop buildings across the nation is the enormous flexibility and creativity inherent in the approach. Using the Stainback Five-Part Public/Private Finance and Development Approach illustrated in this chapter, projects that initially appear to be financially infeasible can be transformed to be attractive to the capital markets and the participating public and private partners. Public and private partners have an enormous arsenal available to them to solve almost any problem that may appear during the predevelopment process. Consequently, neither party should ever give up on a project until they have exhausted the tools included in the five-part approach. Both the public and private partners may need to be creative on multiple fronts in order to solve the inevitable hurdles that will arise during the predevelopment phase of the project.

THE STAINBACK FIVE-PART FINANCE AND DEVELOPMENT APPROACH

The five-part approach to structuring public/private finance and development plans is organized into five optional actions to be taken if the cash flow analysis reveals a shortfall. For projects suffering from major cash flow shortfalls, the key is to combine the most appropriate aspects of each part to create a cumulative effect. The five-part approach (see Exhibit 7.1) includes the following parts:

- Make Productive Use of Underutilized Government-Owned Real Estate Assets
- Use a Creative Combination of Public and Private Sources of Capital and Noncapital Financing

Exhibit 7.1 Five-Part Approach

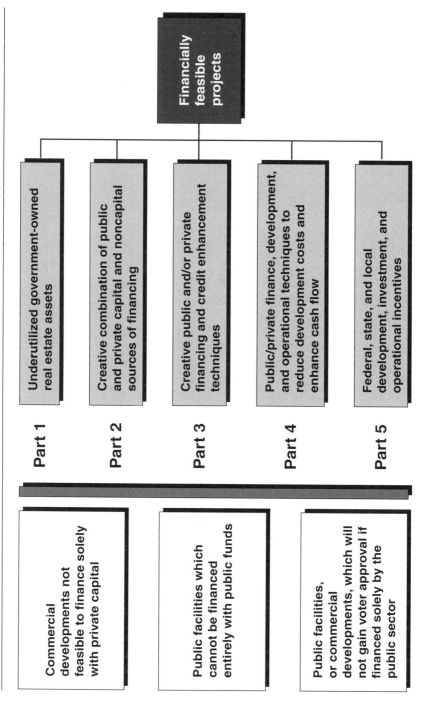

Financially feasible projects

Part 1 — Underutilized government-owned real estate assets

Part 2 — Creative combination of public and private capital and noncapital sources of financing

Part 3 — Creative public and/or private financing and credit enhancement techniques

Part 4 — Public/private finance, development, and operational techniques to reduce development costs and enhance cash flow

Part 5 — Federal, state, and local development, investment, and operational incentives

Commercial developments not feasible to finance solely with private capital

Public facilities which cannot be financed entirely with public funds

Public facilities, or commercial developments, which will not gain voter approval if financed solely by the public sector

- Use One or More Creative Public/Private Financing and Credit Enhancement Techniques
- Use Proven Public/Private Finance, Development, and Operational Techniques to Reduce Land and Building Development Costs and Enhance Cash Flow
- Fully Utilize the Appropriate Development, Investment, and Operational Incentives Available From Federal, State, County, and City Governments

Public and private partners need to realize that one part of the five-part approach may not be adequate to solve the problems that may occur during the predevelopment process. Typically, the answer lies with some combination of the features of each part of the approach.

Part 1: Make Productive Use of Underutilized Government-Owned Real Estate Assets

As described in other chapters, the governments in this country control over $4.5 trillion of real estate. A significant portion of those assets are underutilized, so why not put them to use, by providing them to a public/private partnership, which was formed to finance and develop a needed public facility or a catalytic project that could spur the redevelopment of an important area of a city? These assets could also be a form of investment in a public/private partnership to generate nontax income for the public partner. In addition, public partners should learn to capture all or a portion of the value they create on land adjacent to a public facility financed and developed with public funds. A prime example of this concept is the construction of a convention center. Instead of allowing the private sector to purchase the land adjacent to the new convention center and develop complimentary uses, such as a hotel, urban entertainment center, or support retail space. The government entity or entities that provided the funding of the convention center should leverage the value of city-owned land adjacent to the center by structuring a public/private partnership to develop a hotel and/or other facilities supporting the new center. This would place the government in a position of strength to structure and negotiate a partnership whereby it receives various forms of nontax income from the proposed commercial development.

Strategically located land can be extremely valuable to governments, universities, and school districts. There are a large number of completed public/private development projects whereby the public partner receives either substantial land lease payments over time or the private partner privately finances a needed public facility in exchange for commercially developing government-owned property.

Part 2: Use a Creative Combination of Public and Private Sources of Capital and Noncapital Financing

For most large public/private development projects (those with a cost exceeding $50 million) multiple sources of private and/or public financing are required. The alternative sources of financing may include:

- Equity (cash) issued by the private partner
- Conventional debt issued by the private partner
- Debt secured by the public partner but issued by the private partner
- Debt or bonds issued by the various levels of government or public authorities
- Debt issued by special-purpose development corporations
- Funds available from the various federal government programs
- Subordinated, or soft second mortgages provided by one of the various participating levels of government

Like the overall five-part approach, there may be instances that require some combination of these sources of financing in order to satisfy the required return on investment. Each source of financing has different return on investment requirements. Private sources of financing are typically the most expensive, although the cost of private debt supported in some fashion by the public partner can be very competitive with the cost of publicly issued debt.

In addition to the wide variety of sources of debt and equity, there are a large number of sources of noncapital investments. Noncapital sources of investment do not require any capital funds. Examples of this type of investment include providing the private developer additional development rights to increase the development capacity of the project site, providing land that did not require any investment by public partner, and reducing the parking requirement for a project.

In addition to capital and noncapital sources of financing, there are public/public partnerships, or intergovernmental agreements, whereby the primary public partner joins forces with other government entities to finance all or a portion of the project components assigned to the public partner. The logic behind public/public partnerships is that if a government entity is going to realize tax revenue from the proposed project, it should also share some of the financial burden of the primary public partner. For example, if a city is the sponsor of a public/private development project and the project is going to generate tax revenue for the county and state, both those entities should provide capital and/or noncapital sources on investments in order to facilitate action on the project.

Part 3: Use Creative Public/Private Financing and Credit Enhancement Techniques

There are many types of public/private financing techniques available to public and private partners. New financing techniques or instruments are continually developed in the private capital market and development community. Therefore, it is important to have someone in the public/private partnership that either participates in the capital markets on a daily basis or is otherwise very active in the public/private development arena. It is impossible to list all of the techniques currently available to structure public/private financings, but a few include:

- *Taxable debt secured and paid from selected sources of taxes generated by the project.* Under this financing technique the public and private partners would select the taxes applicable to the project and decide which taxes could be used to reinvest or used to securitize the debt.

- *Tax increment financing.* Tax increment financing (TIF) is often used to finance a portion of the overall project. The source of this financing is the increment of tax revenue generated by the project over and above the tax generated by the project prior to development of the proposed project. In other words, the sponsoring government agrees to freeze the tax at a certain point in time. This serves as a benchmark to measure the amount of new tax revenue generated by the project, which can be used to finance a specific project related to the proposed primary public/private development project.

- *Taxable debt secured by an occupancy guarantee provided by the public partner.* In some instances, the public partner has the legislative power to provide the private partner with a written guarantee to occupy the proposed space once it is completed. This allows the developer to reduce the cost of finance through credit enhancement.

- *Third-party subordinated debt.* There may be instances in which the operator of the completed development provides a portion of the required debt. The private third party not only allows the debt to be subordinated to senior debt issued by other parties, but this form of debt is often guaranteed by the operator or any third party.

- *Community facilities district special tax bond.* Community facilities district special tax bonds in California and other states can serve as another source of debt. This debt can be issued based on a tax levy on the developer leasehold interest and project revenue. Another quality of this form of debt is that the private landowners determine the boundaries of the district. The district can be as small as the proposed project site.

Part 4: Use Proven Public/Private Finance, Development, and Operational Techniques to Reduce Land and Building Development Costs and Enhance Cash Flow

There are numerous techniques available to reduce development costs and/or enhance cash flow if the cash flow analysis of a project reveals a significant shortfall. Although there are many of these techniques (too numerous to list all here) following are several to provide a sense of the creative ways public and private partners can overcome what can initially appear to be insurmountable hurdles to proceed to implementation.

Reduce development costs.

- The public partner provides the project site and delays land lease payments until the private investors achieve a preferred return on their equity investment.

75

- The public partner provides the project site as a form of an equity investment in the partnership and not a land lease.
- The public partner covers the cost of the required infrastructure improvements.
- The parking requirement for the project is reduced, which reduces the private portion of the total development cost.
- The public partner provides the private partner a tax abatement on construction materials.

It should be noted that one of these techniques, and there are others like it, would not require any investment by the public partner, yet by reducing the parking requirement could significantly reduce the cost of the proposed development.

Techniques to enhance cash flow.

- Many public and private partners are exploring the advantages of purchasing energy at a wholesale price.
- Some public partners are forming alliances with energy providers whereby in exchange for a long-term contract, the energy provider reduces energy cost and/or provides an equity investment or provides some form of credit enhancement on the debt.
- Some government entities are providing their private partners with tax abatements, or tax reinvestments, whereby a selected tax generated by the project is actually reinvested in the project. This technique applies only to taxes such as hotel occupancy tax. The logic is that the user of the facility, not the owner, pays the tax; therefore, the impact on the net cash flow is much more than an abatement.
- Depending on how large the cash flow shortfall is, there are operators who will reduce their management fee in the ramp-up years of the project. Typically, the shortfalls occur in years one through five, so a reduction of one or two percentage points in years one through five have a significant impact on the return on investment.

Part 5: Fully Utilize the Appropriate Development, Investment, and Operational Incentives Available from Federal, State, County, and City Governments

There are a multitude of government incentives that apply to the development, investment, and operational aspects of a public/private facility. These incentives are offered to the private sector to reduce development costs, investments, and operational costs. These incentives are available at all levels of government, including federal, state, county, and city governments. In order for private entities to capitalize on these incentives, they will have to complete the necessary research at the various levels of government. There are literally hundreds of incentives available and they vary from government to government, so the following incentives serve only as examples of the types of incentives available:

- Investment incentives:
  - Credit against corporate franchise tax in exchange for new capital investment
  - State and local development bonds
- Development incentives:
  - Public authority guarantee on bond or loan
  - Direct government loan
- Operational incentives:
  - Job creation tax credit
  - Property tax abatement

SUMMARY

Public and private partners have an enormous arsenal of techniques to reduce development costs and enhance cash flow for public/private development projects. If public and private partners have the will, stamina, and creativity, there will be few development projects that will not proceed to implementation because of cash flow shortfalls, as there are so many ways to solve the public/private finance and development puzzle. When the Stainback Five-Part Finance and Development Approach is used, the public and private partners have literally hundreds of ways to reduce the development costs and enhance cash flow of a proposed project. The answer to the most complex public/private finance and development problem is the cumulative effect of combining components of the five-part approach.

Chapter 8

The Developer Solicitation Process

The solicitation of the private partner is often the first time the public partner communicates with the private partner. Therefore, this step in the predevelopment process is critically important. If the government, university, or school district entity is not prepared to communicate with the private partner, the solicitation will more than likely not be received well. Some developers, especially the few focused on the public/private development market, receive one or more requests for qualifications (RFQs) or requests for proposal (RFPs) every week or so. Consequently, it is imperative that the solicitation is well thought out. If not, most developers will quickly review the solicitation and discard it. Clearly, the RFQ and RFP can make or break a public/private development project. This is one of the primary reasons government, university, and school district officials should complete the public/private finance and development process described in Chapter 4 *prior* to issuing any developer solicitation.

Although the public/private finance and development process proposed in Chapter 4 is strongly advocated, government and university officials have a minimum of six other approaches they can use to solicit interest from the private sector.

THE SIX ALTERNATIVE APPROACHES TO SOLICIT INTEREST FROM THE PRIVATE SECTOR

The six basic approaches to generate interest, evaluate private-sector proposals, and select a private partner include:

- Approach One: The three-step RFI/RFQ/RFP process
- Approach Two: The two-step RFQ/RFP process

- Approach Three: The single-step RFP process
- Approach Four: The prequalified developer RFP process
- Approach Five: The sole-source developer method
- Approach Six: The RFQ/negotiate method

The key to all six approaches for government and university officials is to be prepared to communicate with your potential private partner. If the solicitation does not concisely and comprehensively convey the public/private development opportunity, the typical private developer will detect problems, and often quickly determine that the opportunity does not warrant the time and investment required to meet even the minimum requirements of the solicitation.

Before each of the six alternative approaches to solicit interest from the private sector are described, the fundamental information required to generate interest warrants attention. In order for most private developers to be interested in pursuing a public/private development opportunity, the following *basic* items must be addressed.

The following basic solicitation items are essential for a developer RFP. These five categories do not include the additional items that would be included if the sponsoring government or university entity completed the 14 steps included in the public/private finance and development process described in Chapter 4.

These basic solicitation items are organized into five categories:

1. Public Partner Information
2. Demographic and Market Information
3. Information on the Public/Private Development Opportunity
4. Submission Requirements
5. Overview of the Proposed Developer Evaluation and Selection Process

1. Public Partner Information
   - Define the entity managing the proposed public/private development opportunity.
   - Describe the political context of that sponsoring entity. Are there other participating government entities?
   - Describe the goals and objectives of the public partner for the project.
   - Describe any consensus building completed with participating governments, citizen groups, and/or the media.
   - Describe the expected role and responsibilities of the public and private partners.
2. Demographic and Market Information
   - Describe the land, building, and infrastructure program. If a market demand analysis has been completed, be sure to relay the results of the analysis, as well

as who completed the analysis and when. Remember, if a market analysis is older than 15 to 18 months, it will need to be updated by a reputable consultant.

- Describe the demographic and physical context of the proposed project site.

3. Information on the Public/Private Development Opportunity
   - Describe what entity or entities own the project site.
   - Describe in detail the development constraints and opportunities for the site. Addressing issues such as zoning, entitlements, environmental conditions, access to infrastructure, and so on.
   - Describe recent public capital improvements that enhance the value and marketability of the subject property and project.
   - Provide the master plan for the subject property, if any, and/or the context of the proposed project.
   - Describe the vehicular and pedestrian access to the proposed site and its immediate context. If available, provide travel times to nearby activity generators, such as convention centers, employment centers, and transit stations.
   - Address in detail the physical condition of the subject property, such as topography, view corridors, access to utilities, flood plain, and so forth.

4. Submission Requirements
   - Describe the submission requirements of the developer.
   - Describe the major evaluation criteria, preferably weighting the importance of each criterion.

5. Developer Evaluation and Selection Process
   - Provide the estimated schedule to complete the developer evaluation and selection process.

APPROACH ONE: THE THREE-STEP RFI/RFQ/RFP PROCESS

Basically, this three-step process is the same as the RFQ/RFP process, but a request for information (RFI) is issued to solicit ideas and concepts from the private sector prior to issuing an RFQ.

The purpose of issuing an RFI is to obtain an initial reaction from the private sector to the public/private development opportunity and to gain market, economic, and development insights that only companies actively involved in the marketplace will know. In addition, the RFI should ask the private sector whether there are additional issues to be addressed by the public sponsor prior to issuing an RFQ.

The RFI also functions as an announcement of a development opportunity and concurrently as a method to "sell" the opportunity by providing market data, demographics, public improvements, and the like, related to the subject development.

The typical RFI includes the following types of information:

- Project site and context information
- Market demand and supply analysis for the subject building type
- Completed and proposed public capital improvements related to the project directly and indirectly
- The proposed process to form the public/private development partnership
- Request for additional information and/or issues that need to be addressed by the public partner

There are two major problems with issuing an RFI: the time required to develop, issue, and analyze the RFI submittals; and the fact that many developers will not reveal any insights to the project in fear of losing their edge with competitors. Government and university officials should realize that many developers would not provide intelligent and insightful questions because the questions and corresponding answers become available to other developers who may be competing for the opportunity.

APPROACH TWO: THE TWO-STEP RFQ/RFP PROCESS

The two-step RFQ/RFP process has become the most popular developer solicitation process. As shown in Chapter 9, one of the largest problems looming over the public/private development approach is the time required to complete the three-step RFI/RFQ/RFP, or the two-step RFQ/RFP process. Therefore, government and university officials should seriously consider the prequalified developer RFP process, which will be described later in this chapter. By prequalifying developers and limiting the number of RFPs issued to five, or a maximum of seven, government and university officials are able to eliminate the RFQ process and proceed immediately to the RFP process, yet still limit the competing field of developers.

The advantage of the two-step RFQ/RFP process is that the RFQ can be issued to a large and wide spectrum of developers. The RFQ can encompass local, regional, and national developers as well as developers with extensive experience in the subject building type for which the government and university officials may not be aware. The two-step RFQ/RFP process is one that can require 7 to 11 months to complete if properly executed.

Following is an overview of the procedures required to complete the RFQ process alone.

1. Develop the RFQ.
2. Review and approve the RFQ.
3. Establish and document the evaluation criteria used to select a developer.
4. Identify the private-sector companies to receive the RFQ.
5. Produce and issue the RFQ.

6. Give developers the allotted time to prepare their proposals and for the public partner to answer questions posed by the recipients of the RFQ.
7. Complete a preproposal conference.
8. Evaluate developer proposals.
9. Review results of evaluation with the appropriate government or university entities.
10. Announce the short-listed developer teams.

The time required to complete the RFQ stage alone ranges from 12 to 21 weeks. A full and detailed description of the required schedule to complete the RFQ process is provided later in this chapter. The total time required to complete the 10-step RFQ process assumes that Steps 3 and 4 can be completed concurrently with Steps 1 and 2.

THE RFQ PROCESS STEP BY STEP

Step 1: Develop the RFQ

For a major public/private development project or a project critical to the success of redeveloping a downtown area or district, the time required to structure and write a well-written and organized RFQ with graphics can range from two to three weeks. This range assumes that most of the research has been completed. For example, the market demand analysis alone will require a consultant six to eight weeks to complete. For a relatively small project with a total development budget of $5 to $25 million, an RFQ can be prepared in two weeks or less.

Step 2: Review and Approve the RFQ

Once the consultant or internal public-sector group completes a draft of the RFQ, it should be reviewed by key public participants in the developer selection process and other participating government entities. This step should require only one to two weeks.

Step 3: Establish and Document the Developer Evaluation Criteria

The purpose of developing the criteria to evaluate the qualifications of the developers is twofold. This is an opportunity for government or university officials to voice their opinion as to what qualifies a developer with whom they want to form a long-term relationship. What characteristics are important? Address issues such as whether creativity or financial stability is more important. The criteria are the essential ingredient to develop a developer evaluation matrix. Once the public partner receives the developer submittals and it is determined that each proposal satisfies all of the submission requirements, they are simply included in the vertical axis of the matrix. The evaluation criteria are on the horizontal axis. The cells of the matrix contain the assessment as to how well each developer satisfied each criterion. At this point in the RFQ process, the task is to establish and document the evaluation criteria so that the criteria is revealed in the RFQ. The public partner will need to determine the specificity and level of detail of the evaluation criteria.

Step 4: Identify the Private-Sector Companies to Receive the RFQ

The level of difficulty and the time required to complete this step depends on the size of the net cast to find the most appropriate developer as well as whether the public partner has retained a real estate consultant which can rely on their national network of development and construction companies, architects, other real estate consultants, investment companies, and facility management companies.

The primary purpose of issuing RFQs to companies other than developers is to allow business development professionals within those firms the opportunity to present the opportunity to their favorite developer or to assemble a comprehensive team that can provide the sponsoring entity with the expertise to finance, design, develop, construct, and operate the proposed project. If the public partner has to complete research to identify appropriate developers, this should require approximately one to two weeks; otherwise, little or no time is required to complete this step of the process.

Step 5: Produce and Issue the RFQ

This step is simply the graphic production, assembly, and distribution of the RFQ. The time to complete this task is dependent on the level of sophistication desired for the presentation of the RFQ and the number of companies that are targeted. A conservative estimate of the time required to finalize the text and graphics, complete the layout of the document, and reproduce the solicitation and mail it can range from two to three weeks.

Step 6: Answer Questions Posed by the Recipients of the RFQ

Inevitably, the recipients of the RFQ will generate questions in an attempt to clarify the requirements or to gain an edge on their competitors. Either the public partner or their consultant should be available to answer questions posed by the private sector. The public partner has the option of answering questions posed on the phone or fax or require questions to be formally submitted in advance of the preproposal conference (see Step 7).

The time allowed for the private partner to respond to the RFQ typically ranges from three to six weeks. Government or university officials should realize that some developers or related team members may be engulfed in other pursuits or simply be preoccupied; therefore, up to six weeks is warranted. Requiring potential private partners to respond in less than three weeks is not adequate to submit comprehensive proposals.

The allotted time is also highly dependent upon whether the potential private partners are expected to assemble comprehensive teams. If the public partner is requiring the developer to submit only their qualifications, the time frame could be as little as three weeks. If the developer is required to assemble a team, the time allowed to respond to the RFQ should be in the range of four to six weeks.

A comprehensive team required to address all of the predevelopment, development, and operational issues should include the following members:

- A developer(s) with extensive experience with each of the building types included in the proposed development
- Architect
- Urban designer
- Engineers: civil, mechanical, electric, and plumbing engineers, as well as a structural engineer and possibly an environmental engineer
- Construction company
- Real estate attorney(s) (land use, real estate, permit, and corporate)
- Landscape architect
- Investment bank
- Community outreach or consensus planning firms
- Marketing consultant
- Facility manager
- Operator
- Interior designer
- Traffic planner
- Graphic designer
- Public relations specialist
- Leasing and/or tenant-mix specialist

Step 7: Complete a Preproposal Conference

The purpose of a preproposal conference is to provide the public sponsor of the project a forum to achieve one or more of the following:

- Further "sell" the development opportunity to the private-partner candidates.
- Clarify issues raised in the RFQ.

- Answer any written questions submitted by candidates.
- Assess the level of interest demonstrated by the number and types of firms in attendance.
- Provide an opportunity to tour the site and its context.
- Allow networking to occur among the potential participants.

Preproposal conferences at the RFQ stage of the developer selection process are rare but may be appropriate for many large-scale public/private development projects, especially those with a budget exceeding $150 million or pivotal to the redevelopment of a downtown or a redevelopment area.

Step 8: Evaluate Developer Proposals

It is highly recommended that government, university, and school district officials hire an experienced consultant to assist in the evaluation of developer proposals. This is especially true at the RFP stage. The final selection of a developer should be made with the assistance of an objective third party, ideally with extensive experience in evaluating developer proposals.

At this point in the process, the results of Step 3 are essential to an objective and systematic evaluation of the developer candidates. The framework is in place if the public partner is using the developer evaluation matrix—simply fill in the vertical axis with the name of each developer who satisfied the submission requirements and begin inputting the assessment into each corresponding cell of the matrix.

The results of the developer evaluation matrix should be sufficient to develop a short list of developers to be interviewed or to receive an RFP. It is strongly suggested that the number of developers on the short list not exceed five. From the perspective of the short-listed developers, they still have only a 1 in 5 or 20 percent chance of being selected once the RFP process is completed. Even at one-to-five odds, incurring the expenses and man-hours equal to $350,000 to $500,000 or more to submit a competitive proposal is a high-risk investment for any developer.

Suggested Evaluation Criteria for an RFQ

At the RFQ stage, the evaluation criteria should be organized into five categories, as shown in Exhibit 8.1.

Step 9: Review Results of the Developer Evaluation with the Appropriate Government or University Entities

Prior to announcing the short-listed developers who will proceed to the RFP stage, government, university, and school district officials should review the completed developer evaluation matrix with members of the developer selection panel and

Exhibit 8.1   Evaluation Criteria for RFQ Stage

Category 1:   Information on the developer
—History of the firm
—Relevant project experience
—Public/private development experience, especially completed in the last three to five years
—Financial relationships and potential sources of equity and debt
—An overview of the public/private finance plan for up to three recent projects similar to the proposed project
—Of the three recently completed projects, describe any major postdevelopment activities, such as sale of asset, refinancing, or repositioning of equity and/or debt instruments
—Development management experience, especially with the proposed building type or complex
—Pertinent information on the controlling entity, including:
  • The contractual entity that will serve as the ground lessee
  • The parent company
  • The relationship with the parent company
  • Financial stability and strength
  • The financial capacity of the entity specified
  • Joint venture arrangements with investor(s), operators, or construction companies
—Resumes of key individuals who will have significant roles in the development. Require the developer to identify the day-to-day project manager. For most developers, the project manager, not the chairman, chief executive officer, or president of the development company, will be the professional the public partners will interact with daily during the predevelopment and development processes.
—Information about the developer representative who will be responsible for marketing and securing lease commitments from tenants and operators
—References from other public partners, sources of finance, and key members of a typical developer team, such as architects and contractors
—Identify other projects that the developer is pursuing and projects for which the company has been recently selected. The purpose of this information is to assess the capacity of the developer to adequately address the needs of the subject development.

Category 2:   Information and qualifications of key members of the team such as:
—Architect
—Construction company
—Investment bank or investment partner(s)
—Law firm(s)

Category 3:   The developer's initial vision for the project—the character and sense of place and architectural massing proposed

Category 4:   Initial public/private finance concepts

Category 5:   The anticipated working relationship between the public and private partners possibly with other key government or university officials. This step should require only one to two weeks to complete. The review sessions should be arranged concurrently with Step 8.

Step 10: Announce the Short-listed Developer Teams

This step is simply preparing the letters to the five or less short-listed developers selected in Step 9. This task, including the time required to mail the announcement, takes one week or less.

Representatives of the public partner(s) should be prepared to explain to the media and key community groups the method used to select the shortlisted developers and the basis of the selections. The more in-depth and systematic the approach used to evaluate the candidate teams the more objective and accurate the selection will be perceived.

THE SCHEDULE TO COMPLETE THE RFQ STAGE

The time required to complete each step of the RFQ stage is highly dependent upon a wide variety of variables and the approach to each step. Exhibit 8.2 is an outline of each step and the time that should be allotted for each step.

Exhibit 8.2   Time Required to Complete the Typical RFQ Process for a Major Public/Private Development Project

		Schedule (weeks)
Step 1:	Develop the RFQ	2–3
Step 2:	Review and approve the RFQ	1–2
Step 3:	Establish and document the developers evaluation criteria	1 (concurrent with Steps 1 and 2)
Step 4:	Identify the private sector companies to receive the RFQ	1 (concurrent with Steps 1 and 2)
Step 5:	Produce and issue the RFQ	2–3
Step 6:	Give the allotted time to developers to prepare their proposals and for the public partner to answer questions posed by the recipients of the RFQ	3–6
Step 7:	Complete a preproposal conference	1–2
Step 8:	Evaluate developer proposals	2–3
Step 9:	Review results of evaluation with the appropriate government or university entities	1–2
Step 10:	Announce the short-listed developer teams	1
	TOTAL:	13–22 weeks Approximately 3 to 5 months

THE RFP PROCESS

The primary purpose of the developer RFP is to obtain a highly technical and detailed response from developers using the requirements and format required by the public partner.

When developing an RFP, government, university, and school district officials should remember that most developers, especially those that are focused on the public/private development market, are receiving three to five RFPs per month. Consequently, RFPs should be highly organized so that developers can easily find critically important information. They must have a clear and concise description of key information; the text should be straightforward and should include easy to understand tables, charts, and diagrams that summarize pertinent information. An executive summary should be included, which summarizes the development opportunity and the basis for a private developer to make a major investment to complete the predevelopment process and implement the project.

Allow for creativity; consultants assisting government and university project sponsors are increasingly tightening the submissions requirements to the point of not providing candidate developers the opportunity to introduce new concepts for financing, design, tenant mix, development phasing, project delivery, ownership structures, or innovations in operations. While consultants are trying to make sure that developer proposals can be evaluated on an "apples-to-apples" basis, they are not allowing developers the vehicle to share innovations, state-of-the-art concepts, lessons learned, and so on. There is a fine balance here to be achieved, but many developer candidates have the capability to introduce "outside-of-the-box" thinking, which could greatly enhance the public/private partnership or better facilitate action. The RFP should fully allow developers to share their experience and expertise.

Avoid introducing highly technical matters. If government and university officials are constrained by an abnormal amount of regulations, specifications, and/or legislative requirements, they should make the developer aware of these additional hurdles by summarizing these issues, but they should not incorporate attachment after attachment at the RFP stage. These details can be fully addressed after a developer is selected. If the RFP is one or two inches thick, most developers will not want to incur the time and expense of adequately addressing these issues until he or she has been selected. Make them aware of the issues but do not require them to solve these highly detailed issues at this point in the predevelopment process.

The RFP should require developer candidates to address issues in detail. Exhibit 8.3 is a list of the issues that should be addressed by developers.

The level of detail provided by the candidate developers is dependent on several variables.

Perceived or Determined Market Demand

One of the most important factors in determining whether any project is implemented is the demand for the space in the local marketplace. If there is a strong need for ad-

Exhibit 8.3 Issues That the Developer Candidates Should Address

- Public/Private finance plan
- Development phasing
- Development quality
- Total development budgets
- Land, building, and infrastructure program
- Tenant mix
- Economic return to both the public partner(s) and the equity investor(s)
- Master plan
- Architectural concepts
- The proposed character, environment, and public spaces of the overall development
- The specific roles and responsibilities of the key public and private project participants
- The deal structure between the public and private partners for the land and building
- Finance model or cash flow analysis including key assumptions
- Preleasing commitments, or letters of interest from key tenants
- Ownership structure
- Preliminary operation and maintenance program of the building(s) and public spaces
- Predevelopment and development schedules
- Environmental issues
- Traffic and/or transportation issues
- How they will interact with the public partner during the remaining predevelopment and development processes
- Equity and debt commitments

ditional space of the proposed building type, then there will be strong competition among the development community to be selected as the private partner. If the market demand is weak, the public partner will have to present a forceful package describing how the public partner will provide many of the features described in the Stainback Five-Part Finance and Development Approach to the selected developer.

Sense of Competition

Many public/private development opportunities are high-profile developments. These projects are often pivotal for the redevelopment of a city or district. Therefore, these projects receive an inordinate amount of attention among members of the community and the media. Developers want to have a positive impact on their community as well as other cities. Most developers want to do well and do good, so if they have the opportunity to achieve those objectives, they will actively compete to be selected. But for many developers, if they perceive that the level of competition is weak, they will more than likely not put forth as much effort as if they sense that there is a heated competition for a project.

Desirability of the Site

Many project sites for public/private development projects are properties that have never been available for commercial development, for example, U.S. Post Office buildings in large cities. Fifty to 100 years ago, these facilities were an integral part of the heart of the downtown. While these facilities are often civic and/or historic landmarks, they have long outlived their effective use. Post office buildings no longer have to be located on real estate, which is now highly valued. Therefore, the desirability of these sites for commercial development is extremely high.

Level of Importance of the Opportunity for Each Developer

Developers have varying reasons to pursue development opportunities. They range from wanting to enter a new market to being recognized by the community for developing one of the city's finest buildings. If the public/private development opportunity provides the developer the opportunity to achieve that objective, then the developer will expend the level of effort and investment required to be awarded the project.

Level of Importance to Establish a Long-Term Relationship with the Public Partner

Some developers, prior to receiving an RFQ or RFP, have targeted a public partner as an entity with which they want to establish a long-term relationship. More than likely, the developer believes this entity will generate recurring development opportunities. There is a direct correlation between the number of future opportunities and the level of importance of the public partner.

Projected Return on Investment

Most developers can quickly assess the potential upside from a development opportunity. If they perceive that that return on investment can be achieved with minimal risk and in a reasonable amount of time, they will put forth a very competitive effort to be selected by the public partner.

Estimated Likelihood to Be Selected

The odds of being selected must be reasonable or developers will not invest the time and money to compete. They are at risk for their entire investment. If they come in second, they still lose everything. This is why the RFQ phase of the developer solicitation process is so important. Candidate developers must have a sense that they are part of a limited field of candidates or they are unlikely to invest the often enormous amount of time and money required to be competitive.

A STEP-BY-STEP DESCRIPTION OF THE RFP PROCESS USING THE TWO-STEP RFQ/RFP PROCESS

Step 1: Develop the RFP

The RFP should achieve several purposes using the 10 components shown in Exhibit 8.4.

The time required to structure and write a well-written and organized RFP with supporting graphics can range from three to four weeks. Working with an experienced consultant could reduce the time frame to less than three weeks.

Government and university officials should recognize that the RFP is as much a marketing piece as it is a technical document. The RFP should provide developers a strong basis to invest the time and resources required to submit a competitive proposal. Clearly, the proposal effort and cost for developers to respond to an RFP is far greater than responding to an RFQ.

Component 1: Serve as an official announcement of the short-listed developers.   After completing the RFQ process of Approach Two of the two-step RFQ/RFP process, the public sponsor has systematically and objectively selected no more than five development teams to proceed to the technical RFP. Each short-listed developer team now has some comfort that the public partner is willing to form a public/private partnership with one of the five qualified teams. Now the field of developers vying for the project has been reduced to five or less. Each developer has reduced his or her risk of being selected to one in five, or 20 percent. Each developer should feel more comfort-

Exhibit 8.4   Ten Components Necessary in the Development of an RFP

Component 1:	Serve as an official announcement of the short-listed developers.
Component 2:	Continue to convey the basis for the remaining developers to pursue the development opportunity. "Sell" the development opportunity to the marketplace. Share any market analysis completed.
Component 3:	Describe the organization of the public participants.
Component 4:	Share any design work completed to date.
Component 5:	Relay how the public partner(s) will participate in the predevelopment, development, and operational phases.
Component 6:	Describe the submission requirements.
Component 7:	Describe the expectations of the private partner.
Component 8:	Describe the developer selection process.
Component 9:	Describe the evaluation criteria.
Component 10:	Describe the applicable regulations and disclaimers.

able to make the required commitment of time and money to submit a competitive technical proposal. But the public partner should recognize that one or more developers may complete more research and analysis of the opportunity and decide not to proceed to the RFP stage.

Component 2: The RFP should continue to sell the development opportunity. There may be instances in which one or more short-listed developers may have second thoughts about proceeding to the RFP stage of the solicitation process. Consequently, the project sponsor should use the RFP to continue to sell the opportunity as a worthwhile development project to pursue. The public partner should use the RFP to provide developers with an overview of the development opportunity, addressing real estate issues, market highlights, important legislation passed, regulatory hurdles, if any, and the vision for the project. The RFP can also be used to summarize any special legislation passed that facilitates action for this project opportunity. This will demonstrate to developer candidates the level of effort expended by the public partner to be a responsible member of the public/private partnership.

The RFP should be used as a means to amplify the strong market demand for the proposed building uses. Most developers realize that without an objective third party verifying a strong demand for the proposed project, there will be few entities willing to invest in the project.

The public partner should use the RFP as a forum to announce their willingness to structure a fair and reasonable sharing of costs, risks, and responsibilities. In other words, they are prepared to structure a genuine public/private partnership. One of the ways the public partner can demonstrate their commitment to the proposed project is to summarize the applicable capital improvements implemented in recent years, improvements under construction, and improvements proposed in the future. Equally important to investments in capital improvements, the public partner should describe the completed and proposed public facilities directly related to the subject public/private development opportunity.

One of the more important selling points the public partner should convey to developers is the public sponsor's vision for the project. The vision should be described in text, but more importantly, with illustrative color sketches and master plans. If development guidelines have been prepared for the project and/or its immediate context, this too should be shared with developers. If a developer believes the public partner is a strong advocate of the project, but the local community is against it, the developer may not be willing to fight those battles. Consequently, the public partner should use the RFP to describe the consensus among the public entity or entities sponsoring the project and the local merchants—ideally, the consensus among key business and civic leaders.

The bottom line is that the introductory section(s) of the RFP should present a powerful basis for the candidate developers to prepare a highly competitive technical proposal.

Component 3: Describe the organization of the public participants. The RFP stage is the time for the project sponsor to describe the government entity or entities with whom the selected developer will form a partnership. The public partner should describe how the sponsoring entity and other key public participants are organized and the key individuals participating in the predevelopment process. The primary public partner should reveal the strengths and weaknesses of each entity's ability to share the costs, risks, responsibilities, and economic return of the subject project with the developer.

The public partner should also reveal to developer candidates any potential problems in structuring and implementing the project. For example, if there are project approvals that have not been obtained at this point, the public partner should identify each approval and briefly describe both the procedure to obtain the approval and the entities issuing the approvals. All environmental problems with the site should be identified, because remediation costs can be significant. If there are government or private civic groups that are not supportive of the project, these entities should also be revealed to the candidate developers. The developers need to know these hurdles in order to estimate the time required to obtain the subject approvals.

In some instances, the success or failure of a public/private development project can partially hinge upon the completion of one or more capital improvements or nearby civic facility. If these capital improvements or civic facilities are not funded and/or there are anticipated delays, the public partner should provide developers with a realistic prognosis of when these public projects will be completed.

Most developers in responding to an RFP will develop alternative public/private finance and development plans as well as alternative ownership scenarios. If there are limitations for any of the public participants to take an ownership position or provide capital investment or be contractually obligated for a long-term lease, the RFP should clarify this point. Revealing this type of information is only fair to the candidate developers *prior* to making the investment required to prepare a competitive proposal.

Component 4: Share any design work completed to date.   For major public/private development projects, the public entity sponsoring the project should, at a minimum, have completed basic design concepts prior to issuing the RFP. A good public partner should have also completed illustrations that explain not only the plan for the proposed development but also its immediate context. These illustrations should include an urban design plan for the project site and its context. This urban design plan will explain to the developer how the proposed project interrelates to existing major civic facilities, activity generators, and infrastructure projects. Ideally, the public partner should also provide perspective sketches of the proposed development, the desired public spaces, and key pedestrian walkways and amenities.

In addition to visually describing the character of the desired buildings and spaces, the public partner should provide explanatory diagrams that illustrate development factors, such as recently implemented and proposed capital improvements, local and regional vehicular access, and local and regional transportation systems. The public partner should also provide technical information about the project site. This technical information should include land area, right-of-ways, easements, development rights, and required setbacks.

On a more detailed level, the public partner should provide preliminary elevations and sections of the proposed building and/or basic design guidelines for height and massing of the building. Included in this level of detailed information should be an implementation phasing plan for the proposed project, related infrastructure, and demolition, if applicable. It is also appropriate for public partners to provide candidate developers with the results of soil tests and environmental studies.

Component 5: Relay how the public partner(s) will participate in the predevelopment, development, and operational phases. This is a difficult component of the RFP to complete. On the one hand, the public partner must demonstrate to potential private partners how action will be facilitated on the finance, design, development, and approval fronts. On the other hand, the public partner does not want to offer a higher level of assistance than is believed to be required to successfully structure a public/private partnership.

At the RFP stage, the public partner is working with only three to five development teams. This is the time to reveal, at least in concept, how they, and possibly other government entities, will share the costs, risks, and responsibilities required to proceed to the next step of the predevelopment phase. For example, the public partner will better understand what is expected of them after the finance model is completed and the candidate developers have submitted an initial public/private finance and development plan. This assumes that the public partner has *not* completed the Stainback Five-Part Finance and Development Approach.

The RFP should begin to outline how the public partner can assist the private partner. This outline does not require specific actions to be described or any commitments by the public partner. The public partner needs to relay, in concept, how they will assist the selected developer to finance, design, develop, construct, and operate the subject development. Two major types of actions a public partner can take to assist the selected developer are noncapital and capital investments and collaborative support. On the capital investment side, the public partner can cover the cost of demolishing any existing buildings on the site and/or the cost of environmental remediation, and provide direct loans, loan guarantees, and/or credit enhancements when external financing is not adequate to make the project financially feasible. Another type of capital investment is the full or partial utilization of the tax increment generated by the project. Applicable taxes vary from government entity to government entity, but taxes such as sales tax and real estate tax are typically used. In many instances, the use of these two types of taxes can be controversial; therefore, it may be more palatable to government officials and the voters to invest tax revenue generated by tourists, and not the residents of the jurisdiction. These taxes include car rental tax and hotel occupancy tax. The concept behind using tax increment financing should be palatable to government officials and voters, because the tax revenue generated by the project would not occur if the project was not implemented. For most public/private development projects, the tax revenue invested by the public partner is limited to the initial ramp-up years of the project, which could extend from three to ten years. After that, the public partners capture the tax revenue generated over the life of the project, which could be 45 to 50 years or more.

On the collaborative support side, public partners can assist developers on several fronts, such as streamlining the design, development, and construction approval processes; securing entitlements; and optimizing available investment, development, and operational incentives. Another way public partners can assist the selected developer is to provide a moratorium on any new development in the immediate area that will compete with the subject development. The primary public partner should also assign a full-time project manager to represent the public partner(s). This project manager will serve as a single point of responsibility for the public partner(s). This action alone could save the developer a tremendous amount of time and effort throughout the predevelopment process.

On the noncapital investment side, the public partner can provide the project site, additional development rights, and provisions to reduce the number and/or type of parking spaces required by zoning.

In summary, the public partner(s) must convey to the candidate developers that their proposed partnership will be a two-way street—not a partnership whereby the developer incurs all of the costs, risks, and responsibilities. Of course, if the public partner provides some form of assistance, they should expect a share of the gross or net income from the project, or an economic return after the developer receives a negotiated preferred return. The public partner needs to also explain their role and responsibilities during the design and construction phases, as well as their anticipated role once the project is operational.

Component 6: Describe the submission requirements.　An excellent RFP for a major public/private development will require the short-listed developer to describe, in text and graphics, the following:

- The comprehensive team
- The developer's vision of the project
- The estimated total development budget
- The proposed public/private finance plan
- The proposed public/private deal structure
- A development management plan
- A preliminary predevelopment and development schedule
- A preliminary operations program

The comprehensive team.　The developer submittal, in response to the RFQ, has already provided a large amount of information on the qualifications of the team. The primary objective in the technical submittal for the RFP is to provide commitments to use particular individuals and how the team will work together to deliver the project. These include:

- The final comprehensive team to finance, design, develop, and operate the proposed public/private development project

- The organization and interrelationships among the team members—typically, a project team organization chart is part of the developer's submittal
- Identification of the members of the team: development manager, lead designer, lead construction manager, lead investor or investment analyst, and so forth

The developer's vision of the project. In response to the RFP, a developer may arrange for the architect and/or urban designer to develop the following, to illustrate the vision proposed by the developer:

- A detailed description of the land and building program, including parking requirements
- An illustrative master plan
- Plans of key levels of the building—the level of detail is typically equivalent to schematic design (SD) in the architecture industry
- Conceptual building elevation(s) and section(s) illustrating the architectural character and three-dimensional interrelationship of the major spaces can be quite revealing
- Perspective sketches and/or axonometric drawings illustrating the desired pedestrian environment of the particularly important interior and/or exterior spaces
- Use the master plan to illustrate the proposed implementation-phasing plan, ideally tied directly to the projected market demand for the proposed building uses
- Depending on the importance of the project, the public partner may require that the developer provide an outline of the building specifications, which will help the public partner obtain insights into the developer's proposed quality of building materials, equipment, and systems

The estimated total development budget. It is very important for the developer to provide a basic project budget. A basic budget should include all of the major hard and soft costs required to finance, design, develop, and construct the proposed project.

A preliminary total development budget should include 12 to 15 line items, such as:

- Construction costs
- Site preparation cost
- Land cost
- Architectural/Engineering fees
- Fees for other consultants
- Development management fees
- Interest cost during construction
- Fees for obtaining equity and debt
- Reserve funds, if any

Government and university officials should know that soft costs such as fees and interest can add 25 to 40 percent to the estimated hard cost, such as construction costs. Public officials should require candidate developers to submit a total development budget so that there are no surprises as to the actual cost to finance and develop the proposed project.

The proposed public/private finance plan. One of the most important parts of the developer proposal is the detailed description of the proposed public/private finance plan. A good public/private finance plan will address issues such as:

- Investment requirements of the key public and private project participants
- The entity or entities responsible for finance, design, development, and operation of the project once it is completed
- The responsibilities of major public and private participants who are not partners or owners of the project. For example, if the project is sponsored by a city government entity, there may be a role for the county, state, and possibly federal agencies. On the private side, there may be an ownership and/or investment role for the contractor and/or operator. Their roles must be described in detail.

A development management plan. The development management plan will describe the proposed team and methodology for the development team to implement the proposed public/private finance, design, development, construction, and tenanting plan. The candidate developer should identify the specific individuals who will implement the project. The focus will be on the development manager or project manager and how he or she will interact with the public partner(s), key citizen group(s), the media, the development team, and the officer(s) of the development company.

The plan will also address the procedure to secure the required private equity and debt and the likely sources of financing, as well as how the developer will interact with the architect, engineer, contractor, and operator.

Depending on whether the subject project is a public facility or a commercial development, the developer should explain the process to secure leasing commitments from tenants, concurrently addressing the proposed tenant mix and the corresponding building area for each type of tenant. This plan should also address the parking requirements for each tenant and the parking fee arrangements.

The developer should summarize how he or she intends to deliver the quality of building proposed in the proposal, as well as how the day-to-day management of issues will be executed, such as:

- Contract administration
- Scheduling
- Cost control
- Interaction with the public partner(s)
- Obtaining project approvals
- Construction oversight

A preliminary predevelopment and development schedule. Scheduling is often an important component of a public/private development project, because the project needs to open on a certain date. This could be due to a stipulation in the lease, a stipulation in the special legislation requirements for the project, or the fact that in order to proceed with other related developments, this project must be completed by a specific month or season if weather is an issue. Therefore, the graphic illustration of the time required to complete the predevelopment or preconstruction phase, construction, and the preopening activities could be pivotal to the success of that project.

The developer should prepare a month-by-month schedule illustrating the estimated time required to complete the major tasks included in most predevelopment processes. For example, the time required to:

- Complete the three phases of architectural drawings: SD, design development (DD), and construction drawings (CD).
- Secure equity and debt financing for both the private and public partner.
- Obtain key design and environmental approvals.
- Refine the finance model.
- Negotiate the public/private partnership.
- Negotiate contracts with the architect(s), engineer(s), contractor, consultants, and the operator.
- Obtain preliminary leasing commitments from key tenants.
- Prepare the total development budget.

This schedule should illustrate the interrelationships of the tasks and also serve as a management tool to determine when public and private partners should begin and complete key tasks.

A preliminary operations program. Developers should provide their public partner with a conceptual idea of who and how they intend to operate and manage the proposed building once it is completed. The program should include preopening activities and major provisions of an operations and management program. The program should also describe the proposed physical environment to be created, especially the public spaces, the level of security to be provided, and the intended standards of maintenance.

Component 7: Describe the expectations of the private partner. The primary purpose of this section of the RFP is to describe what the public partner expects the private partner to be responsible for during the predevelopment and development phases of the project, as well as the responsibilities once the project is open. This will provide direction for the candidate developers to assemble their team. For example, the public partner should specify whether the private developer is responsible for:

- Market demand study
- Land and building program
- Building design
- Master plan
- Economic impact study
- Structuring and obtaining the required public and/or private financing
- Operations
- Maintenance of either the building and/or the public spaces
- Securing tenants for space not occupied by the public partner
- Building consensus among selected constituents to proceed with the project
- Obtaining design and construction approvals
- Purchasing the project site
- Assembling the land parcels included in the project site
- Remediation of environmental problems, if any
- Taking the lead to prepare the lease agreements and development and/or operational agreement
- Demolition of any existing buildings on the site
- Site preparation
- Traffic improvements

If the private developer is responsible for all of the tasks described above, he or she would have to incorporate the following specialists onto his or her team:

- Urban designer
- Architect
- Market analyst
- Investment banker
- Real estate attorney
- Operator specializing in the subject building type
- Construction company
- Environmental planner and/or engineer
- Traffic planner
- Consultant who specializes in community outreach

If this is in fact the responsibility of the candidate developers, they will be forced to hire all of these specialists in order to be competitive. The fees for this team could easily total several hundreds of thousands of dollars. From the developer's perspective, this investment is at a high risk if he or she is one of five developers short-listed. Again from the perspective of the developer, the odds of being selected is at best 20 percent.

In order to reduce their proposed costs, many developers will request that their consultants provide services on either a wholly or partly speculative basis. An alternative to this arrangement is for consultants to provide their services on the basis of a success fee. In other words, they are only paid all or a major portion of their fee if the development team is selected. Usually, under either scenario, any project-related expenses incurred by the consultant are fully covered by the developer.

Component 8: Describe the developer selection process. The primary purpose of this section of the RFP is to give the candidate developers insight into what is ahead for them before they are ranked number one and are able to work one-on-one with the public partner. This section of the RFP should include most if not all of the following items:

- The number and types of professionals responsible for evaluating the developer proposals. For example, are the evaluators elected government officials, government administrators, staff members, members of an important citizens group, and/or a consultant?
- A schedule of milestone events. For example, approximate time slots should be provided for activities such as deadline for submitting proposals, presentations or interviews of each developer, deadline for submitting questions, preproposal conference, announcement of developer rankings, and announcement of the developer ranked number one.

Component 9: Describe the evaluation criteria. The selection committee will evaluate each response to the RFP and should complete research on the developer's performance on similar projects and the financial capacity of each bidder. This section of the RFP should include a list of the evaluation criteria, such as:

- The developer's experience with similar building types
- Experience with public/private developments, especially in the last three to five years
- Ability of team members to fulfill their stated roles on the development team
- Reported integrity of the developer in prior similar negotiations
- Ability to optimize private participation in the subject project
- Demonstration of structuring and obtaining creative financing
- Responsiveness of the proposed development concept in relation to the public partner's stated objectives
- Level of creativity in responding to the opportunity
- The recent history of key team members working together
- Financial relationships and sources
- Project management of complex development projects
- Proposed contingent and noncontingent economic return for the public partner

- The specific individuals assigned to work with the public partner
- References
- *Optional:* Provide a sense of the level of importance of each criterion, or specify the specific weighting of each criterion. The latter is very helpful for the candidate developers to tailor their proposals, but this level of specificity can be a problem if any of the developers file a protest, because the numerical ranking of the developer proposals will come under scrutiny. One way to avoid this problem is to simply state that one of the evaluation criteria is "other factors deemed relevant by the selection committee."

Component 10: Describe the applicable regulations and disclaimers. This is the public partner's opportunity to specify the conditions and limitations of the RFP. This section of the RFP should include items such as:

- This RFP does not represent a commitment or offer by the public partner to enter into an agreement with a respondent or to pay any costs incurred in the preparation of a response to this RFP.
- The timely responses and any information made a part of the responses will not be returned to the sender.
- The RFP and the selected team's response to this RFP may, by reference, become a part of any formal agreement between the respondent and the public partner resulting from this solicitation.
- Other than as specifically provided in this RFP, respondents are prohibited from contacting any member of the RFP review team concerning this project or response to this RFP and shall be subject to disqualification if they do.
- The respondent shall not offer any gratuities or anything of monetary value to any official or employee of the public partner or any member of the RFP review team for the purpose of influencing consideration of a response to this RFP.
- The respondent shall not collude in any manner or engage in any practices with any other respondent(s), which may restrict or eliminate competition or otherwise restrain trade. Violations of this instruction may cause the public partner to reject the respondent's submittal. This prohibition is not intended to preclude joint ventures or subcontracts.
- All response submitted must be the original work product of the respondent and its consultants. The copying, paraphrasing, or other use of substantial portions of the work product of another respondent is not permitted. Failure to adhere to this instruction may cause the public partner to reject the response.
- The public partner has sole discretion and reserves the right to reject any and all responses received with respect to this RFP and to cancel the RFP at any time prior to entering into a formal agreement. The public partner reserves the right to request additional information or clarification of information provided in the response without changing the terms of the RFP.

- Documents that developers submit as a part of their response will become public records and therefore will be subject to public disclosure.
- *Optional:* Nonexclusivity. The public partner wishes to encourage the best combination of potential development teams. With this objective in mind, all members of a responding team, with the exception of the lead firm, may be listed as development team members on a maximum of three different submittals. The lead development firm will be considered in only one submittal. The public partner reserves the right to ask a lead firm to invite another firm to join their team and incorporate them into their development concept if that particular firm has demonstrated particular expertise in the services they propose to provide.

Step 2: Review and Approve the RFP

Once the internal group within the public partner entity or entities, or the consultant, completes a draft of the RFP, it should be reviewed by key participants involved in the developer selection process and other selected members of the participating public partner entities. This step should require only one to two weeks.

Step 3: Establish and Document the Developer Evaluation Criteria

The evaluation criteria for the RFP will be significantly different from the criteria used for the RFQ. In general, the criteria will be much more penetrating and highly technical. Deciding on the evaluation criteria for the RFP stage is very important because, besides the final interview, this is the last opportunity to evaluate the developer prior to selection of the developer with which the public partner will enter into negotiations. With the exception of dismissing the developer ranked number one during the negotiation phase and proceeding to the developer ranked number two, this is the last opportunity to determine which developer is most advantageous for the public partner.

Each public/private development is different. Each public partner entity(s) has different objectives; consequently, the criteria to evaluate developers will be different in each instance. The following criteria should be viewed as the basic or core criteria to be used in evaluating developer proposals in response to an RFP. The basic criteria to evaluate developer proposals in response to an RFP that is part of a two-step RFQ/RFP process have been organized into 11 categories and are shown in Exhibit 8.5.

Step 4: Produce and Issue the RFP

The public partner and/or their consultant need to prepare a detailed draft of the RFP document. This draft should include all of the graphics required to support the text. The most effective approach to produce the final RFP is to prepare a mock-up of the final.

Exhibit 8.5   The Categories of Criteria to Evaluate
Developer Proposals in Response to RFP

- Team
- Building program
- Design
- Development
- Total development budget
- Public/Private finance plan
- Level of commitments (financing, tenants, and operators)
- Public/Private deal structure
- Development schedule
- Operations and property management
- Subjective criteria

This document should incorporate every aspect of the solicitation, so that it can be turned over to a graphics and/or copy company, which will be responsible for producing the final draft for review. The time required to complete this task is dependent on the level of sophistication desired for the presentation of the RFP. At this point in the developer solicitation process, the public partner is beyond "selling" the development opportunity to candidate developers, so the RFP could be a simple black-and-white unbound document. The estimated range of time to complete Step 4 should be two to three weeks or less. This step should be completed concurrently with earlier steps.

Step 5: Allow Developers to Respond to the RFP and Answer Questions

For a major public/private development project with an estimated construction cost greater than $50 million, developers should be given a minimum of four weeks to prepare their proposal. The larger and more complex the project, the more time short-listed developers should be given to prepare their proposal. The maximum time allowed should be eight weeks.

All questions and requested clarifications by developers should be submitted in writing to the public partner. Ideally, developers should be working with a proposal manager who is serving as the single point of responsibility for the public partner. Developers should be given only two to three weeks to submit their questions. All responses by the public partner will be compiled and returned to all of the short-listed developers by a specified date.

Step 6: Evaluate Developer Proposals

As described in earlier sections, government, university, and school district officials should consider hiring a consultant who has extensive experience managing the developer solicitation process. This allows the public partner to avoid an adversarial relationship with the candidate developers, one of which the public partner will have to negotiate a development agreement. More importantly, the consultant will serve as an objective third party to the public partner and the developer. An outside consultant will also help to depoliticize the developer selection process.

It is highly recommended that the consultant and/or the public partner continue to use a systematic approach in the evaluation of developer proposals. The consultant should be urged to use the developer evaluation matrix, described in Step 8 of the RFQ section of this chapter. In addition to the matrix of information on each proposal, the consultant and/or public partner should also be subjective in their evaluations. For example, the public partner should assess the enthusiasm of each developer to win the project. Assess the level of creativity exhibited by each developer. This type of evaluation can be just as important as the objective and systematic analysis of the developer's finance plan or deal structure. The time to complete this step will be dependent on the level of complexity and scope of the development opportunity, but should be in the range of two to three weeks.

Step 7: Develop Questions for Each Developer Interview

At this point in the developer evaluation process, it is time to meet key members of the entire development team. The procedure to complete the interviews will be described in Step 8. Prior to the actual interviews, public partners and their consultants should develop questions specifically tailored to each developer and questions that may apply to all of the short-listed developers. Having completed Step 6, the public partner and the consultant have completed a detailed analysis of each proposal, so there is a solid foundation to develop penetrating questions to each development team. In addition to asking pointed questions of each development team, the interview should be designed to clarify proposed deal points, detailed data, estimates, assumptions, and projections.

The public partner should invest the amount of time required to develop questions for the different teams, because not only will the results help to select the most advantageous proposal, it will demonstrate to each developer that their future public partner has its act together. The time required to develop questions for each of the short-listed teams depends on the number of short-listed teams and the thoroughness of the developer proposals. Public partners should allow less than one week to prepare questions for each team. To a certain extent, this task can be completed concurrently with Step 6.

Step 8: Arrange and Complete Developer Interviews

The interviews with the short-listed developers are an opportunity for the public partner and their consultants to achieve the following objectives:

- Continue to sell the development opportunity to each development team.
- Assess the chemistry between the public partner and key members of the development team.
- Determine how key members of each team respond to the questions posed by the public partner. In other words, see how they "think on their feet."
- Assess the level of enthusiasm and desire to structure and implement a public/private partnership and deliver the project that the public partner has envisioned.

The public partner or their consultant needs to arrange for the five development teams to be interviewed in one or two days. Developers will want to know the following:

- What the public partner wants the development team to focus on during their presentation
- Who will represent the public partner
- Who will be included as members of the public partner selection committee
- The basic layout of the room
- What presentation equipment is available
- How much time will be allocated for presentation and the question and answer session

Developer interviews are usually scheduled in one or two days in order to accommodate the schedule constraints of members of the public partner. The public partner should allow approximately two weeks to complete Step 8. Most of the two weeks will be consumed by the time required to correspond with each developer. The actual interviews themselves should require only one to two days.

Step 9: Review Results of Evaluation and Interviews with the Appropriate Government or University Entities

The primary purpose of Step 9 is to share the assessment of each developer proposal and corresponding interview with key members of the public partner entity or entities. The format for sharing the results of the analysis of each proposal and interview is typically a combination of the analysis and text describing the subjective observations of the public partner and the consultant. It is highly recommended that the evaluation report include an executive summary.

Assuming that a public partner has hired an experienced consultant, the time required to complete Step 9 should be in the range of one to two weeks or less. Any delays will be the result of tracking down the often wide array of members of the public partner entity or entities and/or checking each developer's references.

Step 10: Rank the Top Three Developers

It is highly recommended that public partners and their consultants rank the top three teams and not select a single development team. The basis for that recommendation is that by ranking the top three developers, the public partner maintains a sense of competition throughout the negotiation process. The number one developer understands that if he or she cannot successfully negotiate a development agreement, the public partner has the right to terminate negotiations and begin negotiations with the developer ranked second. In addition, the public partner may also want to use this sense of competition to ensure that negotiations are completed in a timely fashion. For example, the developer ranked number one should be informed upon selection that he or she has only 90 to 180 days to structure a public/private partnership that is satisfactory to both parties. Clearly, the public partner has the option to extend the time frame, if appropriate. Of course, this is a two-way street, because the public partner must be responsive to the selected developer to maintain the desired schedule.

An interesting alternative to ranking the top three developers and negotiating with the number one developer is for the public partner to select two developer finalists and concurrently negotiate with both. Under this scenario, the public partner maintains a strong sense of competition among the developers and can base the selection of the developer on the negotiated deal structure that is most advantageous to the public partner. This may be the most advantageous method to select a developer for three reasons. First, the public partner has the time to get to know their private partner. Second, each developer is under enormous pressure to structure and negotiate a public/private finance and development plan that is satisfactory to both parties. Third, working concurrently could save a tremendous amount of time, especially when compared to the methodology whereby the top three developers are ranked and negotiations with the developer ranked number one did not produce a successful partnership.

Public officials should realize that there are an increasing number of developers who will not enter into negotiations if the public partner is concurrently negotiating with another developer. Their argument is valid in that they claim the public partner will use the results of their negotiations with one developer against the other in order to better position himself or herself.

The time required to complete Step 10 should be less than one week, assuming this does not include any form of negotiations.

Step 11: Announce the Selected Developer(s)

The announcement of the selected developer(s) is the culmination of a tremendous amount of time and money spent by both the public and private partner, so it should be executed with relative fanfare and enthusiasm. Depending on the scope of the public/private development project, the public partner could arrange for a press con-

Exhibit 8.6 Estimated Schedule to Complete the 11-Step RFP Process

	Schedule (weeks)
Step 1: Develop the RFP	1–2
Step 2: Review and approve the RFP	2–3
Step 3: Establish and document the developer evaluation criteria	2–3
Step 4: Produce and issue the RFP	2–3
Step 5: Allow developers to respond to the RFP and answer questions	6–8
Step 6: Evaluate developer proposals	2–3
Step 7: Develop questions for each developer interview	1
Step 8: Arrange and complete interview of short-listed developers	1–2
Step 9: Review results of evaluation and interviews with key members of the public partner(s)	1–2
Step 10: Rank the top three developers	1
Step 11: Announce the selected developer(s)	1
TOTAL:	18–26 weeks (4.5 to 6.5 months)

ference as the forum to announce the selected developer. At a minimum, the public partner should prepare a press release to be issued to local, regional, and possibly national publications.

The total time required to complete the typical developer RFP process should be in the range of 18 to 26 weeks, or four and one-half months to six and one-half months (see Exhibit 8.6). This estimated time frame can be reduced by completing some of the steps concurrently. For example, Steps 2 and 3 can be completed concurrently. Steps 6 and 7 can also be completed concurrently, and finally, Steps 10 and 11 can be completed in one week if so desired. By completing these steps concurrently, the total amount of time required to complete the developer RFP process can be in the range of 15 to 22 weeks or less than four months to five and one-half months.

APPROACH THREE: THE SINGLE-STEP RFP PROCESS

Up until the last several years, most government, university, and school district officials used the single-step RFP process and issued an RFP without an RFQ. From the perspective of a developer, this may be the most disliked developer solicitation approach, because this single-step process requires a developer to incur the cost and time to prepare a competitive proposal when he or she is potentially one among a large number of developer candidates. The developer has no idea how many developers will submit proposals, nor does the developer know the caliber of his or her competitors. The public partner is asking developer candidates to blindly invest a substantial amount of time and money to prepare a highly detailed and technical response to an RFP. The field of developer candidates could include as many as 15 to 35 development companies. Again, that means each developer is facing enormous odds to be selected. In fact, odds of 1 in 15 or 1 in 35 are equal to 6.7 to 2.9 percent.

If a public partner is facing time constraints, they may elect to use the single-step RFP process. If a public partner issues only an RFP, it is highly recommended that they consider using Approach Four. Using Approach Four, the number of developers receiving the RFP is dramatically reduced to 5 or 7 from the 15 to 35 developers receiving an RFP under Approach Three.

APPROACH FOUR: THE PREQUALIFIED DEVELOPER RFP PROCESS

The logic behind using this approach is simple. The concept is to eliminate the concern developers have with Approach Three, which is that most developers do not want to incur the tremendous amount of time and expense of preparing a highly technical proposal in response to an RFP when they are among a large field of competing developers. Approach Four solves that problem by cutting the field of candidate developers to receive an RFP from 15 or more down to 5. For the public partner, the key to Approach Four is the ability to identify the most appropriate developers for the subject project. If the public partner does not know the development industry well enough to identify five to seven developers who specialize in the proposed type of building, they may want to hire a consultant who specializes in public/private development.

In summary, under Approach Four, the public partner would not issue an RFQ but would issue an RFP to a predetermined list of five to seven developers who specialize in the proposed building type(s) and/or have the financial capacity to obtain the required equity and debt. Once the prequalified developers realize the field of candidates has been limited to five or seven, they will be willing to invest the time and money required to prepare a competitive technical proposal.

APPROACH FIVE: THE SOLE-SOURCE DEVELOPER TECHNIQUE

There will be instances in which a public partner intimately knows or has established a working relationship with a developer so that they feel comfortable working with that developer on a sole-source basis. The public partner should be aware that if they use Approach Five, there may be potential problems, such as a "backlash" from other local developers who feel they are equally qualified; other members of the public partner entity may not have the same level of comfort with the sole-source developer; the local community and media may not like the idea of not creating a competitive environment among the development community; and the media may also question the basis for selecting the sole-source developer.

Clearly, one of the great advantages of Approach Five is the substantial amount of time and expense saved by avoiding the developer RFQ/RFP process. From the perspective of the sole-source developer, Approach Five is the most attractive of the five approaches. Again, there is a significant savings of time and expense if one has the ability to execute a sole-source development opportunity.

APPROACH SIX: THE RFQ/NEGOTIATION METHOD

Maybe the most efficient and effective method of the six methods to solicit developers and negotiate a development agreement is the RFQ/negotiation method. By using this method, the public partner can avoid the lengthy developer RFP process and reduce the amount of time to select a developer by more than 50 percent. The development community greatly appreciates this method because it saves valuable time and significantly reduces predevelopment costs. The public partner should feel comfortable with this method of solicitation, because while it accelerates the developer selection process, the RFQ process ensures that the developer was selected using a highly competitive process. More importantly, this method forges a strong sense of collaboration between the public and private partners. Once the developer has been qualified through the RFQ process, the two parties begin to work together to complete many of the initial fourteen steps included in the public/private finance and development process developed by the author and described in Chapter 4. Working side by side to structure alternative public/private finance plans and jointly determining the most effective ownership and investment scenarios is the best of all worlds for the public/private partnership. The public partner and the developer also jointly complete the other steps included in the process; consequently, the public partner has the opportunity to learn from the developer and the team assembled for the project and vice versa. This method embodies the truest form of partnering between the public and private partners, and can lead to the fairest allocation of costs, risks, responsibilities, and economic return insuring a successful transaction.

Chapter 9

The Precarious Future of Public/Private Development Partnerships

Government, university, and school district officials began using the public/private finance and development approach with frequency in the early 1980s. At that point in time, only a small number of progressive governments were issuing requests for proposal (RFPs) soliciting private investment and expertise to finance, design, develop, and construct government facilities and commercial developments. In the late 1980s and early 1990s, government entities incrementally increased the use of the public/private partnership approach, but while the privatization of services and selling government-owned companies made substantial progress, the public/private real estate industry was experiencing much slower growth.

It was not until 1993 that the public/private development market began to show significant growth. The market has experienced nearly exponential growth over the last seven years. The estimated annual construction volume of public/private development projects in 1999 was approximately $50 billion. At this point in the evolution of the public/private real estate market, the future looks very bright but there are looming problems.

The advantages and disadvantages of the public/private partnership approach to realize needed public facilities and commercial development were described in Chapter 3, but the basis for concern in the future is significant and problems do exist. The predevelopment process for many if not most public/private development projects requires far too much time when compared to the process required for traditional private developments. Many government and university officials are not ready to structure and negotiate public/private development partnerships. They jump from project conceptualization (Step 1) to issuing a developer request for qualifications (RFQ) or RFP (Step 13). The logic behind the thinking of public officials is that they need a building or a building renovation to be completed, so they will offer the opportunity to the private developer community because that is what they do best. By jumping from Step 1 to Step 13, government and university officials are not prepared—they select a developer and begin negotiations without knowing several criti-cally important points, such as:

- What does an objective third party believe is the market demand for the subject building uses?
- What are the total hard and soft costs required to finance, design, develop, and construct the subject building?
- Are the assumptions in the developer's finance model for the subject project ap-propriate for the marketplace and the proposed project?
- What is the level of risk for private equity investor(s), issuers of private debt, and/or issuers of public debt?
- What is the most advantageous ownership and investment position for the spon-soring government or university entity? Has the ownership and investment been structured to primarily benefit the private partner?
- Are there alternative public/private deal structures that are more advantageous to both the public and private partners?
- If there is projected cash flow shortfall in the early years—sometimes called ramp-up years of the project—has anyone applied the multitude of creative finance and development techniques available to reduce development costs and enhance cash flow?
- If there is more than one building use included in the subject project, has anyone explored the financial feasibility of "bundling" the project or building use with weak market demand with the project(s) that appear to generate a strong market demand?

When preparing solicitations, government and university officials, in conjunc-tion with their consultants, are increasing restrictions and the requirements of the private sector, while they should make every effort to facilitate creativity and problem solving by the private sector. In order to win competitive developer RFPs, some private developers, especially those that have been short-listed from a large field to three to five developers, are making promises to government and university officials that they cannot keep. If the sponsoring government or university does not recognize that the promise is not financially feasible, the project is awarded to possibly the wrong developer. This problem is further compounding the potential problems in the future of the public/private partnership industry because the losing developer be-comes quickly disenchanted with the developer RFP process and therefore will shy away from future public/private development opportunities.

In parallel with the lengthy time required to complete the process from project conceptualization (Step 1 of the public/private finance and development process) to applying signatures to the negotiated development agreement (Step 14) is the cost of completing the multitude of studies, designs, meetings, presentations, and so on.

Up until Step 14 of the public/private finance and development process, the selected developer remains at risk. Typically, until the developer successfully negotiates a public/private partnership agreement, he or she can be asked to step aside on grounds that it does not appear that a fair and reasonable deal can be negotiated. The government official has the ability to dismiss the developer ranked number one and begin negotiations with the second-ranked developer. This represents high risk for a developer. For a large project, the time and expense to complete Steps 1 through 14 can include direct and indirect costs in the range of $350,000 to $500,000 plus. This assumes some reasonable hourly rate for the developers' time and the potential opportunity cost of not pursuing and closing another development project.

Many government and university officials and private developers do not understand the enormous flexibility and creativity available for them to solve problems that may arise from time to time. Consequently, some projects never proceed to implementation. As the public/private partnership approach is gaining widespread popularity, the preparation of solicitations (RFQ and RFPs) is improving, but there are still instances of badly structured and/or written solicitations—the basic data on the development opportunity is not provided, the objectives of the sponsoring public entity are not clear, or the requirements of the developer are unclear.

In some instances, it is clear the sponsoring government entity is not prepared and has not completed the basic analyses to determine whether the opportunity may be of interest to any private-sector company. Government officials have issued RFPs for projects and virtually have not offered any assistance or any form of investment to facilitate action by the private sector. Many developers spend only 30 to 45 minutes reviewing RFPs to assess whether they pursue the opportunity. If the RFP does not convey a sense of partnership—sharing the risks, responsibilities, and costs—many developers will simply toss the RFP in the trash. By not using the two-step RFQ/RFP process, government officials create the "horse-race" syndrome for developers. When government or university officials issue an RFP without prequalifying developers, they are asking developers to prepare a lengthy and detailed technical proposal, in open competition with a multitude of developers. From the perspective of the developer, this is often viewed as too much to ask when the field of contenders may reach as high as 25 to 50 developers. In other words, by issuing an RFP without an RFQ, government and university officials are requiring developers to invest a substantial amount of funds, time, and effort to prepare a highly technical and thorough proposal while he or she is in a horse race with 25 to 50 other developers. Simply put, the odds of being selected are 1 in 25, or 1 in 50, which represents high risk for the candidate developers.

THE FUTURE COULD BE VERY BRIGHT, BUT THERE ARE POTENTIAL PROBLEMS

Some of the more promising signs of continued growth in the public/private development industry include the following.

The Estimated Annual Volume of Construction Continues to Increase

A conservative estimate of the construction value of public/private developments in the United States in 1999 was in the range of $50 billion. It is estimated that the value of projects as recently as 1995 was only $25 billion. In that short four-year time span, the public/private development industry grew at an annual rate of 25 percent.

Developers Focus Exclusively on the Growing Public/Private Partnership Market

In 1999, there were still just a small handful of development companies focused *solely* on public/private development projects. These companies include Forest City Ratner, DDR Oliver McMillan, Tower Realty, Inc., Kajima Urban Development, Inc., and LCOR, Inc. There are many other developers implementing public/private development opportunities, but they are concurrently maintaining their pursuit of the traditional commercial development market. These companies include development companies such as Trizec Hahn, Boston Properties, Trammel Crow Company, Hines Interests, Tishman Speyer, and LaSalle Partners.

Public/Private Finance and Development Consultants Are Seeing Much More Demand For Their Services

Again, there are a growing number of consulting firms participating in the public/private finance and development arena, but at this point in time, there are only a few with extensive experience. Ernst & Young formed a public/private development practice in 1996. By mid-1999, this practice had completed nearly 80 engagements. Other consultants primarily focused on the public/private real estate market include the Sedway Group, Keyser Marston, Inc., PRC/Kotin, Inc., Kosmont & Associates, and Hunter Interests, Inc. There are many more consulting firms providing public/private partnership advisory services, but they are focused on services and infrastructure, not the real estate market.

Major Projects in the 1990s Completed Using a Public/Private Partnership Approach

There is a fast-growing list of major projects completed using the public/private finance and development approach. Some of the larger developments under construction or recently completed include the 42nd Street Redevelopment in New York City; the new $1.2 billion Terminal 4 at the JFK International Airport; the $600 million Los Arcos Mixed-Use Redevelopment Project in Scottsdale, Arizona; Yerba Buena Entertainment/Retail Center in San Francisco; and the Denver Pavillion Urban Entertainment Center in Denver, Colorado.

CURRENT PROBLEMS THAT ARE HINDERING THE INCREASING USE OF THE PUBLIC/PRIVATE PARTNERSHIP APPROACH

Time Required to Complete the Developer RFQ/RFP Process

For most public/private development projects, the predevelopment process requires far too much risk, time, and investment. The estimated range of time to complete the traditional developer RFQ/RFP process as described in Chapter 8 is seven to eleven months. For many projects, this time frame grows into two to three years or more! If this trend continues, developers will begin to avoid any public/private development opportunities.

Developer Solicitations Are Not Well Written

Although the quality of most developer RFQs and RFPs is improving, many developer solicitations are poorly written by government and university officials. Government, university, and school district officials should place much more effort into preparing their developer solicitations. In many instances, the solicitation is not well organized. The public partner's objectives for the project are not clear. The level of collaboration is not expressed; consequently, developers perceive that the proposed "partnership" is not genuine and therefore do not respond.

Developer Evaluation and Selection Process Is Not Objective

Many developers are leery that the public/private partnership arena is far too political. They believe the developer solicitation process is only for show. The developer has already been selected on a sole-source basis, but the public partner is required by legislation to use a competitive process to select a developer.

In other instances, a developer based outside the city where the public/private development opportunity exists believes local developers have an inside track to be selected. They believe they will not be playing on a level playing field and consequently decline to participate.

There are also instances in which the public partner is demanding too much from the candidate developers in the solicitation or expecting too much from the selected developer once he or she is selected. In other words, the expectation of the public partner is not in sync with the condition of the marketplace.

Government Officials Are Still Using the Single-Step Developer RFP Solicitation Method

One of the biggest concerns developers have with the public/private development market is the at-risk time and money required to respond to an RFP. The problem is not the competitive environment. It is the idea of having to compete when the field is so large. The odds of being selected in a field of 15 to 25 developers are very high. Typically, that is the number of developers competing when an RFQ or some other means has not been used to narrow the field of contenders. When months of time and several hundred thousand dollars are at risk, this is too much to ask of developers.

Approval Process During the Negotiations Process Requires Far Too Much Time

For many public/private development projects, the completion of the negotiation process is requiring far too much time. The negotiation phase should require only 90 days. This is particularly true if the two-step RFQ/RFP process was used to select the developer. One of the problems compounding the length of time required to complete the negotiation process is the number of approvals required to close a development and/or operations agreement. Public partners should do everything in their power to reduce the number of approvals to conclude negotiations. In some instances, the negotiation phase is requiring nearly a year to complete. This is unconscionable in the context of the fact that the public partner selected the developer based on his or her finance plan. Clearly, this can be a two-way street, in that the developer is to blame for the extended schedule. Public partners should be aware that recently some developers are promising far more than they can deliver in order to be selected, the logic being that once they have been selected, the opportunity is theirs forever. Public partners should consider placing a cap on the time required to complete the negotiation phase. A reasonable range of time is 120 to 180 days. If a development agreement cannot be negotiated in that time frame, then there may be problems that are insurmountable.

Public Partner Is Not Ready to Issue a Developer RFP

One of the most common errors made by public partners is jumping from Step 1 to Step 13. The public partner realizes the need to develop the subject project, but then without completing any analysis leaps to issuing an RFP in order to assess the interest of the development community. The government, university, and school district officials who continue to do this are gradually eroding the credibility of all potential public partners who want to use this creative approach to realize their vision.

Increased Voter Control of the Public Partner

Another trend that may cause additional delays during the predevelopment process is that voters are demanding to have approval rights of any investment by the public partner. Although this concept has merit, the public partner needs to anticipate this action and do everything in their power to resolve this issue prior to soliciting developers. It is not the approval rights that are the problem, it is the time required to complete this action that will set back the timetable to structure the public/private partnership.

Government Officials Do Not Take the Time to Understand the Wide Variety of Alternative Finance and Development Tools Available to Structure a Partnership

The public partner should not rely on the private partner to be the creative force behind structuring the public/private finance and development plans. Government, university, and school district officials should recognize that no one knows their business better than they do. Public partners should be more resourceful and entrepreneurial. They should identify alternative sources of public financing. They should be thinking outside the box when it comes to public finance techniques and ways to reduce development costs and enhance cash flow. For many developers, the public/private finance and development arena is as new to them as it is to the public partner.

Expectations of Government and University Partners Are Often Not in Sync with the Marketplace

Public partners should analyze the market demand for the proposed building uses prior to issuing a developer solicitation. Otherwise, how do they know how to position themselves in the developer community? If the market demand is good, their position is stronger in both the solicitation and negotiation processes.

Public Partners Have a Tendency to Burden Developers with All of the Risks, Responsibilities, and Costs

If public partners have not done their homework on the proposed project, they do not know whether the public/private development opportunity is good or bad. If the public partner attempts to place most of the burdens onto the developer on a weak opportunity, they will lose their credibility with the developer community. The public partner either must complete the appropriate amount of analysis or use the RFQ/ Negotiate Method to solicit developers (Approach Six, described in Chapter 8). This method will at least allow the public partner to work hand-in-hand with the competitively selected developer to complete many of the 14 steps of the public/private finance and development process described in Chapter 4.

Public Partner Does Not Understand the Time and Effort Required to Structure and Negotiate Public/Private Partnerships

One of the primary purposes of this book is to make government, university, and school district officials aware of the tremendous number of man-hours and cost required to submit competitive proposals. For large public/private development projects, it is not unusual for a developer to invest in the range of 350 to 400 man-hours to respond to an RFQ. The number of man-hours to respond to a technical RFP is in direct correlation to the scope and complexity of the opportunity. For a project with a value of $50 million or more, a developer will expend in the range of 1,500 to 2,500 man-hours to prepare a competitive proposal. This excludes the enormous number of man-hours invested by the developer's team of consultants, architects, real estate attorneys, and engineers. In total, the development team could invest in the range of two to three man-years to respond to both the RFQ and RFP. In addition, the development team incurs substantial costs for printing, photography, models, mailing, telephone, and travel costs. Both the man-hours and direct costs are invested at a high level of risk.

Public Partner Does Not Clearly State Project Objectives

It is very important for the public partner to clearly state the primary objectives of the public/private development project. For example, is the purpose of the project to serve as a catalyst for other redevelopment activities? Is the primary purpose to generate new employment opportunities? To generate nontax income for the participating public entities? Or to provide the subject opportunity in exchange for a needed public facility that is privately financed? By stating the objectives clearly, the developer candidates can tailor their finance and development plan to most effectively assist the public partner(s) to achieve their goal.

Misperceptions by the Developer Candidates

The "brain damage" required exceeds the perceived benefits for the developer. If the public/private development opportunity appears to be financially infeasable, developers do not realize the multitude of ways governments and universities can reduce development costs and enhance cash flow, so they do not enter into the developer RFQ/RFP process.

Communication between the Public and Private Partners Is Often Not Clear

The public and private sectors often do not speak the same language and each has varied experiences and expectations, which does not lend itself to a meaningful basis for communication. To correct this problem will require extra effort by both parties and possibly an objective third-party consultant.

Both public and private partners may be required to bend more than they initially thought. After careful analysis, both the public- and private-sector parties may need to make some concessions and assume some risks, bilaterally, that could be acceptable but have not been previously considered. The same could apply to incurring certain costs and responsibilities. Again, one of the great qualities of the public/private partnership approach is the substantial amount of flexibility and creativity available to both parties to structure a deal that is satisfactory to both parties.

The Predevelopment Methodology Is Not Followed

The proposed public/private finance and development methodology described in Chapter 4 is proven to be incredibly valuable to both parties. It does not make much sense not to follow this process step by step. This is one of the only ways to keep both parties on track and focused on the ball.

Both the public and private partners need to be determined and have stamina to structure and negotiate a successful partnership. As stated earlier, the time required to complete the traditional RFQ/RFP process can take 7 to 11 months and several man-years of time. Both parties must have the spirit and determination required to complete the hundreds of tasks included in the predevelopment process. Compounding the situation is the fact that many partnerships must be structured and negotiated in a fishbowl atmosphere, with many public entities, voters, community groups, and the media placing many of the decisions under a microscope to be evaluated from their perspective. The public and private partners need to always remember that they probably could not finance and develop the project without a collaborative effort. Equally important, after billions of dollars of projects have been implemented, the advantages of the public/private partnership approach far outweigh the disadvantages.

Chapter 10

Eight Case Studies

One of the most effective ways to demonstrate the concepts and methodology described in earlier chapters of the book is to provide the level of detail and insights included in case studies. Every public/private development transaction is different. Each public and/or private partner has different project objectives. Most public partners are facing different regulatory constraints and opportunities. The sources of private and public financing will rarely be the same.

Each case study has been organized into the following categories of information:

- Type of Project
- Public and Private Partners
  Primary Public Partner
  Primary Private Partner
  Secondary Public and Private Partners
- Project Participants
  Community Groups
  Merchant Organizations
- Project Scope
  Project Site
  Building Program (including building use and area)
- Project History
- Legislation Driving the Project
- Project Objectives
  Nontax Income
  Leverage the Value of Land to Finance a Needed Public Facility

Catalytic Development to Start the Redevelopment of an Area
Reduce or Eliminate Investment (conserve debt capacity)
- Public Partner's Up-Front Requirements of the Developer
- Type of Developer Solicitation (one of five types)
- Ownership
Landowner(s)
Owner of Proposed Building
- Insights into the Negotiations
Primary Participants
Time Required to Complete
Major Issues
Major Stumbling Blocks
- Basic Deal Structure
- Sources of Finance
Sources of Capital:
    Public
    Private
    Other Sources
Sources of Noncapital Investment:
    Additional Development Rights
    Reduced Parking Requirements
- Types of Incentives
Investment
Development
Operational
- Employment Opportunities
- Approval Process
Key Entities and Why Those Entities
Time Required to Obtain Approvals
Types of Approvals Required

CASE STUDY 1: THE OREGON ARENA (THE ROSE GARDEN), PORTLAND, OREGON[1]

This project was selected as a case study because it is an excellent example of creative financing, the multiple sources of financing, and how well the predevelopment process was organized.

Type of Project

Professional sports arena

Public and Private Partners

Primary Public Partner: City of Portland

Primary Private Partner: Oregon Arena Corporation (OAC). This is a sister corporation to Trail Blazers Inc., which owns the Portland Trailblazers, a National Basketball Association (NBA) franchise. OAC is owned solely by Paul Allen, one of the founding partners of Microsoft.

Project Participants

Public Project Participants: (1) The Metro Council, a regional government that was operating the Memorial Coliseum on behalf of the City. (2) The Portland Development Commission (PDC). PDC was designated as the lead negotiator. PDC serves as the City's redevelopment agency. Influential public, civic, and business leaders appointed by the Portland City Council and the Metro Council formed the "Arena Task Force" (ATF). The OAC retained financial advisors, architects, contractors, lawyers, and an in-house construction management team.

Project Scope

Project Site: The City controlled 20 acres of land adjacent to the existing Memorial Coliseum.

Project Scope: A 20,000-seat arena. There are 14,417 permanent seats and 4,224 portable seats. In addition, there are 1,540 luxury seats. Seating configurations: concerts: 20,000 seats; ice event: 17,500 seats; basketball: 20,300 seats; boxing: 19,500 seats; rodeo: 16,800 seats.

Building Area: 32,000-square-foot floor area.

Physical Features: Ceiling height: 105 feet. Permanent stage: 60 feet by 40 feet. Ice rink: 85 feet by 200 feet.

Source: AudArena Stadium, 1998 International Guide, Amusement Business

Total Development Budget

The total cost of the arena was $262,000,000. The Rose Garden was the largest public/private partnership ever formed in the state.

Legislation Driving the Project

Not applicable

Project Objectives

Public Partner Objectives: In 1991, the City of Portland was facing the effects of a tax limitation initiative known as "Measure 5." Therefore, the City took a fiscally conservative position to avoid any criticism that it was making a "gift" of public funds to a private developer. The City also took a position of minimizing its risks. Consequently, it capped its investment at $34,500,000. These funds were to be used to finance needed infrastructure improvements and a parking garage. Moreover, City officials also required that any cost overruns were the responsibility of OAC, unless the cost overruns were the result of their changes. City officials also took the position that any environmental remediation costs on the project site were to be included in their capped investment of $34.5 million. City officials also required that their investment be paid back from user fees from events in the new arena and the Memorial Coliseum. The estimated time required to recapture their investment was seven to nine years. City officials wanted to create employment opportunities for the underemployed areas of the City. They were also concerned about the liability they will incur in year 61, when ownership of the facility reverts to the City.

Private Partner Objectives: OAC entered negotiations wanting the City to commit to the following:

- Invest the 20-acre property owned by the City.
- Provide a capital investment totaling $34.5 million. This investment was targeted for infrastructure improvements and a parking garage.
- Provide a land lease with a minimum term of 30 years with three 10-year renewal options.

- Protect OAC from the possibility of the City building a competing facility nearby.
- Relinquish control over the construction of both the public and private improvements.
- OAC wanted development rights over the balance of the project site, in order to control the future use of the site.

Public Partner's Up-Front Requirements of the Developer

The Portland Trailblazers organization submitted an unsolicited proposal to the City. Although soon after the proposal was submitted the City officials prepared a list of requirements described in the Project Objectives section of this case study. In addition, the public/private partnership developed a detailed mission statement, describing how they would work together to finance, design, and develop the arena.

Mission Statement

As Partners in the Oregon Arena Project, we shall use all of our experience and expertise, in an atmosphere of enthusiasm and mutual respect, to design and construct the Project in a manner that is mutually beneficial and cost effective for all parties, which meets all the stated objectives of the Owner and provides maximum benefit to the citizens of the City of Portland.

We will use fair, equitable, and efficient processes to accomplish the following goals:

- *Substantially complete the project by October 9, 1995.*
- *Design and build a quality project, which meets the Owner's stated objectives of a world-class facility.*
- *Provide a fair profit for all participants and high value for the Owner.*
- *Achieve completion without claims or litigation.*
- *Fulfill community participation objectives addressing contracting, hiring, training, and community relationships.*
- *Complete the project within the established budget.*
- *Complete the project with no lost time accidents or public liability incidents.*
- *Attain the best possible public relations.*
- *Develop a "project first, me second" attitude by all team members.*

Type of Developer Solicitation

The City did not solicit interest from the private development community, because the owner of the existing NBA franchise proposed to simply negotiate the public/private partnership.

Ownership

The private partner will own the arena for a minimum of 30 years and a maximum of 60 years. The City of Portland owned the project site. They provided the private partner with a long-term land lease.

Insights into the Negotiations

PDC served as the lead negotiator for the public partner. The negotiation phase for this project required nearly two years, from mid-1991 to mid-1993. Both parties were aiming to complete negotiation of the deal structure in one year.

Basic Deal Structure

The public/private finance plan included five traunches of equity and debt.

OAC Responsibilities:
1. Cash equity totaling $46,000,000, which represents 18 percent of the total cost of the project.
2. A first leasehold mortgage totaling $155,000,000. This portion of the financing equals 59 percent of the total project cost.
3. Interest on the unexpended mortgage note during construction totaled $10,500,000, or 4 percent of the total cost.
4. The concessionaire provided a $16,000,000 line of credit during construction and then converted it to a 10-year term obligation after con-

---

"Concession and novelty revenue is another important source of financing revenue for facilities. A significant trend in stadium and arena financing is the sale of the rights to a facility's concession operations. Concessionaire fees provide a concessionaire the right to the concession operations for a specified period of time. The agreement is usually for a specified period of time, and the amount of money paid depends on the specific terms of the agreement. The concessionaire fee represents the capitalized revenue streams that are anticipated to be received by the concessionaire over the term of the agreement."[2]

struction was completed. This investment was in exchange for a long-term operations agreement and represents 6 percent of the total cost of the project. It should be noted that the concessionaire is a sister corporation owned by OAC named Oregon Concessions, Inc.

The cumulative investment by the private partner totaled $227,500,000, or 87 percent of the total cost of the arena and related facilities.

City Responsibility:
5. The City financed public infrastructure improvements and a parking garage. The total cost of these improvements was $34,500,000, or 13 percent of the total cost of the arena and related facilities.

Sources of Finance

Sources of Capital:
1. Paul Allen, owner of OAC, provided the $46 million equity investment.
2. A local bank provided the $155 million first leasehold mortgage.
3. The $10.5 million of interest generated during construction is a result of the other private partner investments.
4. The $16 million investment by Oregon Concessions, Inc. was from traditional banking sources.
5. The $34.5 million investment by the City was financed with Revenue Bonds backed by a 6 percent fee levied on events and parking.

Types of Incentives

No incentives were used in structuring the public/private finance plan.

Employment Opportunities

The City set the following goals for both the public and private improvements:

- Minority enterprises: 10 percent
- Women-owned businesses: 5 percent
- Emerging small-business enterprises: 10 percent

Those goals were exceeded through a combination of efforts:

1. Project components were organized into smaller subcomponents.
2. The outreach program to identify and recruit eligible subcontractors and suppliers was intensified.
3. OAC hired a special consultant to work with interested community and business organizations.
4. A bonding program was established for subcontractors that could not otherwise afford bonds.
5. Apprentice programs were also formed for the various trades working on the project.
6. City staff prepared monthly reports to monitor the achievements of the various programs. These reports were submitted to OAC and the City.
7. OAC adopted the hiring policies and programs that are applicable to all contractors working on the project.

Approval Process

The City of Portland received a proposal from OAC in mid-1991. It is estimated that OAC officials began the preparation of their proposal in early 1991. The time required to evaluate the proposal and negotiate the public/private partnership was two years, or until mid-1993. It is assumed that construction began in the fall of 1993, soon after negotiations were completed. Construction was completed in time to begin the NBA season in November 1995. Consequently, from the time OAC developed their unsolicited proposal to opening day of the Rose Garden required nearly five years.

---

[1]Michael R. Silvey, "How to Execute a Slam Dunk in Public/Private Negotiations: The Oregon Arena Project Experience," *NAIOP's Development Magazine* (Spring 1995).

[2]Martin J. Greenberg and James T. Gray, *The Stadium Game* (National Sports Law Institute of Marquette University Law School, 1996).

CASE STUDY 2: OYSTER SCHOOL/HENRY ADAMS HOUSE, WASHINGTON, DC

This project was selected as a case study because it is a national precedent for many public schools in America. Equally important, this is an excellent example of creativity on two fronts: structuring a payment in lieu of taxes (PILOT) program and optimizing the value of an underutilized real estate asset owned by a public entity.

Type of Project

This public/private development is a combination of a new public elementary school and a luxury apartment building on the site of an existing 73-year-old public school building.

Public and Private Partners

Primary Public Partner: District of Columbia Public Schools (DCPS)
Primary Private Partner: LCOR, Inc.

Project Participants

Public Project Participants: The 21st Century School Fund. This entity is an unincorporated, nonprofit organization established to explore ways to finance the over $500 million of needed improvements and capital projects for the DCPS. The 21st Century School Fund is supported in large part by a grant from the Ford Foundation. Funds provided for this nonprofit organization are conduit through the Washington Parent Group Fund. The 21st Century School Fund has a particularly close working relationship with the Oyster School Community Council (OCC) and specifically the OCC Blueprint Committee, which has been charged with all responsibilities related to the Oyster School building and grounds. The Woodley Park Community Association worked closely with The 21st Century School Fund throughout the predevelopment process.

Private Project Participants: In early 1995, The 21st Century School Fund issued a request for proposal (RFP) to the consulting community to competitively select a public/private finance and development advisor. The lead consultant was Public/Private Development for America (PDA), a company owned by the author. PDA assembled a comprehensive team, which included an architect, contractor, law firm, and engineers. PDA originated the concept of commercially developing a portion of the school site to finance the renovation and/or expansion of the existing school or a new on-site school.

Project Scope

Project Site: The school property is located in the Woodley Park neighborhood of Washington, DC. The legal address is 2801 Calvert Street, NW, Washington DC. The area of the property is 72,714 square feet, or 1.67 acres.

Project Scope: The new on-site school replacing the existing school includes 47,000 square feet of space. The on-site Henry Adams House apartment building includes 211 luxury residential units, or approximately 207,500 square feet. The site is zoned R-5-D. The maximum floor area ratio is 3.5 for all structures. The entire site includes 72,714 square feet. Consequently the maximum allowable gross building area for the property is 254,500 square feet. Therefore, the above-grade program for the apartment building is limited to 207,500 square feet, or 254,500 square feet less the proposed school building program of 47,000 square feet. The actual design for the apartment building included space below grade; therefore, the gross building area was 224,000 gross square feet (GSF). The useable square footage was 211,000.

Project History

The May 4, 1995, issue of the *Wall Street Journal* reported, "The District's financial picture is dismal. It ran a deficit in 1994 equal to $324 million and the estimate this year is $490 million . . ." The article continued, "The schools, despite higher per-public spending than the 40 largest school districts in the country, are a shambles; standardized test scores and attendance have declined every year since 1989; and the average public school is 77 years old." In 1995, there was a $584 million backlog of repairs in the 164 schools in the DCPS inventory.

The Oyster Elementary School was constructed in 1926. It is a well-respected learning institution desperately needing to be rehabilitated and expanded. The OCC went to DCPS and requested the funds to renovate the school and was told the funds did not exist. It was at this point that PDA, in collaboration with The 21st Century School Fund, developed the idea to commercially develop the underutilized nonessential portion of the school site to generate nontax income to finance the renovation of the existing school.

The PDA team developed two alternative master plans for the 1.7-acre school site. In Scheme A, the existing school was rehabilitated and expanded into the three lower floors of the proposed adjacent apartment building. The new apartment building incorporated a media room, gym, and multipurpose room. In Scheme B, the existing school was replaced by a new school and the new apartment building was not connected to the new school building. The PDA team also completed the financial analysis and alternative deal structures between the school district and a developer to be selected on a competitive basis.

The PDA team also completed a study comparing the cost to renovate and expand the existing school to the cost to develop a new school. While the per-unit cost to complete the renovation and expansion was less than the cost to construct a new school, the expansion of the existing school required an additional 6,000 square feet. The total cost for the existing school expansion and renovation was more than the new school.

Concurrently with the PDA team work, a market demand analysis was being completed. The results of this study revealed that the highest and best use of the school site was a midrise luxury apartment building.

Once it was determined that the proposed public/private partnership approach was financially feasible, the next step was to obtain approvals and then issue a developer request for qualifications (RFQ), to be followed by a developer RFP.

In June 1997, the Oyster School restructuring team worked closely with the DCPS to revise the building program requirements. The revised educational specifications provide for 32,495 square feet of interior net program space.

In November 1997, the Fund issued a developer RFP. Developer proposals were due by January 1998. The selection of a developer and negotiations required several months. Negotiation between the public and private partners was completed in the fall of 1999. Construction began in December 1999. The predevelopment phase of this landmark public/private partnership required nearly five years. Nearly 18 months were required waiting for the market demand for residential units to warrant issuing a second developer RFP.

Total Development Budget

The total cost for the new public school, including all hard and soft costs, was $11 million. This cost included atypical payments to The 21st Century School Fund and DCPS. The total development budget for the apartment building and garage was $30,785,359, or $145,902 per unit. The total development budget for both projects was approximately $41,785,359.

Legislation Driving the Project

The District of Columbia City Council approved the concept of dedicating the property tax generated by the private development to repaying the debt associated with the construction of the new school. The owner of the apartment building makes PILOT payments to cover the debt service on the tax-exempt bonds issued for the new school.

Project Objectives

Public Partner Objectives: The overriding objective of The 21st Century School Fund was to generate a sufficient amount of nontax income and tax revenue from the public school property to finance the renovation of the existing school or develop a new school on-site.

The PDA team and The 21st Century School Fund realized the school site had many qualities. First, the school site was close to the Woodley Park-Zoo Metro Rail Station, which would provide commercial tenants with easy access to the City's expansive transit system. Second, the property was located in a highly regarded residential neighborhood. Finally, the site could accommodate a significant amount of additional space. Specifically, the site was zoned to accommodate 254,500 square feet. The new school required approximately 47,000 square feet, which allowed the development of a residential building with 207,500 square feet. The project objectives described in the RFP issued in 1997 were as follows:

- To generate the funding necessary for Oyster School replacement and/or improvements
- To use, to the greatest extent feasible, private-sector practices to facilitate efficient, high-quality construction
- To add to the City's economic base through creative development strategies
- To encourage private capital investment for projects that provide incentive and reasonable expectations of return for developer partners

Public Partner's Up-Front Requirements of the Developer

The developer of the apartment building would also be responsible for the finance, design, development, and construction of the new public school.

Type of Developer Solicitation

The 21st Century School Fund completed the developer solicitation process twice. In 1996, they issued a developer RFP. At that point, the residential development market was weak. Equally important, the interest rate on bonds was extremely high. Consequently, The 21st Century School Fund received a total of only three proposals from the local development community, two of which were deemed insufficient submittals.

In November 1997, The 21st Century School Fund issued a new developer RFP. The prebid conference was held on December 10, 1997. This conference served as a forum for school officials and the Fund to provide developers with additional and more detailed information on the proposed public/private partnership. The deadline for submitting developer proposals was January 30, 1998, or approximately 10 weeks after the developer RFP was issued.

The developer RFP consisted of only 12 pages. It was organized into seven sections:

- Section 1: The Development Partnership
- Section 2: Project Information
- Section 3: Submission Requirements
- Section 4: Proposal Evaluation Criteria
- Section 5: Developer Selection
- Section 6: Statement of Limitations and General Conditions
- Section 7: Supplemental Materials

Insights into the Negotiations

During the time this project was being negotiated, the federal government had formed The DC Control Board to take control of the city government. LCOR Public/Private, Inc. now had three entities with which to negotiate. In addition, a local attorney, working *pro bono,* became a key member of the public partner's team. LCOR had submitted its proposal on January 30, 1998. It was not until early April 1998 that the project was awarded to the developer. During the intervening months, DCPS had required clarifications and a best and final offer (BAFO). Negotiations between the public and private partners required five months.

Basic Deal Structure

The DCPS and the government of the District of Columbia made a portion of the Oyster School property available for "matter-of-right" development via a long-term land lease or subdivision and fee simple sale to the private development community for commercial development. Equally important, the District of Columbia also was willing to dedicate the property taxes from the private development of the site toward financing the construction of the new on-site school. In exchange, the developer was responsible for structuring and implementing the finance, design, and construction of the new school and the apartment building.

Sources of Finance

The new school was financed with an $11 million tax-exempt bond issued by the District of Columbia government. The bond was secured by the PILOT payments and land lease income. The DCPS did not have the authority to issue bonds. The bonds issued by the City were not general obligation bonds. The bonds were not issued until November 1999.

The on-site apartment building was financed with private equity and conventional mortgage financing. The developer structured a joint venture with a major life insurance company.

Types of Incentives

No incentives were used in structuring the public/private finance plan.

Employment Opportunities

Based on the requirements of the developer RFP, there were no special requirements for employment.

Approval Process

The 21st Century School Fund, a key member of the public partner, performed a key role during the approval process by working closely with all of the neighborhood groups to gain support for the design and development of the project.

The DCPS closely reviewed the design for the new school but had only minor input on the design of the apartment building. The City's Planning Department controlled the design process for the apartment building.

Schedule to Complete the Predevelopment and Construction Processes

This school/nonschool public/private partnership has been tried in only one other city in the United States. The 21st Century School Fund was blazing new ground not only for Washington, DC, but also for the nation. When that circumstance was combined with a weak residential market and high rates in the bond market in 1996, this project experienced significant delays. In 1997, this project got back on track. The 21st Century School Fund issued a second round of developer RFPs. This time the market was in much better shape and the Fund received several good proposals from outstanding development teams in January 1998. After careful evaluation of the proposals and initial negotiations, The 21st Century School Fund selected LCOR Public/Private, Inc., one of a small handful of developers in the nation focused solely on the public/private market. The negotiation phase of this project began in May 1998 and was not completed until September 1998. By October 1998, the developer began design work and soil borings. The test borings in the site revealed rock, which caused the redesign of both the school and the apartment structure. After construction documents were completed in the spring of 1999, the competitive bid process began. Around this time, environmental studies revealed oil deposits originating from an adjacent property, which caused more delays. Tax-exempt bonds were finally issued in November 1999. Construction began in December 1999.

Potential Impact of This Project on the Future of Public Schools

In 1990, more babies were born in the United States than at any time since 1961. The 4.2 million births in 1990 was the second year in a row that the annual number of births exceeded the 4 million birth rate that defined the years of the "baby boom" from 1946 to 1964. The year 1990 marked the beginning of the "echo boom," with a rolling growth rate curve that will require an enormous number of new and renovated elementary, secondary, and postsecondary school facilities.

All levels of government are confronted with ever-increasing demands on their funds, so government officials are cutting school budgets. In parallel, taxpayers are beginning to reject proposed bond referendums for new school construction and renovations.

The U.S. General Accounting Office (GAO) completed a report in 1995 that concluded the United States would have to spend $112 billion to repair or upgrade the nation's schools. Schools throughout the nation cannot keep up with the new construction required by the growth in enrollment. Furthermore, The Education Writers Association (EWA) pointed out that year that more than 50 percent of the school buildings in use were built during the enrollment boom of the 1950s and 1960s. While 35- to 45-year-old buildings are typically not a problem, The EWA characterizes those decades as "a time of rapid and cheap expansion. . . ." Many construction experts say the buildings were intended to last only about 30 years.

In summary, the demand for new school facilities far outweighs the ability to finance and develop those facilities. Consequently, school officials should examine the Oyster School/Henry Adams House project to determine whether this approach applies in any of their school district sites. It is an outstanding example of how underutilized school-owned real estate assets could be the instrument to privately finance desperately needed public schools.

CASE STUDY 3: UNIVERSITY OF PENNSYLVANIA'S SANSOM COMMONS DEVELOPMENT, PHILADELPHIA, PENNSYLVANIA

The reasons this project was selected as a case study are threefold: it is a university project for which construction was recently completed; it is a great example of how a public partner changed their ownership position once they understood the potential nontax income they could earn; and the predevelopment methodology used by the University was almost identical to the 14-step methodology proposed in this book. The author served as an advisor to the University in 1996–1997 while with the E&Y Kenneth Leventhal Real Estate Group of Ernst & Young LLP.

Type of Project

An on-campus mixed-use development, which includes a hotel, retail space, restaurants, and bookstore

Public and Private Partners

Primary Public Partner: University of Pennsylvania (Penn)

Primary Private Partner: LaSalle Partners provided development management services for a fee. Williams, Jackson, Ewing, Inc. served as the retail developer.

Project Participants

Private Project Participants:
- In July 1996, the University hired a team of consultants to complete several studies almost concurrently. For master planning, they hired Wallace, Roberts & Todd (WRT). They hired Williams, Jackson, Ewing, Inc. to consult on retail space. Orth-Rodgers & Associates was responsible for traffic planning. In order to provide a basis for the building program, they hired E&Y Kenneth Leventhal Real Estate Group (E&YKL) to prepare a market demand analysis for the hotel. The Public/Private Development Practice of E&YKL was also brought in to: (1) develop alternative public/private finance plans; (2) develop alternative ownership, investment, development, and operation scenarios for the entire development; and (3) manage the developer RFP process.
- The project architect was Elkus/Manfredi Architects Ltd.

- Turner Construction provided preconstruction consultation.
- Penn officials selected the architectural and engineering firms for the project. The development manager had a role in the selection of the architect and associated engineering firms. Barnes and Noble provided interior architectural services for their tenant improvements. Other selected retailers were allowed to have their own architects for tenant improvements. The development manager was responsible for coordinating any overlapping responsibilities. The development manager also assisted Penn officials in selecting a retail management firm. In addition, the development manager was responsible for directing the retail management firm to refine Penn's retail strategy. The retail management firm was responsible for preparing a marketing plan and leasing retail space. The retail management firm was given the option to retain a broker to perform such function.

Project Scope

This vibrant mixed-use development includes a 55,000-square-foot state-of-the-art bookstore, a 250-room luxury hotel and conference center, and 180,000 square feet of retail space. The hotel is known as the Inn at Penn. The bookstore was designed and operated by Barnes and Noble.

Penn owns the project site. The area of the site is 104,108 square feet, or 2.39 acres. The site is bounded by 34th Street, Walnut Street, 38th Street, and Chestnut Street. The Sansom Commons site is strategically located in the heart of University City in West Philadelphia. University City is not only the location for Penn, but also for Drexel University, the University City Science Center, and the Philadelphia College of Pharmacy.

Total Development Budget

The total cost of the project including all soft and hard costs was approximately $48 million.

Legislation Driving the Project

There is no legislation acting as a catalyst for this project.

Project Objectives

Over the last 35 years, Penn has improved the quality of life and image of the University by developing one of America's most attractive urban campuses.

The focus for these improvements has been the central campus area between Walnut and Spruce Streets. The image of the campus to the north of Walnut Street, however, was less positive. This northern precinct had not been integrated with the core campus. The development of Sansom Commons was perhaps the most significant opportunity Penn had to extend the successful resurgence of the core campus to the northern precinct of the University.

The primary objective of the Sansom Commons development was to enhance the quality of life for students by creating an exciting and active "northern gateway" to the campus.

Public Partner's Up-Front Requirements of the Developer

After completing the market demand study; financial analysis; and alternative ownership, investment, development, and operation scenarios, Penn officials decided that the University would own and finance this project. Therefore, the only developer solicitation issued was for development management services. In other words, Penn wanted a developer to manage the design and construction and not obtain financing or take an ownership position. The University retained ownership and approval rights over major decisions affecting the development and operation of the project. The requirements for development management services are far different than the traditional developer role, as will be described in the next section.

Type of Developer Solicitation

Penn officials, in conjunction with E&YKL, developed and issued an RFP for development management services. An RFQ was not issued.

In the RFP, Penn officials were seeking a development manager who would act as Penn's representative in all aspects of the development of the project. The development manager was to be "the team leader for project implementation and responsible for management and supervision of subcontracted disciplines including, but not limited to, architectural and engineering services, retail leasing, hospitality operations, marketing, public relations, and construction management." In addition, the development manager was to "serve as the owner's lead representative and manage the work effort of the development team and general contractor or construction manager during construction." Furthermore, the development manager was expected to have a full-time on-site presence throughout the predevelopment and construction period of the project.

The University also retained a construction manager to provide preconstruction services. The construction manager was selected by Penn, with input from the development manager. The construction manager was responsible for providing budgets, scheduling information, and project oversight. Penn also restricted the construction manager from participating in the construction of the project.

Selected Detailed Information on the Developer RFQ and/or RFP

The following criteria were included in the RFP and used to evaluate development management proposals:

*   Demonstration of understanding of the Sansom Commons project
*   Prior experience working with commercial developments, including hotel and retail development or mixed-use projects in urban settings, especially within a campus setting
*   Proven capability to effectively assess schematic mixed-use development plans
*   Strength of firm's capability as demonstrated by other projects in which a similar role was successfully undertaken
*   The overall strategy to carry out the tasks required, and the strength and backgrounds of the principals involved
*   Proven ability to direct and manage the development of complex projects on schedule and within budget
*   Prior record of performance in obtaining entitlements and permits from agencies in Philadelphia
*   Competitive fee
*   Financial capabilities of firm to provide the services required
*   Creativity of approach to the conceptual development plan
*   The amount of their own time and commitment that principals will devote to this project, the ability of the firm to commit specific personnel for the expected duration of the project, and estimated priority of the Sansom Commons relative to current and future commitments
*   Ability to promptly initiate and complete the project expeditiously
*   Perceived ability to work with Penn

"Submissions should include a list of the Principals of the responding firm(s) and their respective experiences, indicating if any of the responding members of the team have worked together before, and if so, on which projects and their respective roles."

"If the response to this RFP is made by a team, the response must outline specifically what role each firm within the team will carry out in the development management of the project, which firms or individuals will be responsible for various aspects of the development, and how any gaps in expertise will be covered." The submission must include:

1. A list of other projects with which the respondent(s) is currently involved
2. An estimate of the time the firm(s) and the individual members thereof will be able to devote to this project
3. The principal(s) and the on-site manager who will head this project must be identified
4. A listing of business entities related to the respondent
5. Full disclosure of all corporate relationships to other parties which may be involved in the development of Sansom Commons

Proposal Requirements (Included in the RFP)

To assist Penn in evaluating responses, firms are asked to demonstrate an understanding of the project including:

1. A detailed timeline for completion indicating the major components of work to be completed by the development manager
2. A discussion regarding the likely or expected challenges to successful development of the Sansom Commons site
3. A discussion of potential pitfalls and what steps must be taken to anticipate or avoid problems with the management of the development effort
4. Completion of the development budget found in the section so titled. Assumptions related to this budget, other than those found on the budget schedule and within the master plan section, include:
   - Demolition consists only of the removal of the existing asphalt parking lot and sidewalks.
   - All utility connections are available at curb.
   - The site is to be fenced and patrolled during the construction period.
   - The 36th Street plaza will be improved with material similar to that used on Locust Walk.
   - Below-grade conditions are acceptable.
   - No adverse environment conditions exist.
5. Other relevant development issues that should be considered

6. Recommendations for the hotel operators, retail operators/managers, architects, engineers, and other entities with whom the respondents have had recent working experience. Penn welcomes suggestions from respondents for candidates for components of the predevelopment work, including architects, engineers, etc.

7. A critique of the conceptual development program for Sansom Commons

Insights into the Negotiations

The minimal amount of negotiations required was focused on the scope of work for the development manager.

Ownership

The entire mixed-use development is owned by the University. In addition to the University's decision to own the development, they also placed the asset on the city real estate tax rolls as a for-profit venture.

A private company operates the hotel. The retail is managed by a private entity. The bookstore is operated by Barnes and Noble.

Basic Deal Structure

The bookstore, hotel, and retail and associated public spaces were financed using Penn funds and, therefore are owned in their entirety by the University.

Types of Incentives

No incentives were used in structuring the financing for this project.

Employment Opportunities

The construction of Sansom Commons generated 270 jobs. As part of the University's Sansom Common Economic Opportunity Program, a commitment was made to hire West Philadelphia residents. The first phase of development created a demand for 435 full-time employees.[4]

---

[4]Richard Huffman, "Building on Books," *Urban Land* (May 1998).

Approval Process

University officials did not request any of the incentives offered by the Philadelphia Industrial Development Corporation (PIDC) for new hotels near the new convention center. As a result, the economic impact of the project on the city tax base may be greater than that of other proposed hotels. Apparently, the Sansom Commons development "sailed through the public approvals process with minimal delays."

Schedule to Complete the Predevelopment and Construction Processes

In May 1996, Penn officials began hiring their consulting team. By November 1, 1996, Penn issued the RFP for development management services. Written questions for Penn officials were due November 12. Developer proposals were due by November 15. Penn officials along with E&YKL interviewed developers the week of November 18–27. The developer was selected immediately thereafter.

Construction commenced in mid-1997. The bookstore was completed in August 1998. The balance of the development was completed in September 1999.

The entire predevelopment and construction process required only three years and five months.

CASE STUDY 4: THE VA MEDICAL CENTER COMPLEX, CITY OF MEDICINE CENTER, DURHAM, NORTH CAROLINA

Type of Project

The VA Medical Center Mixed-Use Development Complex is a mixed-use development on the campus of the VA Medical Center in Durham, North Carolina. The project is the largest of the new prototype privatization projects for the Department of Veterans Affairs.

The Durham VA Medical Center (VAMC), with 1,500 employees, is a 502-bed referral, teaching and research facility providing tertiary and extended care. Since its opening in 1953, the VAMC has been closely affiliated with Duke University Medical Center, which is located directly across the street. There are 213,000 veterans in the primary service area. In 1996, the VAMC's operations included 8,900 inpatients and 154,600 outpatient visits, with a total budget of $130 million.

The original hospital opened in 1953, and now the VAMC provides general and specific medical, surgical, and psychiatric inpatient and ambulatory services, and serves as a major referral center for North Carolina, southern Virginia, northern South Carolina, and eastern Tennessee. The VAMC functions as a regional referral center for radiation therapy, neurological disorders, therapeutic endoscopy, kidney and pancreas transplant, and other procedures. It is also a referral center for high-risk open-heart surgery.

Research at the VAMC covers a broad range of activities conducted by 100 funded investigators working on 250 projects. This effort is currently the sixth largest VA research group, with a VA budget of $6.5 million, and a total budget of about $11 million. The facility is host to a Gerontological Research, Education and Clinical Center, Research and Development Unit, and a Health Services Research and Development Field Station.

The research is presently being performed in eight different VAMC buildings, including the main VAMC building. New clinic construction at the hospital has enveloped the principal research building within the hospital clinical space. The present configuration of research space (including animal research) was undesirable.

In addition to the space in the main VAMC hospital building that became available for ambulatory care resulting from the relocation of research space, the VAMC required approximately 14,000 square feet for ambulatory care space for general medical uses and routine office management of primary care, ambulatory, medical, and surgical patients.

The VA also used the enhanced-use leasing authority as a mechanism to address the VAMC's parking problem. The VAMC had parking for 1,242 VA users (VA employees, patients, and visitors), which included a 998-space parking garage completed in 1989, and 244 surface parking spaces at various sites on the VAMC campus. It was projected that 100 additional parking spaces should be provided.

LCOR selected this public/private opportunity because the privatization effort at the Department of Veterans Affairs clearly indicated the federal government's entrepreneurial approach in solving the financial problem's facing the country's veterans. Congress mandated that the VA utilize and leverage its real estate assets in order to raise the required dollars to fund clinic expansion and medical research programs. LCOR also pursued this opportunity because of its desire to build a long-term relationship with the VA as well as with Duke University and Duke University Medical Center, which are strategically located across from the Durham VA Medical Center. Finally, LCOR recognized this opportunity as an in-fill urban site that has been under federal control for almost 40 years in what is otherwise a relatively suburban community.

Public and Private Partners

The primary public partner is the Department of Veterans Affairs in Washington, DC. The project will specifically benefit the Durham VA Medical Center as the secondary public partner. Additional secondary public partners include Duke University. The primary private partner is LCOR North Carolina LLC, an affiliated subsidiary of LCOR Public/Private, a national development company.

Project Participants

Key community groups include the Durham Chamber of Commerce, the Crest Street Community Association, Triangle Transit, the City of Medicine, and the American Cancer Society.

Project Scope

The original scope of the project incorporated three acres of property at the intersection of the Fulton and Erwin Streets, otherwise known as the heart of the City of Medicine. This intersection is the center of one of the finest medical institutions on the East Coast with national and international reputations. The City of Medicine is home to four hospitals that annually cover 1.7 million outpatient visits and serve more than 270,000 inpatients each year; more than $600 million is spent annually on medical and health-related research in Durham County, and one in every three Durham citizens is employed in the field of medicine, pharmaceuticals, or biotechnology. Duke University Medical Center, part of the Duke University Health System, has consistently ranked among the top 10 U.S. health systems, has attracted more than $213 million in sponsored research in 1998, and its School of Medicine ranks as one of the largest and best medical schools in the country. Duke University has 11,000 students, 21,300 employees (including Duke University Medical Center), and has 1.8 million visitors annually.

Due to innovative planning and the committed goal to provide the VA with the maximum amount of economic value to the public partnership, the project size expanded to five acres.

The building program incorporates the following uses, offering a flexible development program that can expand or contract to meet the existing market conditions at time of development. The project was phased in order to build upon and leverage the asset value of the public partner over a 10-year period from the execution of the Memorandum of Understanding to the final Certificate of Occupancy of the seventh building:

Development Program—City of Medicine Center Campus

Office Tower One	150,000 square feet
Pediatrics and Bone Marrow Transplant Center	30,000 square feet
Hotel	130,000 square feet
Office Tower Two	240,000 square feet
Office Tower Three	300,000 square feet
Retail Building One	10,000 square feet
Retail Building Two	30,000 square feet
VA Clinic	19,000 square feet
VA Research	40,000 square feet
VA/LCOR Garage	2,000 spaces

Authorizing Legislation

In 1991, the United States Congress enacted legislation authorizing the Secretary of VA to enter into long-term agreements called *enhanced-use leases.* The enhanced-use leasing concept is a revenue-generating approach to asset management. (The legislative authority is 38 U.S.C. 8161 et. seq., "Enhanced-Use Leases of Real Property.") The lease allows for non-VA uses on VA property in the form of services, activities, or facility development provided that such uses or activities are not inconsistent with the VA's mission. As well, the lease's overall objective must enhance the VA's mission and programs. In return for entering into an enhanced-use lease with a private developer, the VA may obtain any combination of monetary consideration, services, facilities, or other benefits from the operation of the non-VA uses so long as the benefit is determined by the VA Secretary to be "fair consideration."

Project Objectives

The objective of the overall Enhanced-Use Program is to generate nonappropriated revenues for the direct benefit of local VA hospitals and medical centers. In addition, and specifically related to this project, the public partner's objectives were to generate funds from the leases in order to provide services to veterans. One component was to have the developer provide up to 14,000 square feet of clinic space in order to improve and expand the existing clinic facilities that directly serve veterans in the Carolinas and Virginia. A second component was to provide up to 50,000 square feet of medical research office and dry laboratory space to consolidate research functions and enhance research programs that benefit veterans on a long-term basis as well as future patients who frequent these regional medical centers. The VA's minimum objective was to relocate approximately 20,000 square feet of research space, which was located in the main hospital building, into new space. The VA also desired to obtain, on a no-cost basis, additional on-site parking for 100 VA users (VA patients, employees, and visitors) and improve parking for current VA users through the management of an existing surface and structured parking facility and any future parking facility. The Department's final objective was to obtain periodic ground lease rental payments as part of the consideration for the enhanced-use lease, with the understanding that ground lease rent would be applied by VA toward any VA costs resulting from its use of space or services in the mixed-use development. The VA also benefited from cost savings (estimated up to 30 percent) due to its ability to structure these improvements outside of the federal procurement, design, and construction process. The use of an enhanced-use lease resulted in reduced time needed to structure and execute this development, resulting in additional significant cost savings. The national and international benefits from research conducted on the campus and in conjunction with Duke University Medical Center are not readily quantifiable.

Public Partner's Up-Front Requirements of the Developer

LCOR prepared a proposal including site plans, architectural elevations, and renderings at a cost of approximately $150,000. Once selected, approximately two years of predevelopment activities were required by the developer at a total cost of approximately $1 million prior to commencement of construction. This included business planning, site planning, development and lease agreement negotiation, economic modeling, environmental and geotechnical testing, engineering, preparation of feasibility studies (traffic, parking, market), development of schematic designs, preparation of conceptual and detailed construction budgets, and commencement of marketing activities.

Type of Developer Solicitation

LCOR responded to a competitive RFP issued by the Department of Veterans Affairs.

Ownership

The parcels of land and the existing garage will continue to be owned by the federal government but will be subject to a master development and lease agreement. Upon commencement of construction, a site-specific enhanced-use lease will be entered into with the developer for a 75-year term. The private partner will own the buildings during the term of the lease. At the expiration of the lease term, ownership of the assets will revert to the Department of Veterans Affairs unless the enhanced-use lease is extended.

Insights into the Negotiations

Primary participants in the negotiation included the Washington-based VA Office of Asset and Enterprise Development, the Durham VA Medical Center, and LCOR. The award to the developer was made in May 1998. A Memorandum of Understanding was executed within two months. The Memorandum of Understanding defined the VA's requirements, detailed how the VA properties would be best utilized to achieve VA objectives, and addressed all business terms including a selected financing strategy to implement the development of the project. The parties negotiated the development and lease agreements within an additional 10 months. The enhanced-use lease specified that the developer would be responsible for planning and designing all VA space requirements to be provided to the Department under the terms of the lease. It further stipulated that the developer would be fully responsible for financing, planning, developing, managing, and maintaining the development complex and generating revenues from commercial activities and other permitted uses within the development complex. As part of the consideration for the enhanced-use lease, the lease provided for periodic ground lease rental payments, which were applied by the VA toward all VA costs resulting from its use of space and services in the development complex. Major issues included performance milestones, protection of federal assets including lease subordination, phasing of development, impact of construction on the current and future operation of the VA Hospital, and timing of delivery of clinic and research facilities developed for the Durham VA Medical Center as part of the consideration provided by the developer. Major stumbling blocks included agreement on operational policies and financial responsibility involving the existing garage facility and the replacement of both surface parking and existing research buildings prior to completion of newly constructed buildings.

Basic Deal Structure

The VA Medical Center provided three acres of property for development by the private sector. As consideration for the enhanced-use lease, LCOR committed to construct a 19,000-square-foot clinic facility in the existing hospital and up to 40,000 square feet of research space (research office and wet and dry laboratory). The final consideration will depend on the final implementation of the private-sector development program, which was and continues to be market driven. Development will occur over an eight-year time frame. As construction of each building occurs, dollars will be set aside to fund the VA facilities. Once sufficient funds are reserved, based on a square-footage formula of buildable space in each private-sector building, construction of the VA facilities will also occur. In addition, the local VA Medical Center will share in net proceeds generated by the existing garage over the initial 75-year lease term. Allocation of these funds will be directed to the VA facility fund until all facilities are constructed, at which time all remaining funds generated will flow through directly to additional VA programs on a local level, including funding employee benefit programs such as child day care, health and wellness programs, and other such activities authorized by the Durham VA Medical Center Director's Office.

Sources of Finance

Capital for this project was provided almost entirely by the private sector. Non-capital investments included additional development rights on two parcels that were not originally incorporated but were required in order to provide the VA the maximum consideration requested in the original RFP. Due to the nature of the total development program incorporating over 2,000 parking spaces, shared parking solutions for all tenants resulted in an overall 25 percent reduction in parking spaces, with a project savings of $5 million.

Types of Incentives

While the VA did not contribute a cash investment, the VA did provide control of its specified parcels, which allowed LCOR, with its development expertise, to leverage the unique location of the VA property. Because market demand ultimately determined the scope and timing of this development, the VA's ability to provide sufficient time for LCOR to implement its program was a crucial element of the VA's "investment" in this project. The VA also assigned its ability to directly debit monthly parking charges from VA employees' paychecks, which improved the existing parking garage operation. Access to VA security, trash removal, and consolidation of energy plant services were additional incentives provided by the VA. The VA also encouraged VA affiliates located in the Durham market to relocate its offices to the private developments constructed on the VA campus. Finally, because the VA land will remain under federal ownership, the development was not subject to local jurisdiction and was therefore exempt from zoning regulations, site plan approval requirements, and building permits.

Financing Techniques

The developer and its team of investment bankers arranged a combination of bond financing, conventional private debt, and equity. The nature of tenants, which included the University and Medical Center; public companies; the federal government, with short-term two-year revolving leases; start-up biotech venture capital–funded research companies; and both national credit and local retail tenants, required a comprehensive, complex, and flexible menu of financing alternatives. Challenges included lease subordination issues, depth of Durham office market, collateral issues relating to private expansion of an existing federal garage facility, and convincing the finance markets that short-term two-year VA leases will be automatically renewed (based on a core mission-critical use determination).

Employment Opportunities

This public/private project will create 1,525 construction-related jobs and 2,400 permanent jobs, including employment in sophisticated and highly technologically advanced medical research.

Approval Process

In order to create this federal partnership, the VA secured support of the local community prior to the issuance of the RFP, including various stakeholders and adjacent community associations. Public hearings were held to determine potential impact on veteran services, employees, local commerce, and the community. Because the project was not subject to approvals from the local jurisdiction, only the approval by the State of North Carolina Department of Transportation was required for improvements to the existing infrastructure. The Secretary of the VA must approve the business plan supporting all enhanced-use lease projects once they have been approved by the Office of Management and Budget. Final approval on the project requires a 60-day approval process when Congress is in session. The overall approval process occurred simultaneously with the predevelopment effort conducted by LCOR.

CASE STUDY 5: RUTGERS STATE UNIVERSITY, NEW BRUNSWICK, NEW JERSEY

Type of Project

University Center at Easton Avenue is a 12-story mixed-use project consisting of student housing, retail space, and shared parking facilities. The City of New Brunswick, New Jersey, is the seat of Middlesex County and is also the home of Rutgers University.

Public and Private Partners

This university development is the successful result of a public/private partnership, which combined the efforts of a major university (Rutgers University), a regional hospital (Robert Wood Johnson University Hospital), and an urban city (New Brunswick, New Jersey) with the development expertise of a major national real estate developer (LCOR, Inc.). The primary public partner was Rutgers University; the secondary public partners were the Housing and Urban Development Authority of the City of New Brunswick and Robert Wood Johnson University Hospital.

Rutgers is the State University of New Jersey and has experienced tremendous growth since its founding. Today, the University has an enrollment of over 48,000 students, 33,000 of which are located at the New Brunswick campus. The University is the largest employer in New Brunswick and one of the largest employers within Middlesex County.

Rutgers has a vested interest in the future of New Brunswick and wanted to ensure that the City continues to be favorably viewed by prospective faculty, staff, and students and their families. Rutgers also recognized that its students were creating problems in the city's neighborhoods, thus creating a public relations problem for the University.

The University had a need for additional student housing as evidenced by very strong demand for its existing units. Rutgers also required additional parking within close proximity to the campus. The existing on-campus housing stock consisted almost exclusively of typical dormitory facilities and was among the oldest in the entire University system. Rutgers officials recognized the recruiting value of having an attractive, modern housing facility to show prospective students and their families.

Robert Wood Johnson University Hospital is a major teaching hospital located in New Brunswick. The hospital has been expanding its services and presence in the region and, as a result, its parking facilities were at full capacity during the day. The hospital recognized that future growth was dependent on expansion beyond its current city block location and began acquiring buildings and vacant land. Similar to Rutgers, Robert Wood Johnson University Hospital officials also realized the importance of its host community being favorably viewed by prospective staff and patients and their families. The hospital also needed to ensure that its facilities were capable of accommodating an increased volume of staff and visitors. Additional parking was an area that was deemed especially important to the hospital.

The City of New Brunswick believed that its downtown commercial district was deteriorating because the bulk of the student population was located too far away, and the students did not have a "downtown orientation."

Project Participants

At the outset, New Brunswick officials were involved in nearly all meetings with the other participants. Through the city's attendance and active involvement, institutions realized that the city would be very supportive of a project that fulfilled mutual goals. Among the attendees at the various meetings were the mayor, city economic development officials, city planning officials, city engineering officials, and city attorneys.

Initially, all meetings with Rutgers were attended by University representatives from the finance, housing, planning, and public relations departments. Meetings with hospital officials were attended by representatives of the finance, administration, and life safety departments. Meetings with special focus groups to evaluate the proposed plans were also conducted by the developer with student representatives.

Project Scope

The $55.2 million public/private partnership project is a mixed-use development designed to house 672 university students. The project is located on a unique triangular site on Easton Avenue and Somerset Street in New Brunswick. The building program includes:

900-space parking garage	304,600 square feet
Retail space	20,700 square feet
Student/Faculty health club	6,400 square feet
168-unit student housing	237,000 square feet

Project History

New Brunswick has experienced the benefits and challenges of having Rutgers within its borders since 1766. New Brunswick benefits from the presence of Rutgers in many ways, including international recognition from a major university; a large, stable economic base from the university's students, faculty, and staff; and an educated workforce desirable to potential employers. Conversely, Rutgers is also either directly or indirectly responsible for deterioration of the city's owner-occupied housing stock as units are rented to students; inflated rents from students resulting in reduced opportunities for local residents to locate affordable housing; and students living in the city's neighborhoods creating problems related to overcrowding, noise, and illegal parking.

Legislation Driving the Project

This multipartnership project was authorized under state and city procurement and redevelopment legislation.

Project Objectives

Driving the creation of this development was the need to achieve a number of competing objectives from the New Brunswick community. These objectives were identified by each stakeholder as follows:

City of New Brunswick:
- Neighborhood revitalization by improving the affordability of housing within the city and increasing the number of owner-occupied residences
- Decreased student overcrowding and parking problems in its neighborhoods
- Revitalization of its downtown district through creation of a link between the downtown and student populations
- To provide an improved, active streetscape in an area that was being underutilized
- Creation of an attractive structure in a very prominent and central location

Rutgers University:
- Increased supply of available student housing
- Increased supply of available parking in close proximity to the campus

- To attract students previously living in off-campus housing into Rutgers' housing by providing an affordable and attractive alternative
- To increase Rutgers' competitive edge for prospective students by providing an affordable and attractive housing alternative
- To provide student housing and parking in an affordable, safe, and attractive environment

Robert Wood Johnson University Hospital:
- Increased supply of available parking in close proximity to the hospital
- To complete the assemblage of the entire block adjacent to the hospital (of which Robert Wood Johnson was already the majority owner) for future growth
- To provide parking in an affordable, safe, and attractive environment

Public Partner's Up-Front Requirements of the Developer

LCOR was responsible for the preparation of the initial conceptual designs, including:

- Developing requirements for consultants, anticipated dates of retention, and lines of responsibilities for all development team members
- Preparation of outline budgets and schedules
- Developing project approval approaches
- Developing an overall construction strategy

Type of Developer Solicitation

Rutgers University issued the RFP for the University Center project.

Ownership

University Center is owned by the Housing and Urban Development Authority of the City of New Brunswick. However, because each participant was interested in owning their respective component(s) at the end of their lease term, the building was structured as a condominium from inception. Each participant was granted the option to purchase their respective component(s) upon the expiration of their lease (and the corresponding full amortization date of the bonds) for nominal consideration.

Insights into the Negotiations

LCOR negotiated a development management agreement with the City of New Brunswick Housing and Urban Development Authority.

Basic Deal Structure

The City of New Brunswick, through its Housing and Urban Development Authority, became the owner of the project to facilitate redevelopment incentives and to ensure the lowest cost of financing. Rutgers became the lead tenant for student housing components, parking for students, and the Student Fitness Center. Robert Wood Johnson University Hospital became a secondary tenant for hospital parking. The City of New Brunswick guaranteed the lease up of all remaining retail space. LCOR, as development manager for Rutgers and the City, coordinated the entire predevelopment, development, financing, marketing, leasing, and construction components of the University Center project.

Sources of Finance

The University Center ownership position was accomplished by the Housing and Urban Development Authority of the City of New Brunswick issuing $55.295 million in tax-exempt financing on behalf of the project. Security for the debt was in a variety of forms:

- Long-term lease with Rutgers for 100 percent of the residential area, parking area, and fitness center
- The required lease payments match the debt service attributable to the respective components over the term of the financing.
- Sublease from Rutgers to Robert Wood Johnson University Hospital for approximately 600 parking stalls. The lease payments proportionately match the required lease payments by Rutgers for its parking units.
- Guarantee was provided from the City of New Brunswick for the debt service attributable to the project's retail area.

Types of Incentives

Because the City of New Brunswick desired to have a project developed to solve many of the problems that it believes result from the University's presence, the City offered the following assistance:

- Condemnation power to assist in site assemblage
- Zoning revisions/variances that permitted a project of sufficient size and scope
- Tax-exempt financing if appropriate guarantees were secured

Employment Opportunities

Employment opportunities were generated in the fields of construction, retail, operations, and management.

Approval Process

LCOR was responsible for managing the approval process. Project approvals were required by the City and the University, both of which were active participants and important stakeholders in the process.

CASE STUDY 6: JFK INTERNATIONAL AIRPORT, TERMINAL 4—INTERNATIONAL AIR BUILDING, JAMAICA, NEW YORK

Type of Project

The JFK International Air Terminal 4 project (JFK IAT) is a transportation development project incorporating the operation and redevelopment of an existing airport passenger terminal. The project incorporates construction of the terminal headhouse, east and west concourse structures, and landside and airside facilities. Within this overall program is a 100,000-square-foot retail center located inside the terminal.

LCOR pursued this public/private opportunity because JFK was the first privatization effort of a major airport in the United States. It is also one of the largest public/private developments ever to be undertaken in the history of the country. LCOR determined that the ability to create a unique financing structure coupled with the technical capability and operating expertise would be crucial elements in securing this award. LCOR also recognized the economic opportunity associated with operating the International Arrivals Terminal while the redevelopment and new terminal expansion was underway. Finally, LCOR was interested in pursuing a long-term relationship with the Port Authority of New York and New Jersey as well as pursuing other airport privatization and airport-related development projects throughout the country.

Despite limited prior experience in developing and operating airport facilities, the Terminal 4 development opportunity was immediately appealing to LCOR. Upon reviewing the RFQ, the company determined that Terminal 4 presented significant barriers to entry, a major and immediate development requirement, and very attractive market dynamics. Specific considerations included:

- Terminal 4 would be very large and complex, requiring LCOR to lead a comprehensive development management approach involving multiple principals and an unusually large, diverse team of consultants.
- The process would require significant senior staff resources and creative solutions in all areas of the project—design, construction, financing, leasing, operation, and public involvement.
- It would be expensive to pursue and close, limiting potential competition.
- Airlines providing origination and destination service to JFK would have limited opportunity to choose alternative terminal facilities; they would be "captive" to Terminal 4.

- LCOR enjoyed a good relationship with the staff of the sponsoring public-sector entity (Port Authority of New York and New Jersey) based on previous project work.
- The complicated design and construction work to be performed would be best managed by a local developer with access to the most experienced design/construction team.
- Such a privatization transferring total responsibilities for design, construction, financing, and operations had not yet been executed for passenger terminal facilities in the United States. Responding to the RFP would present significant challenges rarely, if ever before, faced by even the "established" players in the airport development business worldwide.

Public and Private Partners

The primary public partner is the Port Authority of New York and New Jersey. The primary private partner is JFK IAT LLC, which consists of national real estate developer LCOR, Inc.; international airport operator Schiphol USA, an affiliate of Amsterdam-based Schiphol; and worldwide investment bank Lehman Brothers.

Project Participants

Participants in the JFK project include major airlines, existing airport retail tenants, and potential future Fifth Avenue tenants.

Project Scope

The project is located in New York at the John F. Kennedy International Airport. The project is the cornerstone of a multibillion-dollar program undertaken by the Port Authority to reconstruct much of Kennedy Airport. The new IAT will be easily expandable to meet the growing needs of the New York region. The new terminal will also offer shopping, dining, and entertainment options for travelers and airport employees.

The building program includes:

Floor area		1,499,689 square feet
Headhouse	1,036,789 square feet	
Concourses	462,900 square feet	
Number of gates at completion		16 (expandable to 32)

Number of hardstands at completion		10
Number of ticketing positions		108 (expandable to 144)
Available parking		2,305 spaces
Total retail space		100,000 square feet
Number of airplanes to be served		75
Public seating		5,108 seats
Food court and retail area	800 seats	
Boarding area at gates	4,380 seats	

Legislation Driving the Project

The Port Authority did not require the enactment of special legislation to authorize this development project. In fact, it was an act of Congress that authorized the Port Authority, a bi-state agency, to enter into contractual agreements, including the development of Terminal 4.

Project Objectives

The Port Authority had several objectives in mind when it determined the need to redevelop Terminal 4. These included:

- Securing private expertise and private capital for infrastructure investment
- Gaining operational expertise and efficiency in terminal management
- Enabling the replacement of the existing terminal without incurring recourse debt
- Reestablishing JFK as the premier international gateway to the United States

Terminal 4 was one of a series of costly improvements that the Port Authority programmed for JFK Airport. As the overall operator and sponsor for the airport, the Port Authority wanted to ensure that this project was of a world-class signature facility. However, an underlying goal was to remove itself from day-to-day terminal operations.

LCOR recognized that perhaps the single most important element in achieving the Port Authority's specific program objectives for the project was the true concept of "partner." With its understanding of the Port Authority's goals, limitations, and commitment to a fair solicitation process, LCOR had the confidence to invest the resources necessary to develop a winning proposal. LCOR also recognized the value of inviting key Port Authority staff to participate actively in the formulation of the project's development plans and deal/financial structure. The points below are the fundamental "partnering principles" that were applied to Terminal 4 throughout the solicitation, award, and closing stages of the project:

- Nurture an environment that is conducive to achieving the highest degree of cooperation possible between the public- and private-sector participants.
- Include Port Authority staff and consultants in the team's working groups covering design, construction, operations, financing, and due diligence.
- Develop a 100 percent comprehensive response to RFP that showcases the value-added potential of the development team.
- Prepare a format of response that is professional, clean, and easily understood despite the complexity of the proposal.
- In the proposed business plan, recognize value created or delivered by the Port Authority versus value created by JFK IAT. Also, provide meaningful participation in net cash flow to align public- and private-sector interests across all areas of the project—construction costs, financing costs, revenues, and operating expenses.

Public Partner's Up-Front Requirements of the Developer

LCOR was responsible for preparing extensive design drawings and it was responsible for engaging legal counsel to create complex legal and financial transactional agreements. Cost associated with this up-front effort approached $30 million. This included various predevelopment activities that were required prior to financial closing.

Type of Developer Solicitation

LCOR responded to an RFQ and subsequently an RFP issued by the Port Authority of New York and New Jersey.

Insights into the Negotiations

Extensive negotiations on each aspect of lease documents, development documents, and financial closing documents resulted in a seven-figure legal cost prior to closing. It was the complexity of the transaction that created a financial structure and operational plan that led to LCOR's success in securing the project.

Completing negotiations successfully was a direct result of LCOR's ability to distinguish the value of its proposal from the competition. After acquiring a thorough understanding of the project's challenges and a team capable of addressing them in unique ways, the Terminal 4 team developed a plan that offered many unique advantages to the Port Authority.

- Design—all-new facility, at same cost. The Port Authority and competitor proposals combined renovated and new project elements.
- Operations—staffed critical management positions with venture staff and outsourced everything else to third-party contractors pursuant to competitive bidding resulting in a more productive, less costly staff.
- Construction—developed phasing schedule that saved months off the construction schedule, accommodated continued operations with less disruption to passengers and airlines, and saved the money that supported an all-new facility. Having intimate knowledge of construction costs on the airport allowed the team to be more aggressive with cost estimates.
- Program—included a large, centralized, branded retail court featuring major duty-free store as its centerpiece.
- Revenue—established market-based pricing that offered cost certainty to airlines and more profit potential to the venture and the Port Authority.

Basic Deal Structure

The $1.2 billion project was privately financed by the JFK International Air Terminal LLC partnership. The project will be developed, managed, and operated by the partnership under a 29-year lease assignment from the Port Authority. LCOR and its partners succeeded in obtaining the right to redevelop and operate the terminal under the terms of a lease with the Port Authority for 25 years after substantial completion of the new facility. Under LCOR's innovative design and development program, the existing International Air Building will be completely demolished and replaced with a new state-of-the-art 1.5 million-square-foot International Air Terminal ("IAT") to be completed by the summer of 2001. Redevelopment will be staged to provide for continued operation of the terminal, which services over 6 million passengers per year.

Sources of Finance

The LCOR team provided $15 million equity for this project. The balance of required funds was arranged through Lehman Brothers and Citicorp Securities, Inc. as lower-cost debt.

Working with the Port Authority and its investment banking team, LCOR and its partners designed a unique financing structure involving a $15 million equity contribution from the partnership and a $932 million tax-exempt bond issue, which, when combined with interest income and rental income from IAT during construction, provided full funding for the redevelopment of the facility. The innovative tax-exempt bond issue was the first project-based air terminal financing to be completed without benefit of anchor leases from major airlines and is entirely nonrecourse to the Port Authority and achieved investment-grade rating from three rating agencies. Payment of principal and interest on the bonds are guaranteed by MBIA Insurance Corporation to achieve an AAA rating. When completed, this highly visible public/private venture will have provided the Port Authority and the City of New York with a brand new $1.2 billion state-of-the-art terminal facility with only a nominal investment from the Port Authority for the adjacent roadway and infrastructure.

The LCOR finance team structured investment-grade, nonrecourse financing with no required support from the Port Authority, airlines, or the venture. The competition required minimum traffic guarantees from the Port Authority or long-term airline leases to be in place prior to closing. LCOR also accommodated the accelerated repayment of bonds in the event the Port Authority's right to operate JFK Airport is not extended by the City of New York. LCOR convinced the Port Authority of the value of subordinating returns typically paid senior to debt service in order to achieve the lowest cost of capital for the project and to maximize total return to its public partner.

Types of Incentives

Because the terminal is publicly owned and financed, the only incentives received were saving on sales taxes on construction-related material. No additional incentives were provided by the City of New York, the State of New York, or the Port Authority.

Employment Opportunities

This public/private project will create 5 million man-hours in construction work during the development and construction period.

Approval Process

The Port Authority retains jurisdiction for development approval for improvements to the airport. The only additional approvals required related to security and facility jurisdiction by the Federal Aviation Administration. The schedule of partnership approval milestones is as follows:

April 19, 1996	Memorandum of Understanding
May 1, 1997	Notice to Proceed
May 13, 1997	Financial Closing
February 10, 2000	West Concourse w/5 gates
May 8, 2001	Date of Beneficial Occupancy
April 8, 2002	Project Completion

CASE STUDY 7: U.S. SOLDIERS' AND AIRMEN'S HOME, WASHINGTON, DC

Type of Project

This public/private development involved the preparation of a business plan for the mixed-use development of 130 acres of federally owned property in the District of Columbia, as well as asset management of existing facilities. The development plan calls for office, retail, residential, hotel, golf course, and historic redevelopment.

At the conclusion of the business plan phase, the developer had the right to negotiate its role as a development manager. The developer chose to submit an offer to lease the 49-acre North Capitol campus and to retain its exclusive asset management rights on the main campus.

Public and Private Partners

The public partners are the United States Soldiers' and Airmen's Home (USSAH) and the Armed Forces Retirement Home (AFRH) Board. The primary private partner is LCOR, Inc.

Project Participants

Twenty-three veterans' associations, representing 10 million veterans across the United States, were in the key position to conduct a strong liaison role in helping the USSAH successfully achieve its goals. Veteran support, which brought a tremendous amount of knowledge and experience, not only helped support the Home's position but helped create higher visibility for all veterans. Defending the existence and future financial viability of the Home means defending the rights of all veterans for whom the USSAH was originally created and for whom it has continued its mission.

The USSAH Community Relations Plan involved foundations including the National Trust for Historic Preservation; universities; federal agencies, including the Federal National Mortgage Association (Fannie Mae); museums, leadership from Wards 1, 4 and 5; district leadership including the Mayor's Office, the City Council, the Department of Housing and Community Development, the Chamber of Commerce Marketing Center, the People's Involvement Corporation, and the WMATA Community and Development Departments; and private citizens such as local religious and institutional leaders.

The institutions of the surrounding neighborhood partnered in a cooperative arrangement called the Neighborhood and Community Initiative (NCI), with the single mission to improve the communities they serve. The neighborhood improvement initiative was undertaken at the urging of the Children's National Medical Center, the Washington Hospital Center, Providence Hospital, Howard University, Children's Hospital, the USSAH, the Veterans Affairs Hospital, the National Rehabilitation Hospital, Catholic University, and Trinity College.

Project Scope

The project scope is as follows:

OPTION 3a—35-Year Buildout	Square Feet/Unit	Gross Acres
New Development		
Office/Medical	650,000 square feet	12.5
Parking (structured)	2,275 cars	
University Village (incl. cloverleaf site)	615,000 square feet	16.5
Parking (surface)	1,034 cars	
Senior housing	280,000 square feet	10.9
Parking (surface)	275 cars	
Student housing	140,000 square feet	7.8
Parking (basement—single level)	225 cars	
Hotel	225 rooms	2.2
Parking (structured)	250 cars	
Retail	10,000 square feet	(incl. w/in office area)
Parking (structured)	50 cars	
Open space/park/garden		6.3
Adaptive Reuse		
North Gate House		.3
South Gate House		.4

Authorizing Legislation

The contract between LCOR and the AFRH required that LCOR propose legislative authority, which would be required so that the business plan could be implemented. Based on this requirement, the plan evaluated the benefits of ground lease structure from a legal and financing standpoint and also evaluated the benefits of a financial structure that minimized capital investments but maximized the returns through the reversion of assets at the end of the lease period. The plan also reviewed the enhanced-use lease legislation authorized by Congress. Finally, the plan evaluated the contingent environmental liability and impact to the AFRH Trust Fund.

Project History

Established nearly 150 years ago as an asylum for old and disabled soldiers, the USSAH has evolved into one of the country's most dedicated efforts of continuing care retirement environment. The realization of the U.S. Military Asylum (USSAH) culminated after more than two decades of frustrated efforts by Jefferson Davis, Robert Anderson, and, most notably, General Winfield Scott. The dream of creating what was to become the United States Soldiers' and Airmen's Home finally reached fruition when General Scott returned victorious from the Mexican War, with $150,000 paid by the City of Mexico in lieu of ransacking. Scott was able to pay off his troops, buy supplies, and offer the remaining money to Congress to establish what became known as the Soldiers' Asylum. Since that time, the Home's history has been spattered with periods of financial difficulty and threats of closure.

Late in 1851, the 256-acre Riggs estate (in northwest DC) was purchased as a permanent location for the Home. Over the years, additional land was bought from adjoining landowners. The largest parcel of 272 acres belonging to W. W. Corcoran was purchased in 1872. Since then, a significant amount of the total acreage has been given to the District of Columbia and other agencies for purposes including the Veterans Affairs Hospital, the Washington Hospital Center, and North Capitol Street. Currently, the Home sits on 325 acres of parklike land.

Historically, operational funding has come from the soldiers (and later, airmen) themselves. A permanent trust fund was established and supported by monthly active-duty payroll deductions of 25 cents (at a time when the average pay of a soldier was $11 per month). Current withholding is 50 cents. Additionally, fines and forfeitures from military disciplinary actions, interest from the trust fund, and resident fees provide the principal support for the Home today.

The Armed Forces Retirement Home Act, Public Law 101-510, which took effect in 1991, created one of the most significant changes for the Home. This new law established the AFRH, which combined the USSAH and the U.S. Naval Home in Gulfport, Mississippi, under unified management of the Armed Forces Retirement Home Board (AFRHB). Regulations for resident eligibility/resident fee, operating funds, and oversight are now standardized for both homes. As an independent federal agency, the AFRH administers an advisory board appointed by the Secretary of Defense in each home.

Although the homes are excellent examples of "the military taking care of its own," relying on funding from the contributions of active-duty servicemen and women is a double-edged sword. Congressionally mandated military downsizing has since left its mark. Since 1990, funding from the active-duty pay deductions and fines and forfeitures has dropped 39.1 percent, a total of approximately $142 million. The Home now operates at an annual deficit of $8 to $10 million due to the downsizing of the military and increased health care costs. At this rate, insolvency will occur in 2004.

The USSAH has since initiated actions to reduce its operating costs, including cutting the number of residents by more than 800, reducing staff by 24 percent, and closing two dormitories. The AFRH has attempted to increase income by increasing resident fees at both homes, by establishing an Armed Forces Retirement Home Foundation, and by setting up a voluntary retiree allotment. Most importantly, the AFRH has supported an increase in the active-duty military deduction from 50 cents to $1. The increase has not yet been implemented.

Congress has also given the USSAH permission to use its excess land in order to generate income. In 1998, the AFRH contracted with LCOR, Inc. in a public/private venture to evaluate options and opportunities to provide the Home with much-needed income.

Background

In the mid-1980s, the National Capital Planning Commission (NCPC) recognized the need to develop a carefully thought-out plan to ensure the orderly development of Washington's Monumental Core. It had become evident to the Commission that without such a plan, the Mall's distinctive openness would soon disappear due to a flood of new museums and memorials being constructed and those yet proposed. The NCPC proceeded to prepare several studies exploring alternatives to overbuilding the Mall. These studies evoked intense debate at the time about the merits of open space versus new development in the heart of Washington. In the end, the NCPC made preserving and enhancing the open space around the Mall the cornerstone of its new plan, and locating new museums and memorials outside the Mall the principal tool for achieving that goal.

In 1992–1993, the NCPC invited a team of prominent architects, urban designers, economists, and transportation planners to review the staff's initial studies. The consultants commended the concept of preserving Washington's ceremonial core, but also urged that the whole city, not just the federal enclave, should be considered in this plan. Thus, what began as a federal facilities study evolved into a new vision for an expanded Monumental Core. Perhaps the single most critical idea was a simple axial diagram showing the Capitol as the center of Washington, with bold lines radiating north, south, east, and west. This single diagram defined the plan by enlarging the traditional boundaries of the Monumental Core. Unlike earlier plans, this plan, "Extending the Legacy," goes beyond the Mall and expands the definition of *federal interest* to include adjacent neighborhoods, waterfronts, parks, and gateways. Of significance to this document and this effort, the bold line extending north from the Capitol along North Capitol Street terminates at the United States Soldiers' and Airmen's Home, entrusting the development of the site with a major role in the future of the city.

Project Objectives

Project objectives included:

- Creating a single vision for the entire campus
- Ensuring that the Home benefits from and contributes to the synergy of new development created on the existing campus
- Maintaining the Home's image and purpose intact and separate from any new development
- Preserving and integrating into the plan historic architecture, artifacts, and landscape elements
- Creating a vision for the whole neighborhood
- Compatibility with its neighboring uses
- Capturing the imagination of the community and those overseeing its implementation
- Generating long-term revenue to the Armed Forces Retirement Home Trust Fund, which will improve financial conditions and ensure the viability of the USSAH

Development Team

After being selected in a competitive process, LCOR:

1. Determined the disciplines required to thoroughly analyze potential alternative disposition and revenue opportunities open to the AFRH

2. Issued an RFQ utilizing a process similar to the one in which LCOR was selected
3. Interviewed over 100 firms
4. Selected a team of 34 firms
5. Directed team members to concentrate on a specific campus so that work could be completed in a timely manner

The disciplines required for the business plan included market feasibility, land use counsel, site planning, environmental law, architecture, landscape architecture, specialty architecture (historic, university, and senior housing), historic preservation, traffic engineering, civil engineering, general construction, structural and mechanical, electric, and plumbing (MEP) engineering, investment banking, real estate marketing, additional legal counsel (health care, environmental, tax increment and investment tax credit financing), marketing, and public relations.

Specific development strategies designed to maximize the use of undeveloped assets and existing facilities along with appropriate financing methods were identified. Plans for land use, conceptual development, and asset management were prepared.

The team met on a weekly basis both in its entirety and in specific subgroups. LCOR and team members also held additional relevant meetings with designated constituents throughout the seven-month business planning process. Over 150 meetings were held to:

- Identify existing conditions
- Analyze land uses
- Determine market needs and demand
- Evaluate site planning alternatives
- Establish golf course constraints and opportunities
- Review and recommend alternative financing structures
- Identify environmental conditions and restrictions
- Analyze civil engineering solutions
- Understand historic conditions and ramifications
- Recommend preservation concepts, plans, and feasibility
- Create design guidelines and covenants
- Create landscape and streetscape scopes of work and design
- Study architectural sensitivity choices and alternatives
- Prepare development and construction schedules
- Evaluate existing health care operations

The team was organized with LCOR at the helm to coordinate, direct, analyze, and evaluate the team's efforts and disciplines for the North Capitol campus, the main campus, and existing facility operations. Team members for the main campus were further organized into three specific disciplines, which included adaptive reuse of existing facilities, renovation of historic structures, and development opportunities on undeveloped land.

Each campus was assigned a distinct design team responsible for identification of existing conditions and recommendation of alternative solutions. These disciplines included site planning, architecture, general construction, and engineering. Both campuses were analyzed in depth by the remaining professional firms responsible for their respective specialized disciplines.

The challenges that faced LCOR dictated the formation of such an extensive development team. It is believed that only a public/private partnership could understand and respond to the Home's need. The private sector is able to bring resources and solutions that the Home most likely cannot create or implement on its own.

One of the challenges has been to determine land values, income streams, market feasibility, and potential development plans for property, which has remained under federal ownership for over 150 years, located in a currently challenging neighborhood.

A second challenge has been to expeditiously draw up real plans, which could be implemented immediately based on an inevitable deadline foreboding insolvency for the Home. Real, yet flexible, plans needed to be put in place in order to generate income to offset an $8 to $10 million annual loss and to replenish the AFRH Trust Fund.

Basic Deal Structure

A ground lease program was utilized to protect the assets of the USSAH. Under a ground lease, the AFRH, as lessor, would grant a long-term lease to a developer, who would make physical improvements in the property. At the end of the lease term, the improved property would revert back to the lessor.

The AFRH required that the ground lessee covenant that it would not exceed a minimum construction loan to value ratio and bond improvements for the benefit of both the lender and the ground lessor. The ground lease contained detailed design and development covenants. The number of buildings, minimum parking, square footage and height of improvements, expected use of the improvements, minimum square footage (per pad and entire project), and total investment budget were set forth as a standard against which to measure subsequent review and approval. The USSAH has the right to review and comment on design plans.

The plan summarized the estimated results of each asset's preliminary financing structure and *pro forma* forecast. The data reported include: (1) the amount of debt and equity required, based on the general project assumptions detailed previously and the estimated cost of each asset; (2) the estimated average annual debt service coverage during the first 10 years and the estimated internal rate of return on equity investment, based on the project costs and operating assumptions separately identified for each type of major asset; and (3) estimated ground lease payments to the AFRHB.

Value to the AFRHB was measured for all assets as the gross amount, the average annual amount, and the present value of income streams projected to be received by the AFRHB. Each income stream was first calculated over the 35-year analysis period (2002–2036). The present value of each forecast income stream would then be calculated as of January 1, 2000. In addition, a "residual value" of each asset was calculated by applying a 10 percent capitalization rate to the projected net cash flow of the asset in 2036, and discounting this amount back to the January 1, 2000, present value date.

Four types of income streams were estimated:

1. Base ground lease payments, which are fixed annual amounts and therefore relatively predictable

2. Participating ground lease payments in the form of either or both: (a) profit sharing as a defined percentage of net income after debt service and reserves, or (b) surcharges paid by users of the facilities or other income. The amount of profit sharing has been determined individually for each asset, depending on that asset's projected financial condition and the attendant financing requirements.

3. Contribution by each property management company (including the hotel manager) of one-half percentage point of its annual property management fee

4. Estimates of "second curve" income that would derive from various personal services provided by the property management company to the employees and residents of the facilities located on the USSAH campuses

Financing Techniques

The financing plan assumed that each type of facility would be financed separately, rather than through a unified "master trust" arrangement. This type of financing plan enabled the most economically attractive assets to benefit from the lowest market rates and ensured that no nonproductive, deficit-producing assets are developed on the USSAH property.

The financing of each asset was assumed to fund estimated costs and fees relating to developing and designing, constructing, and furnishing the facility, including a contingency allowance as well as allocated off-site improvement costs.

The financing spread assumed for each type of asset was composed of two components: (1) a credit spread that was sized depending on the type of asset and the underlying security for the financing, and (2) a 100-basis-point interest rate cushion that adjusted for current historically low interest rate levels. Based on the project cost and operating assumptions for each facility, the financial analysis assumed that a target 20 percent internal rate of return on equity must be achieved for any asset that includes equity in its financing structure.

Four types of financing structures were used:

1. Taxable real estate/project financing for the office, retail, and hotel assets
2. Taxable lease financing for the federal office building and embassy facilities (including embassy staff housing)
3. Taxable developer financing for single-family and multifamily residential housing and the golf course
4. Tax-exempt revenue bond financing for the University Village, student housing, residential housing, and Continuing Care Retirement Community

Tax increment financing.   In April 1998, the District of Columbia City Council enacted the Tax Increment Financing Authorization Act of 1998 ("TIF Act"). The TIF Act creates a new source of financing for certain eligible development projects in the District of Columbia.

In general, tax increment financing targets undeveloped or underdeveloped properties that are not realizing their potential as sources of economic activity and tax revenue. The concept of TIF is to permit the project sponsor to pledge the incremental increase in real property taxes and sales taxes generated by a project to secure additional financing. The financing is then repaid through the future tax revenues.

From the standpoint of the project sponsor, TIF functions like a grant: the sponsor generally receives the TIF proceeds up front, and the proceeds are repaid through real property and sales taxes generated by the project. The District, for its part, benefits from the new direct taxes generated by the project, which are not pledged to support TIF, by spin-off economic activity, and by all of the new direct taxes once the TIF debt is repaid. Because the fundamental principle of TIF is that it will be used only to the extent necessary to finance projects that will not otherwise move forward, both the project sponsor and the District benefit through TIF.

The business plan:

- Outlined the key criteria that a project must satisfy to be eligible for TIF
- Summarized the process for obtaining approval of a TIF application
- Discussed the potential use of TIF proceeds
- Described the key limitations relative to using TIF in connection with the redevelopment of the USSAH
- Provided a general description of several alternative models for the use of TIF by the USSAH
- Listed the benefits of TIF from the perspectives of all concerned parties
- Described the process that has occurred and will need to occur in order for TIF to work for the USSAH

Three models for using TIF, which may be used independently or in concert with one another, were considered:

1. The first model used the sales tax increment created by on-site development of retail uses to fund streetscape improvements and other public amenities in the areas surrounding the USSAH.
2. The second model used future real estate tax and sales tax increments generated by one or more broad geographic areas to fund improvements in those areas or in nearby areas.
3. The third model used future real property tax increment created by on-site development to fund the streetscape improvements and public amenities.

Investment tax credit financing. The business plan discussed the potential availability of the benefits of the rehabilitation tax credit for federal income tax purposes in connection with the redevelopment of the USSAH's historic core. Several buildings on the USSAH campus potentially qualified as certified historic structures for which appropriate rehabilitation expenditures may be undertaken.

In general, the requirements to qualify for the 20 percent rehabilitation tax credit include:

- The rehabilitation must be of a certified historic structure, which must be either listed in the National Register or located in a registered historic district, and certified by the Secretary of the Interior as being of historic significance to the district.
- The Secretary of the Interior must certify that the rehabilitation is consistent with the historic character of the property or the district.

- Qualified rehabilitation expenditures (i.e., those expenditures that qualify for the credit) generally include amounts incurred that are chargeable to a capital account for depreciable real property. Thus, expenditures on a sidewalk, a parking lot, or landscaping are not qualified rehabilitation expenditures. Also excluded are expenditures for the enlargement of an existing building.

Unlike the typical transaction in which the sponsor of a rehabilitation tax credit project would purchase the real property to be rehabilitated, the owner of the USSAH campus will continue to be the federal government. Although the federal government would obviously realize no direct benefits from a rehabilitation tax credit, the use of a long-term ground lease should allow a private developer or other entity to take advantage of the rehabilitation tax credit. One must, however, structure the ownership and use of the historic buildings correctly to qualify for the rehabilitation tax credit.

Employment Opportunities

The fiscal impact of the first phase of main campus redevelopment is greater than that of the second phase, due, in part, to a more current timing sequence and greater construction and renovation activities, which occur in the first phase. The second phase is potentially developed over a much longer time period, producing an independent, lower fiscal impact. The remaining 10-year period of the 35-year development plan was not projected in this analysis.

The fiscal impact model separates economic impact between construction and operational periods, using commonly accepted multiplier effects derived from input/output tables. The proposed new development and revitalization produce both direct and indirect jobs of 28,057. The total projected value-added annual wages and new employment generated by these activities at USSAH's project is almost $700 million.

The development options for the North Capitol campus offer a wide range of incremental advantages for the District. The first two options provide less dense development with more residential components. These options produce nominal returns to the city, because there is very limited commercial development. The last option, which is the highest and best use option for the North Capitol campus, produces an increment in wages in excess of $58.5 million.

Approval Process

A study of development permits and approvals required to commence construction of new facilities indicated in the USSAH business plan was conducted. The time frames given for the actual permit approval processes depend on adequate up-front communication with the agencies during the design phase so that the permit phase is streamlined.

Permit Type	Agency	Time Limit
Plan approval	National Capitol Planning Commission	30–90 days
Approval of water/sewer/storm	DC Water & Sewer Authority	1–2 months
Approval of erosion/sediment control design	DC Department of Consumer & Regulatory Affairs (DCRA)	2–3 months
Approval of stormwater management design	DCRA	2–3 months
Permit for public space work	DC Department of Public Works (DPW)	1–3 weeks
Approval of water meter locations	DPW	1–3 weeks
Environmental assessment	National Environmental Protection Act (NEPA)	6–9 months
Building permits	DCRA	6 months
Approval of access points and traffic signals	DPW	4–6 months
Approval of plans for health care/ skilled care buildings	DC Department of Health & Human Resources	30 days
Grading permit	DCRA	2–3 months
Wetlands permit	Army Corps of Engineers	3 months
Approval for falcon habitat	U.S. Fish and Wildlife Service	30 days
Permit for removal of underground fuel storage tanks and contaminated soil	DCRA	30 days
Permit for removal of asbestos-containing materials	DC and EPA Region III	2 weeks
Approval of traffic queue and air quality impact analysis	DCRA	2–3 months
Coordination with electric utility	Potomac Electric Power Company (PEPCO)	Ongoing
Coordination with natural gas utility	Washington Gas	Ongoing

Schedule to Completion

1999	Secure Congressional Authorization
2000	Implement Community Relations Plan

2001	Initiate Phase I Approval and Permitting
1999–2000	Execute Ground Leases
1999–2000	Initiate Phase I Marketing, Design, and Financing
2000–2001	Commence Phase I Horizontal Construction
2000–2001	Commence Phase I Vertical Construction

CASE STUDY 8: WHITE FLINT METRO STATION, NORTH BETHESDA, MARYLAND

Type of Project

This is a mixed-use residential, office, and retail transit-oriented public/private development.

Public and Private Partners

Primary Public Partner: Washington Metropolitan Area Transit Authority (WMATA)
Primary Private Partner: LCOR, Inc.

Project Scope

The White Flint East Mixed-Use Development will be developed on a 32.4-acre tract located on the east side of Rockville Pike to the east of the White Flint Metro Station. This major parcel is part of the North Bethesda/Garrett Park Sector Plan and has been designated for development under the Transit Station Mixed (TSM) zone. This zone will allow for up to 2,800,000 square feet of development, evenly split between commercial and residential uses. The LCOR plan provides for both high density at the metro station and appropriate open spaces for both the residential and commercial components.

The development has been divided into two distinct parts. The western portion, adjacent to the metro station, contains approximately 18 acres and is bounded on the west by the metro station and tracks. This is part of the County's urban design plan for the area. This portion provides for the commercial and "Main Street" retail development and the location of the 1,000–1,500-car WMATA parking garage along with the appropriate kiss and ride area and 10 bus bays. Metro employee parking for 110 cars is also provided in this garage.

The garage has been located at the northern portion of the site, with the main access from Old Georgetown Road. The focal point of the site is a four-building office complex of over 1,000,000 square feet, ranging in size from 18 to 24 stories over a multilevel underground parking structure for over 2,500 cars. Special lighting, signage, and various paving materials will all help to create a sense of place for this prominent location.

The remaining 14 acres to the east contain over 1,300 residential units in four high-rise luxury rental apartment buildings.

A summary of the program for the site follows:

Site size: Approximately 32.43 acres

Residential: 1,338 high-rise rental apartment units in four phases:

Freestanding retail 200,000 square feet

Office/First-floor retail: 1,204,000 square feet, in four office buildings.

Structured parking facility: A four-level parking garage with 1,000–1,500 parking spaces for WMATA patrons and 110 Metro employee parking spaces. Other Metro facilities constructed along with the garage would include:
- Bus terminal facility with 6 sawtooth and 4 parallel bus bays
- Kiss and ride area with 30 short-term parking spaces

Project History

The WMATA issued a general solicitation for 30 sites in 1996. This was one of the premier sites, a prominent, strategically located site in an urbanizing area. WMATA's underlying goal is to generate transit revenues and increase ridership.

Total Development Budget

Total project cost for the White Flint East Metrorail Station Project is estimated at $350 to $400 million.

Authorizing Legislation

No special legislation was required.

Project Objectives

- Development, which could occur rapidly, based on both land use and market considerations
- Significant increase in WMATA ridership and the revenues related thereto
- Significant increase in Montgomery County's real estate tax base

Public Partner's Up-Front Requirements of the Developer

- LCOR will be responsible to rezone the property
- LCOR will own and develop all phases of the project, incurring all expenses of marketing, construction, etc., on a long-term land lease from WMATA.

Type of Developer Solicitation

The WMATA issued a general request for proposal solicitation of 30 sites in March 1996. The proposal was due in July 1996, and the award was issued in June 1997. A $100,000 bond was requested at the time the RFP response was submitted.

Insights into the Negotiations

Negotiations were lengthy and required a substantial legal budget.

Sources of Finance

Conventional debt and equity sources will be used to finance the development.

Types of Incentives

No incentives were used in structuring the public/private development.

Employment Opportunities

Hundreds of construction and permanent jobs will be created by this project.

Approval Process

The project must be approved by Montgomery County and the Federal Transit Administration.

Schedule to Completion

The project will be completed in phases over an 8–10 year period.

Financial Proposal

The following financial structure was created for the White Flint East Metro Station:

Form: Unsubordinated long-term land lease between the
                     WMATA, as land lessor, and LCOR, Inc. or its assigns,
                     as land lessee.

Developer Request for Qualifications

DOWNTOWN "CITY" CONVENTION CENTER
HEADQUARTERS HOTEL

A MAJOR CONVENTION CENTER HOTEL TO SUPPORT
THE CONVENTION CENTER
AND DOWNTOWN "CITY"

Issued By:
"City" Downtown Management Corporation on Behalf of
Civic Center Department, City of "X"

Request for Qualifications Prepared By:
"City" Downtown Management Corporation

Date: _____

NOTICE OF REQUEST FOR DEVELOPER QUALIFICATIONS

Sealed responses containing development team qualifications for a Convention Center Headquarters Hotel will be received by the "X" Downtown Management Corporation, 9999 Smith Ave., Suite 999, City, State, Zip, prior to 5:00 P.M. on Date: _____.

The Request for Qualifications (RFQ) document may be obtained from Mr. Jones, President, "X" Downtown Management Corporation, 9999 Smith Ave., Suite 999, City, State, Zip, (999) 999-9999.

A pre-response conference will be held at 10:00 A.M. on September 30 at the Convention Center. Respondents are not required to attend, but are encouraged to do so.

All respondents will be required to comply with City Council Ordinance No. 78-1538, passed August 9, 19XX, relating to Equal Employment Opportunity Contract Compliance.

The City reserves the right to reject any or all responses to this RFQ, to advertise for new RFQ responses, or to accept any RFQ response deemed to be in the best interest of the City.

A response to this RFQ should not be construed as a contract nor indicate a commitment of any kind. The RFQ does not commit the City to pay for costs incurred in the submission of a response to this RFQ or for any costs incurred prior to the execution of a final contract.

Date: _____

Signature of Appropriate City Manager or Director

Contents

Selection Procedure

Overview
Time Frame
Schedule

Submission Requirements—RFQ Phase

Criteria for Selection

Submittal Instructions

Conditions and Limitations
Minority and Women Business Enterprise Requirements

INTRODUCTION

The City of "X" seeks to strengthen its position among the nation's leading convention center destinations and continue the redevelopment of the downtown area as one of the premier cultural, entertainment, and trade centers in the United States. City leaders recognize that one of the major components needed to make "X" an attractive convention destination is the addition of a major hotel within walking distance of the George R. Brown Convention Center. Mayor John Smith and the City of "X" Administration have taken a very proactive and decisive approach toward bringing this project to fruition, providing the impetus needed to push this development ahead.

Downtown "X" is well known throughout the world as the heart of an international city, the nerve center of the world's oil and gas industry with an increasingly service-oriented economy, and a spectacular collection of world-class commercial architecture rising out of the gulf coastal plain. The investment to create and maintain the heart of the nation's fourth largest city has been immense. Downtown "X" has a daytime population approaching 140,000 people, with approximately 56 million square feet of gross space, including buildings ranked among the most famous in the world.

The Vision

The "X" Convention Center is located in the southeast fringe of downtown "X." The closest modern commercial development is approximately 1,000 feet from the Convention Center. The Center is well designed and, given its size, can compete effectively with the largest convention and trade show venues in North America. The Center's location was purposely selected outside the downtown core to allow for development of a sufficiently sized Center. Future expansion is possible, as are other compatible land uses within the perimeter of the Center. Due principally to the downturn in "X's" economy during the early and mid-1980s, the land between the core of downtown and the Center has not experienced significant development. Moreover, the hotel supply near the Center severely contracted during the same period, seriously undermining the City's ability to compete for national convention business.

The City's goal is to get a major hotel development team to build a world-class convention center headquarters hotel and associated developments, which will allow "X" to compete effectively on a national level for convention and tourism business and help to link the Convention Center to downtown. The overall goal is one of creating a tourist- and pedestrian-friendly urban campus to evolve around the Convention Center. A significant first step toward this goal is to expand the number of economically supportable hotel rooms in downtown, within walking distance of the Convention Center.

Background

In January 19XX, the City of "X" celebrated the opening of the million-square-foot, state-of-the-art Convention Center, the nation's tenth largest, located in downtown

"X." Although the Convention Center is one of the nation's most functionally advanced convention facilities, consistently winning high reviews from meeting planners and association executives alike, its growth has been constrained by a lack of convention-oriented hotel rooms near the Convention Center. At present, a large convention, which can be comfortably accommodated at the Convention Center, must transport a significant portion of its delegates by bus to hotels outside the downtown area. This substantially increases the cost of holding a convention in "X," as well as lowers delegate enjoyment and satisfaction. "X" has lost numerous major citywide conventions for this reason alone.

The Convention Center Headquarters Hotel

The most frequently stated reason for an association not booking a convention in "X" is the lack of a large convention-oriented hotel near the Convention Center. When the convention hotel issue was previously addressed in 19XX, there were 133 associations that would not book in "X" without the convention hotel, with estimated delegate spending of over $900 million. Numerous associations have joined this list since 1988 and since the Convention Center's opening; the Center has experienced a decline in the number of annual citywide events. The Convention Center users are most concerned that the hotel is within walking distance of the Convention Center. Therefore, their willingness to consider "X" as the city to host their event is severely affected by the absence of conveniently located, high-quality hotel rooms. The City has determined that in order to increase utilization levels and capitalize on the full potential of the Convention Center, a world-class convention center hotel must be developed on a site near the Convention Center.

The City's goal is to provide an overall convention package that attracts major national conventions and enables the Convention Center to fully achieve its envisioned community benefit. In an effort to bring more and larger conventions and trade shows to "X" and to positively impact the City's and State's economy, the City's leadership is strongly committed to promoting the development of a major convention headquarters hotel to support the Convention Center and to serve as an economic catalyst for downtown and the region. An independent accounting firm, under contract to the City in 19XX, projected the total economic output of the Convention Center to increase by over $100 million at opening to nearly $150 million 10 years later with the construction of a hypothetical 1,200-room Convention Center Headquarters Hotel.

As evidence of leadership's commitment, earlier this year, the state legislature approved a comprehensive package of progressive legislation that conveys a series of financial incentives and inducements, which are presented later in the RFQ, to stimulate the development of a Convention Center Headquarters Hotel.

The City of "X", "Y" County, and State of "Z" are enthusiastic about the opportunity to do business with qualified parties capable of developing the Convention

Center Headquarters Hotel and related developments with the overall goal of enhancing economic development efforts downtown and throughout the entire city.

Statement of Authority

The "X" Downtown Management Corporation, in association with the City of "X," has the right to solicit this RFQ and facilitate development of a contractual relationship with a developer/operator. This solicitation is being undertaken pursuant to recent legislation related to headquarters hotel development.

Solicitation Process

In order to allow broad participation by the development community, and in anticipation of strong interest emanating from this solicitation process, the City has elected to conduct a three-phase development solicitation procedure for the selection of the developer(s) consortium or consortia:

Phase I: Request for Development Qualifications
Phase II: Detailed Request for Proposals—Short-Listed Teams
Phase III: Recommendations and Negotiation of Terms and Conditions with the Selected Team(s)

OWNERSHIP AND FUNDING REQUIREMENTS

Ownership Requirements

To be eligible to benefit from the tax "rebates" under recently approved legislation, a municipality or a municipally sponsored, nonprofit corporation must own the Convention Center Headquarters Hotel. For this purpose, the City of "X" is creating a corporation that will have all the powers of a local government corporation and a nonprofit corporation pursuant to Art. 1528L and Art. 1396 of the "State" Revised Civil Statutes Annotated. The corporation will have the power to receive refunds, rebates, and abatements of taxes paid on a qualified hotel project as provided to it under House Bill 2282, Acts of the "State" Legislature, Regular Session, 19XX. It is expected that the corporation will be served by a board of directors composed of nine to eleven members, which will be appointed by the mayor with the approval of City Council.

The corporation and/or the City may enter into a development agreement concerning the Convention Center Headquarters Hotel with the developer/operator team selected through this solicitation and evaluation process. The economic benefits associated with the design, development, and operation of such type of property can be assigned in its entirety or shared with the selected developer team. This legal ownership requirement does not preclude an interested party who would wish to undertake development of a Convention Center Headquarters Hotel without the participation of a municipally sponsored local government corporation. However, in such instance, the financial incentives package would not be available.

Convention Hotel Legislation

During May 19XX, House Bill 2282, designed to encourage developers to construct a Convention Center Headquarters Hotel in cities of 1.5 million or more, was approved by the state legislature. The purpose of this legislation is to permit all state hotel occupancy taxes and state sales and use taxes collected at a convention center hotel (must be located within an Enterprise Zone and within 1,000 feet of the convention center complex to be deemed a "Qualified Hotel Project") to be rebated to the municipality or a municipally sponsored local government nonprofit corporation that owns the hotel(s) during the first seven years after such "Qualified Hotel Project" is open for initial occupancy. The tax rebate applied to taxes collected only at such hotel. By the legislation, a Convention Center Headquarters Hotel, properly situated and owned, will be a "Qualified Hotel Project" and be an eligible business and project under the meaning of the "State" Enterprise Zone Act, Chapter 2303, "State" Government Code. Final approval of a proposed project will be made by the "State" Department of Commerce and/or the State Comptroller.

H.B. 2282 also permits local taxing entities, such as the City, County, and Metropolitan Transit Authority, to rebate the local hotel occupancy tax, local sales and use tax, local mixed beverage tax, and local property taxes for a period of up to 10 years. Granting of these rebates is discretionary on the part of each taxing unit. The following table presents a summary of the fiscal incentives that may be available to the selected developer team:

Taxing Entity	Category	Rate
State	Hotel Occupancy Tax	6.0%
	Sales Tax	6.25%
County	Hotel Occupancy Tax	2.0%
	Beverage Tax	1.50%
	Property Tax	0.60032%
Local School Districts	Property Tax	1.384%
Metro	Sales Tax	1.00%
City	Hotel Occupancy Tax	7.00%
	Beverage Tax	1.50%
	Sales Tax	1.00%
	Property Tax	0.63%

Based on projections prepared for the Convention Center Headquarters Hotel, these combined fiscal incentives could range from $6 million to $10 million annually. Actual incentives would depend on actual results from operations. Each development team should conduct their own calculations to arrive at their estimate of fiscal incentives. A copy of H.B. 2282 is provided in the Appendix.

Project Capital Funding

The selected developer team will bear the responsibility of identifying and securing the necessary long-term capital funding for the construction of the proposed Convention Center Headquarters Hotel. For the purpose of this RFQ, respondents should address potential financing options, including a capital structure suggested for the project. At this RFQ stage, financing options only need to be conceptualized. Short-listed development teams invited to participate in Phase II, the detailed proposal submission phase, will be required to present a detailed financing program.

The municipally sponsored, nonprofit corporation may consider a number of debt structure alternatives as may be proposed by the respondents, from which the optimal approach will be selected at a later stage. The corporation may serve as the legal issuing conduit for debt financing, which may be potentially structured as a tax-exempt or a taxable transaction.

Site Attainment

The City does not control a site targeted for the development of the project. H.B. 2282 mandates that development must occur within 1,000 feet of the Convention Center complex and be within a state-approved Enterprise Zone to qualify for tax rebates, refunds, and abatements. The City is not bound to any specific site, and indeed, the proposing teams are free to consider and submit any sites they wish. It is not incumbent on each responding development team to demonstrate how it proposes to gain access to the selected site as a condition of responding to this RFQ. However, incorporating information on site preference and plans to obtain its control will enhance possibilities for inclusion of the developer team in the short list for Phase II. Short-listed teams will be required as part of Phase II to select a development site and demonstrate an ability to gain development control over it.

During the RFP stage (Phase II), it will be incumbent on the proposer to verify site ownership and legal boundaries to determine if the proposed hotel project site qualifies for tax rebates, refunds, and abatements.

"CITY" MARKET DESCRIPTION

"City" Regional Profile

The Convention Center is situated in the middle of an eight-county, 7,400-square-mile "City" region County Metropolitan Statistical Area (CMSA) with a 19XX population estimated at 3,902,800. Economic projections predict the regional population to reach 4,041,000 by 19XX; 4,367,000 by the year 19XX; and 5,258,000 by 19XX. These estimates were prepared by "Smith" Consultants.

"City" boasts a stable and growing economy, having overcome the difficult years of the early to mid-1980s. In May 19XX, "City" surpassed the previous record job count set in March of 19XX, more than regaining the jobs lost in the 19XX–19XX recession. Since the bottom of its recession, "City" has gained nearly 300,000 jobs—more than any other metro area except Chicago–Gary–Lay County. Among the large metro areas, "City's" 20 percent net gain for that period trails only the growth rate for Seattle–Tacoma. Houston's economic momentum is even more impressive, occurring at a time when other major U.S. cities are dealing with job losses and recessionary conditions.

The region has diversified significantly since the early 1980s, in response to the recession of that decade, with health care industries and service sectors accounting for much of the growth. Diversifying sectors, according to University of "X's" Center for Public Policy, averaged 8 percent annual growth between 19XX and 19XX. From 19XX to 19XX, these diversifying sectors accounted for half of all new jobs in the economic base. Most of "City's" economic diversity is being led by growth in the service sector. Large corporations are a major element of the regional and downtown economy, with 16 Fortune 500 companies and 10 Fortune Service 500 companies in 19XX, located in "City."

"City" is the third largest port by tonnage in the United States, handling more than 125.3 million short tons of cargo in 19XX. In 19XX, it was first in foreign tonnage, handling 67.6 million short tons of foreign cargo. "City's" international orientation is represented by 54 foreign consular offices. Over 120 firms' headquarters in 21 foreign nations maintain business representation here, including over 50 foreign banks. Passengers at "City's" two airports increased by 6.7 percent for a total of 27,582,300 million in 19XX. "City" is eighth among U.S. cities in international passenger volume and remains among the lowest-cost U.S. air hubs in the nation. Direct air service links "City" to over 100 cities in the United States and to more than 20 international markets.

A fully developed freeway system radiates in all directions of downtown. The Convention Center site is located on "U.S. 00" with average daily traffic of 146,000 vehicles per day, and crosses Interstate "00" with average daily traffic of approximately 185,000 vehicles per day, and Interstate "00" with 107,000 vehicles per day. Rush hour is now being aided by mobility improvements, including a total of 58 miles of transit ways—the most of any U.S. city. METRO, "City's" transit authority, will construct $200 million worth of improvements in the downtown area in the next six years as part of the Better Bus Plan currently under development.

INSERT MAP OF MARKET AREA

"City" offers high quality-of-life attributes, a low cost structure, abundant cultural and recreational resources, quality public education, good weather, and easy access to public services. All these attributes make "City" a very desirable destination for business relocations and start-ups. Housing is very affordable in "City." Housing costs for a mid-management standard of living were 6 percent below the national average for 1992 and 32 percent below the average of 20 metropolitan areas with 1.5 million in population.

"City" today offers a valuable mix of resources for economic growth—a vast pool of technological and engineering knowledge needed in a wide variety of fields, universities and colleges that offer the potential for joint ventures with business, a skilled labor force and good labor availability, low business costs and living costs, and a tradition of cooperation between the private and the public sectors.

Downtown "City" Profile

"City's" downtown is approximately 1.5 square miles in area, containing approximately 50 million square feet of commercial, special, and general-purpose office space and approximately 4 million square feet of government-owned buildings. The daytime office population was estimated at 137,038 in 19XX by the University of "City's" Center for Public Policy. Downtown is the home of major corporate headquarters including: Company A, Company B, Company C, Company D, Company E, and Company F. With the inception of branch banking under "City" law, major banks began to concentrate many operations formerly performed in branches to their downtown headquarters. Downtown is the home or regional home office of Bank A, Bank B, Bank C, Bank D, and Bank E. Major law and accounting firms are located downtown because of their business relations with major corporations. While there has been consolidation of corporate functions in "City" over the past few years, downtown has fared well. Downtown has not lost any major corporate headquarters to other business centers and has added several in the past decade, notably "A" Corporation and "B" Corporation. Numerous international firms maintain offices within downtown.

At one time, downtown was the dominant retail center of "City." However, this position has changed as retail stores have followed a suburbanizing population. Today, less than 1.5 percent of the region's retail space is in downtown. Yet 1.03 million square feet remain devoted to retailing, with the 205,000-square-foot "Smith's" flagship store on Main Street and the 185,000-square-foot "City" Shops, which is near the Convention Center on the east side of downtown, serving as principal anchors. Over 200,000 square feet of mostly service retail space may be found in "City's" unique tunnel system. Retail hours cater to downtown office workers. The retail sales trend in downtown is up somewhat, and a recent study by Urban Marketing Collaborative estimates that the downtown market is underserved and has the potential to expand by 40 percent. At present, there is limited nighttime shopping opportunities in downtown.

Downtown "City" has a uniquely developed, 5.5-mile, principally privately owned tunnel and skywalk system connecting over 40 million square feet of space within downtown. This climate-controlled, well-designed, safe, and carefully maintained environment allows pedestrians to move quickly and comfortably through the downtown area.

Presently, downtown has the highest visitation rate of any area in the "City" region, with an estimated 40 million annual visits. Of these, 35 million are work related, 7 million government or business related, and 8 million related to downtown civic, educational, cultural, religious, or entertainment attractions. At 8 million nonbusiness visits, downtown serves as the largest attraction in the region.

In 19XX, there were approximately 830,000 trips per day entering or leaving downtown. Because downtown is the seat of city and county governments, large numbers of daily visits are made. In 19XX, 70,000 of these trips were made by bus and the rest by private automobiles. There are over 75,000 parking spaces in downtown, with 29 percent in garages. Future transit development calls for significant improvement of the city streets as well as new transit centers, freeway connections, and bus circulation patterns as part of Metropolitan Transit Authority ("METRO"). These improvements will positively impact at least 13 streets in the downtown area with improved street pavement, sidewalks, transit patron shelters, lighting, landscaping, street furniture, and other amenities. Great care is being taken to ensure that improvements provide the best possible transit environment, pedestrian streetscape, and business support services as a part of this program. Two streets designated for extensive improvements are "North" and "South," which, in an improved state, will provide excellent connections from the Convention Center to retail shopping, downtown hotels, and recreation facilities along these streets. The capital budget for street improvements is approximately $100 million in the downtown area, and construction is expected to begin in 19XX. The federal government has already approved the basic scope of the project pending completion of preliminary engineering, which is currently underway.

In addition to the transit improvements previously mentioned, which will dramatically improve streets and transit throughout downtown, several other transportation projects will greatly enhance access to downtown in general and the Convention Center area in particular. First, preliminary design work is underway to extend the "City" Toll Road into downtown, thus providing a direct link from the airport to downtown. Second, a new interchange is planned to provide direct connectors to the east side of downtown.

Downtown is where most large outdoor public events are produced. Virtually every weekend, fun runs, bicycle races, parades, or festivals attract thousands to downtown. The Thanksgiving Day Parade was nationally broadcast to 13 million viewers for the first time in 19XX and attended by 700,000. The largest event downtown is the "City" International Festival. Each spring, this 10-day arts and entertainment extravaganza attracts a total of over 1 million visitors.

"City's" downtown skyline is a well-known visual feature, which attracts the at-

INSERT PHOTOS OF EVENTS IN DOWNTOWN

tention of residents and visitors alike. The Convention Center Hotel would be uniquely situated at the foot of this skyscraper. Similarly located is the Theater District. Operational year-round, it draws 1.6 million visitors to its nearly 700 performances, and also features restaurants serving daytime, evening, and weekend patrons. The District has 10,482 seats in four theaters: Theater A, Theater B, Theater C, and Theater D. "City" is one of only four U.S. cities with permanent companies in all the major performing arts: grand opera, ballet, theater, and symphony. The Theater District project is a collaboration formed by the arts organizations, the Civic Center Department, and Central "City," Inc., to create an entertainment district around the theaters and cooperatively promote the area and its activities.

The ongoing redevelopment of the "Smith" Convention Center as an entertainment attraction with theaters, nightclubs, and additional restaurants is expected to attract people into downtown for additional leisure time activities when it opens in 19XX. The "Smith" Convention Center was decommissioned as a convention center in 1988 when the "New" Convention Center opened in downtown. The City has also decommissioned the 115,000-square-foot "City" Coliseum to be redeveloped as a civic/educational/entertainment attraction effective December 19XX. A request for proposal (RFP) for this five-acre site was recently prepared and distributed by the City. The site is expected to be a major location of day and night activity.

Flanking the Theater District is the Bayou, a living waterway connecting to the Ship Channel. The Bayou is being redeveloped as a part of a 25-year master plan, stretching from the west side of downtown to the port. Redevelopment efforts include parks, as well as a substantial investment in hike-and-bike trails. A feature of the redevelopment is the construction of the park in the Theater District. Walks connecting the Bayou along the Parkway were opened in 19XX.

The Square, the historic district in the north end of downtown, which has been on the National Register since 1983, is being revitalized as a tourist/entertainment area for "City." Under the auspices of the Square Historic District Project (a revitalization office jointly funded by the City and downtown interests), several major improvements have been made in the past year. The focal point is the park, which has been redeveloped as an "art park." In addition, the Greater "City" Convention and Visitors Bureau recently moved its headquarters to the area and is heavily involved in promoting additional events and street fairs in this area of downtown. Several new restaurants and bars have opened, and more are expected in the coming year.

Convention Center Area Description

Two nodes of development activity are present in the immediate site area. These areas, currently and increasingly over time, will influence the Convention Center and the headquarters hotel.

"City" Center is located west of the Convention Center. It is a large-scale, mixed-use development started in 1970 and situated on land that borders the Convention Center site area. It has a total of 5 million square feet of office space, a 400-room hotel, 200,000 square feet of retail and convenience food service, and 5,000 parking spaces. A total of five office towers are present, four of which are approximately 90 percent leased. The fifth building's occupancy stands at 50 percent because its anchor tenant relocated in a consolidation move. The retail space is approximately 92 percent leased. "City" Center has approximately 20 acres of undeveloped land, six of which have been landscaped to serve as a park joining the Convention Center and "City" Center.

The other major adjacent development is Chinatown, located immediately west of the Convention Center. The Chinatown district consists of 154 acres: 102 acres are devoted to private and public development; 52 acres are roadbeds and right-of-ways. It has its own development entity, the Chinatown Community Development Corporation. The area is in a start-up mode but the foundations of development have been laid in the zone as the area has Oriental restaurants, stores, businesses, and warehouses. A redevelopment plan has been prepared, and it is expected that the large Oriental population in "City" will contribute to the successful implementation of most elements of the plan.

Downtown Development Planning

The 1990s are an exciting time for downtown "City." The City has repositioned itself in response to changes in lifestyles, technology, government, development trends, and the economy. Generally, the results have been the enhancement of office niche markets such as banking, accounting, law, transportation, and government, which make up the overwhelming majority of the downtown economy. Other industries have generally evolved into support services for the business day office market.

During 19XX and 19XX, "City" Downtown Management Corporation engaged in the production of a Downtown Development Plan. The purpose of this plan was to develop a realistic revitalization program to ensure downtown's continued growth and prosperity and to contribute to the attraction of convention groups and tourism. An integrated downtown development strategy has been proposed by the "City" Downtown Management Corporation recommending programs, incentives, and developments that can stabilize, reinforce, diversify, and expand downtown's economy, and which:

- Respond to the needs of the fundamental industries in a period of transition and thereby protect investments in facilities that serve those industries
- Refocus on other downtown industries to identify opportunities for expansion as support for the office market and for independent economic growth
- Seek opportunities for synergy between industries and with other areas of the City
- Augment the entertainment and recreational venues within downtown

This strategy will preserve and enhance investment, employment, and property values within downtown and in the entire inner city. In addition, it will increase employment, help improve inner-city neighborhoods, improve the City's quality of life, and help foster a better image for the City as a whole. The plan recommends incremental, market-based changes that harness the power of market trends, build on current strengths, and optimize natural assets to help downtown remain the diversified, vital, prosperous, exciting heart of a growing international city.

INSERT MAP OF DOWNTOWN

INSERT AERIAL MAP OF DOWNTOWN

CONVENTION AND TOURISM PROFILE

Overview

Conventions, trade shows, and tourism are increasingly important businesses in "City." The City offers an excellent combination of easy access via "City" airports; the state-of-the-art Convention Center, along with several other excellent convention and assembly facilities; a variety of cultural and entertainment options; an extremely hospitable workforce; and low local rates for hotels and activities.

On September 26, 19XX, a major celebration marked the opening of "City's" Convention Center. With a total building area of approximately 1.2 million square feet, the Convention Center can host numerous events simultaneously and, in fact, comprises several facilities. These facilities feature 470,500 square feet of exhibit space (371,500 of which are on one floor), a 3,600-seat general assembly hall, and the largest grand ballroom in the state. In the near future, the Convention Center will have telescopic seating for events that can accommodate up to 8,000 attendees. State-of-the-art communications, plumbing, and electrical systems make the Convention Center a national leader in convention and trade show services.

Through the year 2000, the Convention Center is expected to meet occupancy projections estimated during the planning phase of the Convention Center. It is projected to host 30 to 35 conventions and trade shows annually. The Convention Center has consistently met this goal since its inception. Many of the events held today are regional and state events. When the Convention Center first opened, the City attracted several national conventions, which have been difficult to rebook without the appropriate lodging facilities needed for events of this magnitude. It is anticipated that national conventions will return to the Convention Center once a major headquarters hotel opens.

"City" also has the Arena, located approximately five miles from downtown, which is a part of the Arena complex. With 1.2 million square feet of interior exhibit space, this complex can host some of the nation's major shows, especially when an additional 400,000 square feet of exterior exhibit space is considered. The Arena itself has 160,000 square feet of floor area and a seating capacity of 66,000.

Based on Convention and Visitors Bureau records, in 19XX "City" hosted 351 conventions in the Convention Center and citywide hotels, with 554,279 delegates pumping approximately $341 million into the "City" economy. An additional $78 million was spent by the 1.1 million attendees to 24 special events and 77 public shows. Total visitor traffic in "City" in 19XX was estimated at 8.5 million visitors. Conventions have already been booked beyond the year 2000, and the City has undertaken an aggressive stance in attracting trade shows and conventions. The opening of a Convention Center Headquarters Hotel is expected to create over $100 million of additional annual economic impact. This revenue growth is anticipated to come to "City" by inducing in-house demand to visit the City by further penetrating the national convention market.

The following table presents an overview of competitive attributes of "City" and regionally competitive destinations in the convention center industry.

City	Population	Hotel Rooms Citywide	Hotel Rooms Downtown	Convention Center Exhibit Space	Convention Center Meeting Space
City A					
City B					
City C					
City D					
City E					
City F					
City G					
City H					

Competitive Assessment

The convention business is a very competitive segment of the travel and hospitality industry, the largest industry in the world. Four Sunbelt cities are the principal competition for "City." City "A" is the top competitor, followed by City "B," City "C," and City "D." Cities "E" and "F" are also extremely competitive and frequently prevail over "City" for business. Cities "G" and "H" can also be considered key competitors with "City."

All the main competitors have significantly higher inventory and quality in their downtown rooms:

"City"
Number of downtown hotels:
Number of rooms:
Hotels with more than 1,000 rooms:
    N/A

City "A"
Number of downtown hotels:
Number of rooms:
Hotels with more than 1,000 rooms:
    Hotel 1
    Hotel 2
    Hotel 3
    Hotel 4

City "B"
 Number of downtown hotels:
 Number of rooms:
 Hotels with more than 1,000 rooms:
  Hotel 1
  Hotel 2
  Hotel 3
  Hotel 4

City "C"
 Number of downtown hotels:
 Number of rooms:
 Hotels with more than 1,000 rooms:
  N/A

City "D"
 Number of downtown hotels:
 Number of rooms:
 Hotels with more than 1,000 rooms:
  Hotel 1

Presently, "City" has a package of hotels that includes Hotel 1, Hotel 2, Hotel 3, Hotel 4, Hotel 5, Hotel 6, and Hotel 7. Because only Hotel 1 is within walking distance of the Convention Center, attendees to conventions must use chartered shuttle bus service within downtown at a significant cost, which is ultimately absorbed by them. Moreover, the inconvenience of moving thousands of people imposes an additional unidentifiable cost on organizers and attendees. Of "City's" major competitors, only City "C" requires such extensive busing.

Compared to other cities in the region, "City" now has the fewest convention-quality rooms in its downtown. City "B" offers more than 10 times the number of hotels, with approximately seven times the room capacity. City "B" offers five times as many hotels with three times the capacity.

Convention Center Expansion Plans

As part of the original master plan, the City contemplated future expansion of the Convention Center. The existing Phase I would be subsequently followed by the addition of Phases II and III, each containing approximately 300,000 square feet of exhibition space and ancillary meeting space totaling a minimum of 50,000 to 60,000 square feet for each phase. The City's objective has been to develop a facility large enough to host multiple events simultaneously or back to back. There are no immediate plans for construction and development of the additional phases. Actual expansion of the Convention Center will be dictated by demonstrated business expansion for convention and trade activity.

To be prepared to execute the projected expansion, the City has been gradually acquiring the necessary real estate over the last 10 years in order to eventually double the 11 acres currently accommodating the first phase of the Convention Center. The entire site for Phase II is already owned by the City and is presently used as parking space. Approximately 80 percent of the property needed for Phase III development has been acquired to date, with plans to steadily acquire the remaining parcels specified in the master plan. Land acquired to date or earmarked for acquisition is equivalent in size to four blocks for each of the two phases.

The site to be dedicated for Phase II is bounded by "A" Avenue, U.S. Highway "A", "B" Avenue, and "C" Avenue. Property being accumulated for Phase III expansion is bounded by "D" Avenue, "C" Avenue, "E" Avenue and U.S. Highway "A."

The City has astutely provided for a self-funding Convention Center operation. The room tax for the City flows through the Civic Center Department, a portion of which is further allocated to the Greater "City" Convention and Visitors Bureau. The Convention Center is accumulating capital and will be poised to execute an expansion once a headquarters hotel is developed and convention and trade show business warrants an expansion.

Greater "City" Convention and Visitors Bureau

The goal of the Greater "City" Convention and Visitors Bureau (GCCVB) is to make "City" a premier, recognizable convention and tourism destination. In 19XX, the GCCVB welcomed its new president, moved to new offices in downtown's historic square, increased its budget by 97 percent from $4,452,418 to $8,775,820, recruited new leadership in several key GCCVB departments, increased its goals, enlarged its membership base, and developed an award-winning advertising campaign. This turnaround in the GCCVB positioning, staff quality, and level of funding further validates the City's intense desire to become a major national and international player in the convention and tourism industry.

During 19XX, the GCCVB booked 300,000 room nights for 19XX and 350,000 room nights for future years. Convention sales goals for 19XX to 19XX include generation of 600 leads and the booking of more than 500,000 room nights. Longer-range future plans include generation of 900 sales leads per year and 1 million room nights by fiscal year 19XX–19XX, and to have the GCCVB host one major convention meeting planners industry event.

The goal of the GCCVB's tourism sales department is to convince domestic and international travel professionals to include "City" as part of their consumer travel packages. The department generates sales for area hotels for both tour group and leisure travel business through direct sales, participation at industry trade shows, sales missions, and familiarization programs.

For 19XX and 19XX, the tourism group will launch a new $3 million national and international advertising and promotion campaign designed to foster a new image for "City" as a diverse and culturally rich city.

The successful development and opening of a Convention Center Headquarters Hotel is fundamental to the attainment of the Greater "City" Convention and Visitors Bureau goals.

"CITY" HOTEL MARKET OVERVIEW

The information on the "City" hotel market presented below is based on information contained in a study prepared for the Civic Center Department by an independent accounting firm. Neither the "City" Downtown Management Corporation, the Civic Center Department, the "City," nor any of its instrumentalities makes any representations or warranties with respect to the completeness or accuracy of this information.

Historical and Current Market Conditions

The "City" hotel market has been emerging from a prolonged slump caused by the decline of the energy industry during the early to mid-1980s, combined with overbuilding and overfinancing of hotel properties. Steady improvements have occurred during the last few years, and it is expected that this positive trend will continue.

In 19XX, the "City" hotel market consisted of approximately 33,200 rooms in 150 hotels. For the third consecutive year, "City" hotels achieved annual occupancy rates above the national market at 62.5 percent, with a $61.61 average daily room rate. Following an economic slump and concurrent hotel glut of the early 1980s, hotel demand in "City" has been increasing since 19XX, except for a dip in the first half of 19XX as a result of the Gulf War and the ensuing recession. Average room rates have been improving since January 19XX. However, hotel rates in the "City" market are among the lowest reported average rates among the major cities in the nation. The low comparable room yield has frustrated previous attempts to add a Convention Center hotel.

Based on a study commissioned by the City, citywide hotel occupancies are anticipated to increase from an estimated 62.5 percent in 19XX to a stabilized level of 70 percent by 19XX. Citywide average room rates are expected to outpace inflation for the next several years, recovering some of the ground lost during the early to mid-1980s. Estimated average rates are expected to grow from $61.61 for 19XX to $79.50 by 19XX.

It is anticipated that with the addition of a Convention Center hotel and with the strong tourism campaign developed by the GCCVB, the mix of hotel demand will show continued growth in the corporate group, convention, and leisure segments.

Downtown "City's" Hotel Market

As shown on the map on the following page, the hotel market in downtown "City" is made up of only five properties despite a strong and stable economy in the CMSA, which is positively impacting hotel demand in downtown. No new hotel development has been seen in the last 11 years, and no additions to supply are presently contemplated to the best knowledge of the City. Current hotel properties are scattered throughout downtown and contain approximately 2,100 rooms.

Except for a dip in the first half of 1991 during Operation Desert Storm and the subsequent recession, hotel demand in "City" has increased steadily since 19XX while average room rates have been improving since 19XX. Downtown hotel occupancy during 19XX averaged 59 percent while daily rates averaged $84.50.

The lack of a convention center headquarters hotel and the closure of several downtown hotels, resulting in a 2,000-room net loss since the mid-1980s, has left "City" with a hotel supply that is considered inadequate to attract major conventions. "City's" loss of competitiveness occurred at a time when other cities were discovering the significant economic benefits that healthy convention trends could bring to the City's economy.

The small supply of available downtown hotel rooms has been continuously cited by convention planners as a negative factor in "City's" convention sales efforts. Based on reported bookings at the Convention Center and interviews with area hotel operators, it is estimated that only 2 percent of the City's total occupied hotel rooms, approximately 175,000 room nights, originate from conventions hosted at the Convention Center.

INSERT MAP OF EXISTING HOTELS

POTENTIAL DEVELOPMENT SITES

The City has not decided on the hotel site for the proposed Convention Center Hotel. Various undeveloped parcels considered suitable for the convention hotel development have been identified and analyzed with respect to their attributes. Desired site attributes include the following:

- Location near the Convention Center, within 1,000 feet of a governmentally owned convention center and within an Enterprise Zone, in order to comply with approved legislation for a qualified hotel project
- Location that optimizes the downtown and Convention Center integration, balances the distance from the downtown core, and is close enough to key commercial demand generators to penetrate demand
- Capacity to develop a world-class convention center headquarters hotel and ancillary development

A map identifying the 1,000-foot area surrounding the Convention Center and the City's Enterprise Zone 1 is illustrated. The area inside the dotted black line represents the land parcels qualifying for the approved tax rebate benefits.

During the RFP stage (Phase II), it will be incumbent on the proposer to verify site ownership and legal boundaries to determine if the proposed hotel project site qualifies for tax rebates, refunds, and abatements.

INSERT MAP OF ENTERPRISE ZONE #1

FINANCIAL INFORMATION

Results from a Recent Headquarters Hotel Study

An independent accounting firm has recently prepared a set of assumptions for a Convention Center Headquarters Hotel based on a preliminary schedule of development costs. The analysis also presented information about occupancy, average daily rates, and financial performance of the hotel. A 1,200-room hotel was assumed. There has been no evaluation completed for phasing multiple properties or mixed-use developments. Proposers are encouraged to consider such options as they may enhance project returns. Presented below are excerpts from that report.

> *It is noted that the information was prepared for internal purposes only and should not be relied upon as a representation of achievability. It is incumbent upon the Proposer to complete its own verification and analysis. This material is presented solely for informational purposes.*

Development costs cited in the report were estimated based on consultations with hotel construction and development professionals regarding recent and current costs at the time these estimates were being developed during 19XX. Development cost analysis reflects only the City's and its advisors' best judgment at the time of its preparation during 19XX and is presented herein only to provide a point of reference on the potential development costs associated with this project. Based on preliminary cost estimates, total development costs for a standard four-star hotel having 1,200 rooms and a 1,000-car parking garage are shown below.

Downtown "City" Convention Center Headquarters Hotel

Item	Total Cost	Per Room Cost*
Site acquisition and preparation	$10,500,000	$8,750
Construction	92,565,832	77,138
Furnishings	18,000,000	15,000
Equipment	7,080,000	5,900
Professional services	6,070,496	5,058
Financing/Administration	2,550,000	2,125
Preopening costs	6,000,000	5,000
Contingencies	6,613,316	5,511
Construction interest	14,570,744	12,143
	$163,950,389	$136,625

*Based on a hypothetical 1,200-room hotel.

Estimated Results from Operations

Based on a series of key assumptions, results from operations for the proposed Convention Center Hotel were projected by an independent accounting firm. It was as-

211

sumed that the hotel will be operated as a first-class, 1,200-room convention center hotel, having a 20,000-square-foot ballroom, 18 meeting rooms, approximately 5,000 square feet of retail space, a full complement of food and beverage outlets, and a 1,000-car parking garage. Following is a summary of some of the key assumptions made in order to arrive at the project results:

Occupancy Estimates

The proposed Convention Center Hotel is expected to attract guests from a wide variety of sources and compete with hotels all over "City" and the United States for various types of guests. Hotel demand was classified into four primary demand segments according to the type of traveler expected to stay in the proposed hotel.

- **Convention Center**—groups utilizing the Convention Center for conventions, meetings, trade or public shows, and special events
- **Commercial**—individuals and groups of less than 10 people traveling for business reasons, usually on company expense accounts
- **Group**—people traveling for either business or pleasure and booking a block of 10 or more rooms at one or more hotels
- **Tourist/Leisure**—defined as individuals or small groups visiting the City for non-business reasons

The proposed 1,200-room hotel is expected to achieve annual occupancy rates of 49 percent in 19XX, increasing to a stabilized level of 62 percent by 19XX.

Average Daily Rates

Average daily room rates for the proposed Convention Center Hotel were estimated in constant 19XX dollars for each market segment for the first five years of operation, then adjusted for the anticipated effects of inflation throughout a full 10-year analysis period. The table presented below summarizes the estimated average daily room rates for each market segment and the average room rate.

Estimated Demand and Occupancy Rates for Proposed 1,200-Room Hotel

Year	Commercial	Group	GRB	Tourist/Leisure	Total	Occupancy
19XX	43,133	67,392	66,385	7,500	216,410	49%
19XX	45,263	77,720	103,845	8,300	234,628	54%
19XX	47,393	83,484	112,035	9,200	252,112	58%
19XX	48,564	85,968	120,330	9,400	264,262	60%
19XX–20XX	49,736	88,128	123,060	9,600	270,524	62%

Estimated Average Daily Room Rates

Year	Commercial	Group	Convention	Tourist	Average Room Rate
19XX	$117.00	$ 92.25	$100.25	$59.75	$ 99.75
19XX	125.25	99.50	106.75	68.25	106.50
19XX	134.00	107.25	113.50	78.50	114.50
19XX	139.75	111.50	119.25	81.50	119.00
19XX	145.25	116.25	124.25	84.75	123.75

Cash Flow and Gap Analysis

The following four exhibits present information from the financial analysis performed by the independent accounting firm. Exhibit A.1 presents a summary of operating results for the proposed hotel. The statement of net operating income before debt service and income taxes was developed based on assumptions made on departmental and nondepartmental revenue and expense items as well as on the premise that the hotel will be affiliated with a first-tier hotel company, managed and staffed by competent personnel, and advertised and promoted aggressively to the public.

Adjusted Cash Flow Position Analysis

This section presents the investment gap estimates, identifies and quantifies possible tax revenue sources to finance these gaps, and summarizes the net funds available to the developer or investor after applying these tax revenues.

Exhibit A.2 presents the gap between estimated income available for debt service and debt service costs as calculated for the 1,200-room hotel. These estimates were based on the development costs presented earlier, the projected net operating income before debt service and income taxes, and interest cost ranging from 6 percent to 10 percent. The investment gap is defined as the hotel's anticipated annual shortfall after debt service.

Exhibit A.3 summarizes estimated tax proceeds that could be available to support debt service payments for the proposed hotel. The analysis assumes tax rebates from County, City, and State jurisdictions. City and County legislation authorizing the tax rebates has not been approved to date.

Exhibit A.4 presents an adjusted net position after debt service, assuming the tax rebates are received. The analysis assumes an 8 percent interest cost for the debt financing of the hotel development. The analysis shows the attainment of a net surplus beginning in the second year of operations. Net surplus begins to trend down after the year 2002 once the term of the financial incentives available from the State expire.

Exhibit A.1 Summary of Operating Results for a Hypothetical 1,200-Room Hotel (in thousands)

	19XX		19XX		19XX		19XX		19XX		2000		2001		2002		2003		2004	
	Amount	%	Amount	%	Amount	%	Amount	%	Amount	%	Amount	%	Amount	%	Amount	%	Amount	%	Amount	%
REVENUE																				
Rooms	$21,587	58.0	$24,988	58.6	$28,867	59.3	$31,447	59.3	$33,477	59.2	$34,830	59.2	$36,250	59.3	$37,670	59.3	$39,226	59.3	$40,781	59.3
Food and beverage	13,690	36.8	15,474	36.3	13,690	35.6	13,690	35.6	13,690	35.6	13,690	35.6	13,690	35.6	13,690	35.6	13,690	35.6	13,690	35.6
Telephone	1,076	2.9	1,213	2.8	1,076	2.8	1,076	2.8	1,076	2.8	1,076	2.8	1,076	2.8	1,076	2.8	1,076	2.8	1,076	2.8
Rental and other income	647	1.7	749	1.8	647	1.8	647	1.8	647	1.8	647	1.8	647	1.8	647	1.8	647	1.8	647	1.8
Minor operated departments	215	0.6	249	0.6	215	0.6	215	0.6	215	0.6	215	0.6	215	0.6	215	0.6	215	0.6	215	0.6
	$37,215	100.0	$42,673	100.0	$44,495	100.0	$47,075	100.0	$49,105	100.0	$50,458	100.0	$51,878	100.0	$53,298	100.0	$54,854	100.0	$56,409	100.0
DEPARTMENTAL COSTS AND EXPENSES																				
Rooms	$6,109	28.3	$6,626	26.5	$6,109	26.5	$6,109	24.8	$6,109	24.4	$6,109	24.1	$6,109	24.1	$6,109	24.1	$6,109	24.1	$6,109	24.1
Food and beverage	10,957	80.0	12,246	79.1	10,957	79.1	10,957	78.9	10,957	78.9	10,957	78.9	10,957	78.9	10,957	78.9	10,957	78.9	10,957	78.9
Telephone	807	75.0	910	75.0	807	75.0	807	75.0	807	75.0	807	75.0	807	75.0	807	75.0	807	75.0	807	75.0
Minor operated departments	204	95.1	237	95.1	204	95.2	204	95.2	204	95.0	204	95.1	204	95.1	204	95.1	204	95.1	204	95.1
	$18,077	48.6	$20,019	46.9	$18,077	46.9	$18,077	45.5	$18,077	45.2	$18,077	45.1	$18,077	45.1	$18,077	45.1	$18,077	45.1	$18,077	45.1
GROSS OPERATING INCOME	$19,138	51.0	$22,654	53.0	$26,418	53.0	$28,998	55.0	$31,028	55.0	$32,381	54.9	$33,801	54.9	$35,221	54.9	$36,777	55.0	$38,332	55.0

UNDISTRIBUTED OPERATING EXPENSES

Line item	1	2	3	4	5	6	7	8	9	10	11
Administrative and general	$3,950 11.0	$4,189 10.0	$3,950 9.0	$3,950 9.0	$3,950 8.6	$3,950 8.6	$3,950 8.6	$3,950 8.6	$3,950 8.6	$3,950 8.6	$3,950 8.6
Management fees	1,116 3.0	1,280 3.0	1,116 3.0	1,116 3.0	1,116 3.0	1,116 3.0	1,116 3.0	1,116 3.0	1,116 3.0	1,116 3.0	1,116 3.0
Marketing	3,436 9.2	3,566 8.4	3,436 7.4	3,436 7.4	3,436 7.3	3,436 7.3	3,436 7.3	3,436 7.3	3,436 7.3	3,436 7.3	3,436 7.3
Energy costs	1,651 4.4	1,773 4.2	1,651 3.8	1,651 3.9	1,651 3.8	1,651 3.7	1,651 3.7	1,651 3.7	1,651 3.7	1,651 3.7	1,651 3.7
Property operations and maintenance	2,312 6.2	2,448 5.7	2,312 5.1	2,312 5.3	2,312 5.1	2,312 5.0	2,312 5.0	2,312 5.0	2,312 5.0	2,312 5.0	2,312 5.0
	$12,465 33.0	$13,256 31.0	$12,465 28.0	$12,465 28.1	$12,465 27.6	$12,465 27.6	$12,465 27.6	$12,465 27.6	$12,465 27.6	$12,465 27.6	$12,465 27.6

FIXED CHARGES AND OTHER DEDUCTIONS

Line item	1	2	3	4	5	6	7	8	9	10	11
Property taxes	$1,615 4.3	$1,679 3.9	$1,615 3.6	$1,615 3.4	$1,615 3.3	$1,615 3.3	$1,615 3.3	$1,615 3.3	$1,615 3.3	$1,615 3.3	$1,615 3.3
Insurance	773 2.1	804 1.9	773 1.7	773 1.6	773 1.6	773 1.6	773 1.6	773 1.6	773 1.6	773 1.6	773 1.6
	$2,388 6.4	$2,483 5.8	$2,388 5.3	$2,388 5.0	$2,388 4.9	$2,388 4.9	$2,388 4.9	$2,388 4.9	$2,388 4.9	$2,388 4.9	$2,388 4.9

PROJECTED NET OPERATING INCOME BEFORE RESERVE FOR REPLACEMENT, DEBT SERVICE AND INCOME TAXES

1	2	3	4	5	6	7	8	9	10	11
$4,285 11.5	$6,915 16.2	$4,285 20.3	$4,285 21.6	$4,285 22.3	$4,285 22.3	$4,285 22.3	$4,285 22.3	$4,285 22.3	$4,285 22.3	$4,285 22.3

RESERVE FOR REPLACEMENT OF FIXED ASSETS

1	2	3	4	5	6	7	8	9	10	11
$372 1.0	$853 2.0	$372 3.0	$372 4.0	$372 4.0	$372 4.0	$372 4.0	$372 4.0	$372 4.0	$372 4.0	$372 4.0

PROJECTED NET OPERATING INCOME BEFORE DEBT SERVICE AND INCOME TAXES

1	2	3	4	5	6	7	8	9	10	11
$3,913 10.5	$6,062 14.2	$8,411 17.3	$8,358 17.6	$10,330 18.3	$10,749 18.3	$11,190 18.3	$11,626 18.3	$12,111 18.3	$12,589 18.3	$12,589 18.3

This analysis was prepared for a hypothetical hotel and is restricted to internal use only. The information has not been verified, and representations about its accuracy are not being made.

Exhibit A.2 Investment Gap Analysis for a Hypothetical 1,200-Room Hotel

Assumed Interest Rate: 6.0% Estimated Development Cost: $163,950,389

	1995	1996	1997	1998	1999	2000	2001	2002	2003	2004
Net operating income	$3,913,000	$6,062,000	$8,411,000	$9,358,000	$10,330,000	$10,749,000	$11,190,000	$11,626,000	$12,111,000	$12,589,000
Debt service	$11,910,817	$11,910,817	$11,910,817	$11,910,817	$11,910,817	$11,910,817	$11,910,817	$11,910,817	$11,910,817	$11,910,817
Shortfall	($7,997,817)	($5,848,817)	($3,499,817)	($2,552,817)	($1,580,817)	($1,161,817)	($720,817)	($284,817)	$200,183	$678,183

Assumed Interest Rate: 8.0% Estimated Development Cost: $163,950,389

	1995	1996	1997	1998	1999	2000	2001	2002	2003	2004
Net operating income	$3,913,000	$6,062,000	$8,411,000	$9,358,000	$10,330,000	$10,749,000	$11,190,000	$11,626,000	$12,111,000	$12,589,000
Debt service	$14,563,292	$14,563,292	$14,563,292	$14,563,292	$14,563,292	$14,563,292	$14,563,292	$14,563,292	$14,563,292	$14,563,292
Shortfall	($10,650,292)	($8,501,292)	($6,152,292)	($5,205,292)	($4,233,292)	($3,814,292)	($373,292)	($2,937,292)	($2,452,292)	($1,974,282)

Assumed Interest Rate: 10.0% Estimated Development Cost: $163,950,389

	1995	1996	1997	1998	1999	2000	2001	2002	2003	2004
Net operating income	$3,913,000	$6,062,000	$8,411,000	$9,358,000	$10,330,000	$10,749,000	$11,190,000	$11,626,000	$12,111,000	$12,589,000
Debt service	$17,391,734	$17,391,734	$17,391,734	$17,391,734	$17,391,734	$17,391,734	$17,391,734	$17,391,734	$17,391,734	$17,391,734
Shortfall	($13,478,734)	($11,329,734)	($8,980,734)	($8,033,734)	($7,061,734)	($6,642,734)	($6,201,734)	($5,765,734)	($5,280,734)	($4,802,734)

Exhibit A.3 Estimated Tax Revenues for a Hypothetical 1,200-Room Hotel

	1995	1996	1997	1998	1999	2000	2001	2002*	2003*	2004*
CITY TAX REVENUE										
Hotel occupancy tax (7%)	$1,511,090	$1,749,160	$2,020,690	$2,201,290	$2,343,390	$2,438,100	$2,537,500	$2,636,900	$2,745,820	$2,854,670
Beverage tax (1.5%)	39,870	44,970	50,235	54,780	58,320	60,660	63,075	65,610	68,235	70,950
Sales tax (2%)	312,560	353,700	396,820	432,700	460,640	479,080	498,220	518,140	538,880	560,440
Property tax—city	438,535	455,914	474,107	492,843	512,665	533,302	554,754	576,749	600,101	623,996
Total city tax revenue	$2,302,055	$2,603,744	$2,941,852	$3,181,613	$3,375,015	$3,511,142	$3,653,549	$3,797,399	$3,953,036	$4,110,056
LOCAL SCHOOL DISTRICT TAX REVENUE										
Property tax—CISD	$187,944	$195,392	$203,189	$211,218	$219,714	$228,558	$237,752	$247,178	$257,186	$267,427
Property tax—HCED	542,948	564,465	586,989	610,187	634,729	660,279	686,838	714,070	742,982	772,567
Total school district tax revenue	730,892	759,857	790,178	821,405	854,443	888,837	924,590	961,248	1,000,168	1,039,994
COUNTY TAX REVENUE										
Hotel occupancy tax (2%)	$431,740	$499,760	$577,340	$628,940	$669,540	$696,600	$725,000	$753,400	$784,520	$815,620
Beverage tax (1.5%)	39,870	44,970	50,235	54,780	58,320	60,660	63,075	65,610	68,235	70,950
Property tax—county	224,057	232,936	242,231	251,804	261,931	272,475	283,435	294,673	306,604	318,813
Total county tax revenue	695,667	777,666	869,806	935,524	989,791	1,029,735	1,071,510	1,113,683	1,159,359	1,205,383
STATE TAX REVENUE										
Hotel occupancy tax (6%)	$1,295,220	$1,499,280	$1,732,020	$1,886,820	$2,008,620	$2,089,800	$2,175,000	N/A	N/A	N/A
Beverage tax (11%)	292,380	329,780	368,390	401,720	427,680	444,840	462,550	N/A	N/A	N/A
Sales tax (6.25%)	976,750	1,105,313	1,240,063	1,352,188	1,439,500	1,497,125	1,556,938	N/A	N/A	N/A
Total state tax revenue	2,564,350	2,934,373	3,340,473	3,640,728	3,875,800	4,031,765	4,194,488	0	0	0
TOTAL TAX REVENUE										
Total city tax revenue	$2,302,055	$2,603,744	$2,941,852	$3,181,613	$3,375,015	$3,511,142	$3,653,549	$3,797,399	$3,953,036	$4,110,056
Total county tax revenue	695,667	777,666	869,806	935,524	989,791	1,029,735	1,071,510	1,113,683	1,159,359	1,205,383
Total school district tax revenue	730,892	759,857	790,178	821,405	854,443	888,837	924,590	961,248	1,000,168	1,039,994
Total state tax revenue	2,564,350	2,934,373	3,340,473	3,640,728	3,875,800	4,031,765	4,194,488	0	0	0
Total	**$6,292,964**	**$7,075,640**	**$7,942,309**	**$8,579,270**	**$9,095,049**	**$9,461,479**	**$9,844,137**	**$5,872,330**	**$6,112,563**	**$6,355,433**

*Approved state legislation limits availability of tax rebates to the seven-consecutive-year period commencing the first year of operation. Therefore, total tax revenue available to cover shortfall from operations is reduced.

This analysis was prepared for a hypothetical hotel and is restricted to internal use only. The information has not been verified, and representations about its accuracy are not being made.

Exhibit A.4 Adjusted Cash Flow Position Analysis for a Hypothetical 1,200-Room Hotel

	1995	1996	1997	1998	1999	2000	2001	2002*	2003*	2004*
Total Tax Revenue										
	$6,292,964	$7,075,640	$7,942,309	$8,579,270	$9,095,049	$9,461,479	$9,844,137	$5,872,330	$6,112,563	$6,355,433
Projected Shortfall (8% Interest Rate Scenario)										
	$10,650,292	$8,501,292	$6,152,292	$5,205,292	$4,233,832	$3,814,292	$3,373,292	$2,937,292	$2,452,292	$1,974,292
Net (Deficit)/Surplus										
	($4,357,328)	($1,425,652)	$1,790,017	$3,373,978	$4,861,757	$5,647,187	$6,470,845	$2,935,038	$3,660,271	$4,381,141

*Approved state legislation limits availability of state tax rebates to the seven-year period commencing the first year of operation. Therefore, total tax revenue available to cover shortfall from operations is reduced.

This analysis was prepared for a hypothetical hotel and is restricted to internal use only. The information has not been verified, and representations about its accuracy are not being made.

SELECTION PROCEDURE

Overview

The City has the responsibility for selection of a developer for the downtown Convention Center Headquarters Hotel project. A Selection Advisory Panel will be appointed by the mayor.

Staff support for the Selection Advisory Panel will be provided by the Civic Center Department of the City and "City" Downtown Management Corporation. Other City departments and outside consultants will be involved, as appropriate.

Statement of Qualifications for the Development of the Convention Center Hotel will be due November 16 and must be prepared in conformance with the guidelines that follow. A $10,000 submittal fee payable to the City of "X" Civic Center Department must be submitted with the statement. This submittal fee will be refunded in its entirety to those proposers who are not short-listed for Phase II of the selection process, the preparation of a formal, detailed proposal. Short-listed teams not selected as the project developer when the outcome of the evaluation process is announced will be entitled to receive a full refund as well. A Pre-Response Conference will be held on September 30 at 1:00 P.M. at the Convention Center. Participants should call (999) 999-9999 to confirm attendance and obtain specific room location. Proposers are not required to attend but are encouraged to do so. Potential proposers are encouraged to indicate interest so that the City can provide follow-up correspondence that may assist proposers. After a review of the RFQ responses by the Selection Advisory Panel, clarification may be requested, and proposers may be asked to make a presentation to the Panel during the week of November 22. Unless requested by the Panel, no additional information can be submitted by the respondent after the November 16 due date. Requests for additional information or clarification will be copied to all team members who attend and properly register at the Pre-Response Conference or write to receive information by October 10, 19XX.

Time Frame

Each response to this RFQ will be evaluated by the Selection Advisory Panel, after which a selected number of proponents will proceed to the detailed submission phase. Each response to this RFQ shall be subject to the same review and assessment process. One or more project developer(s) will be recommended.

Schedule

September 8, 19XX	RFQ issued
September 30, 19XX	Pre-Response Conference
October 10, 19XX	Last day for written questions to be received

November 16, 19XX   Qualifications submissions due by 5:00 P.M.
December 5, 19XX   Short list announced
February 25, 19XX   RFP response due by 5:00 P.M.
March 27, 19XX   Developer(s) recommended for negotiations

The City reserves the right to extend or otherwise modify the above-presented calendar. If and when such changes in the schedule occur, notice will then be given to proponents still involved at that stage of the process.

SUBMISSION REQUIREMENTS—RFQ PHASE

A three-phase process has been established by the City for soliciting developer participation in the development of the Convention Center Hotel. Phase I involves the RFQ. The intent of this phase is to identify teams who have the proven capacity, track record, and interest to develop a Convention Center Headquarters Hotel in downtown "X." In order to minimize the out-of-pocket costs incurred by respondents, a reduced amount of information is being requested during the first phase. The intent is to obtain substantiated evidence of performance capacity to complete an undertaking of this magnitude, along with verification of prior or present involvement in the development and operation of headquarters hotels.

Phase II, the RFP phase, will require preparation and submission of detailed project and participant information that will provide sufficient basis for the City to assess the project feasibility and the practicality of financing, identify required inducements from the City and the extent of the City's involvement, and determine the character and scale of the project.

Phase III will involve the recommendation by the Section Advisory Panel of a developer team(s) from the short list and the negotiation of terms and conditions with the selected developer team.

The Submission Requirements and Selection Criteria sections that follow address only the RFQ phase. Requirements for the subsequent RFP phase will be made available at the appropriate time to the short-listed candidates.

The following are the submission requirements for Phase I:

1. Transmittal letter
2. Developer information
   - Name of contact person(s) for correspondence and notification purposes
   - Legal name/names of principal officers, authorized representative to work with City
   - Summary of qualifications, list of completed projects, relevant experience
   - Prior experience with governmental entities
3. Hotel management company
   - Number, types, and geographic location of hotels under management
   - Principals of company
   - Project lead person
   - Comparable projects managed
4. Hotel chain (if use of independent management is contemplated, please state)
   - Project lead person
   - Comparable chain-affiliated properties
5. Architect information and general contractor (contractor information is optional for this stage)

- Principals of firms
- Firm background
- Qualifications on comparable projects

6. Hotel facility
   - Statement of project concept
   - General characteristics with initial details of proposed development
   - Project marketing and management

7. Project financing (optional with RFQ submission)
   - To the extent project financing is addressed and identified, substantially or conceptually, the project team could receive a higher rating in the evaluation process depending on the level of commitment relative to the project financing. Submission of detailed financing information will be mandatory for the RFP submission of short-listed teams.

8. Land control/site identification
   - Selected project site and method to obtain control
   - To the extent a project team is able to submit a controlled site at the RFQ stage, which is considered suitable for project development, they will receive stronger consideration. Control of a suitable site will be a requirement for Phase II.

9. Special conditions
   - Any and all special conditions that developer may propose to offer or to ask City as part of the proposal. If selected for the short list, developer would have to elaborate as to costs, terms, payment amounts, conditions, timing, and such other pertinent factors.

10. Statement on expected policy for Minority and Women Business Enterprise participation

It is the interest of the City to encourage the best combination of potential teams. With this objective in mind, all members of a responding team, with the exception of the lead developer, may be listed as members on more than one but no more than three different proposals. A developer of one team may submit as a support group to another group but will not be considered for multiple lead developer submittals. For instance, a lead developer in one project team may submit as a landowner or investor on another team.

CRITERIA FOR SELECTION

The Selection Advisory Panel will thoroughly evaluate each response to this RFQ on the basis of development team experience, project concept, project management, economics and financial capability, participation of minority- and women-owned enterprises, and ability to develop the Convention Center Headquarters Hotel.

The principal criteria for Phase I will be identifying teams qualified through both experience and financial capability. For Phase II, the short-listed respondents will be asked to prepare and submit project information in much greater level of detail and to propose a schedule for development. Specifically, for the Phase I responses, the Panel will review submissions in accordance with the selection criteria listed below.

40%	Experience of development team; emphasis on similar projects
35%	Financial capability, level of financial commitment, and economic impact to the City
10%	Minority/Women/Disadvantaged business participation
15%	Miscellaneous—control of site, completeness of project team, other issues

SUBMITTAL INSTRUCTIONS

Developer shall prepare one original and 12 copies (excepting large-scale drawings and exhibits if included in package) of a qualification response in 8½" by 11" format. Proposals must be organized following the Submission Requirements section headings noted on pages 221 and 222 and must include at least the requested information. The City reserves the right to request additional information during the RFQ review period.

Responses must be submitted not later than 5:00 P.M. on November 16, 19XX. The response must be bound and sealed when submitted. The response material must be submitted by mail or delivered to:

"City" Downtown Management Corporation

9999 Smith Ave., Suite 9

City, State, Zip

The envelope must state "RFQ Response—Convention Center Headquarters Hotel Due 5:00 P.M., November 16, 19XX."

Questions concerning the RFQ should be directed to Mr. Jones at (999) 999-9999. Questions or clarifications relating to definitions or interpretations of this RFQ or about operations of the Convention Center must be submitted in writing on or before October 10, 19XX, to Mr. Jones, "City" Downtown Management Corporation, 9999 Smith Ave., Suite 9, City, State, Zip.

Responses to questions and clarifications received in writing prior to the Pre-Response Conference will be made in writing and distributed to all properly registered attendees at the Pre-Response Conference or to those who request information in writing by October 10, 19XX. Oral explanations or instructions shall not be considered binding on the City.

Respondents will be notified in writing of any change in the specifications contained in the RFQ. Neither the City, "City" Downtown Management Corporation, Central "City," Inc., nor any of their officers, agents, or employees shall be responsible for the accuracy of any information provided to any proposer as part of this RFQ. All proposers are encouraged to independently verify the accuracy of any information provided. The use of any of this information in the preparation of a response to this request is at the sole risk of the proposer.

Conditions and Limitations

This RFQ does not represent a commitment or offer by the City to enter into an agreement with a proposer or to pay any costs incurred in the preparation of a response to this request. The responses and any information made a part of the responses will not be returned to proposers. This RFQ and the selected firm's response to this RFQ may, by reference, become a part of any formal agreement between the proposer and the City resulting from this solicitation.

The proposer shall not offer any gratuities, favors, or anything of monetary value to any official or employee of the City, "City" Downtown Management Corporation, or Central "City," Inc., for the purpose of influencing consideration of a response to this RFQ.

The proposer shall not collude in any manner or engage in any practices with any other proposer(s), which may restrict or eliminate competition or otherwise restrain trade. Violation of this instruction will cause the proposer's submittal to be rejected by the City. The prohibition is not intended to preclude joint ventures or subcontracts.

All responses submitted must be the original work product of the proposer. The copying, paraphrasing, or otherwise using of substantial portions of the work product of another proposer is not permitted. Failure to adhere to this instruction will cause the response to be rejected.

The City has sole discretion and reserves the right to reject any and all responses received with respect to this RFQ and to cancel the RFQ at any time prior to entering into a formal agreement. The City reserves the right to request clarification of RFQ data without changing the terms of the RFQ.

The proposer must furnish a Certificate of Authority, signed by the chief executive officer or managing partner of the company, with its response. The Certificate must list the specific officers who are authorized to execute agreements on behalf of the company.

Minority and Women Business Enterprise Requirements

It is the policy of the City to stimulate the growth of local Minority and Women Business Enterprises (Disadvantaged Business Enterprise), to encourage the full participation of Minority and Women Business Enterprises in its procurement activity, and to afford them a full and fair opportunity to compete for all City contracts. The Minority and Women Business Enterprise participation goal for this project is 15 percent.

1. The successful proposer must ensure that Minority and Women Business Enterprises, as defined in the Minority and Women Business Enterprise Ordinance No. 84-1309 passed August 22, 1984, have a full and fair opportunity to participate. In that regard, the successful proposer shall take all necessary and reasonable steps to meet the Minority/Women/Disadvantaged Business Enterprise (M/W/DBE) goal for this contract.

2. The successful proposer and any subcontractor shall not discriminate on the basis of race, color, national origin, or sex in the performance of this contract.

3. The successful proposer will be required to provide documentation of having met the M/W/DBE goals or good faith efforts if the M/W/DBE goals have not been met. Evidence of good faith efforts is outlined in Section E, Contractor Respon-

sibilities of the Bidder Requirements for Minority and Women Business Enterprise Program, available from the Director of the Affirmative Action Division of the mayor's office.

4. The successful proposer's performance in meeting the M/W/DBE participation goals during project development and operation may be monitored by the Affirmative Action Contract Compliance Division of the mayor's office or other parties.

Phase II Developer Request for Proposals

A Major Convention Center Hotel to Support the
Convention Center and Downtown

Issued By:
Downtown Management Corporation on Behalf of
Civic Center Department, "City"

Request for Proposals Prepared By:
Downtown Management Corporation

November 30, 19XX

November 30, 19XX
Mr. Chairman
"City" Downtown Management Corporation
9999 Smith Ave., Suite 9
City, State, Zip
Subject: Convention Center Hotel Phase II—Requests for Proposals

Dear Mr. Chairman:
Following up on the letter sent to you last week by the mayor, the enclosed information is requested of your team in proposals for a major convention center hotel. The

general approach as set forth in the request for qualifications (RFQ) dated September 10, 19XX, applies to this request for proposal (RFP). As such, the Phase II proposal due date, February 18, 19XX, at 5:00 P.M. is the due date for your team's response. An original and 12 copies are required at the following address to the attention of Mr. Jones, along with a $15,000 submission fee check:

"City" Downtown Management Corporation
9999 Smith Ave., Suite 9
City, State, Zip

Questions and requested clarifications will be received in writing and sent to Mr. Jones's attention until 5:00 P.M., December 15, 19XX. Responses to such questions, clarifications, and addenda will be returned to all teams by December 23 and will be addressed to the contact person identified in the RFQ response.

All respondents will be required to comply with City Council Ordinance No.78-1538, passed August 9, 1978, relating to Equal Employment Opportunity Contract Compliance.

"City" reserves the right to reject any or all responses to this RFP, to advertise for new RFP responses, or to accept any RFP responses deemed to be in the best interest of the City.

A response to this RFP should not be construed as a contract nor indicate a commitment of any kind. The RFP does not commit "City" to pay for costs incurred in the submission of a response to this RFP or for any costs incurred prior to the execution of final agreements.

We look forward to working with you.

Sincerely,

Mr. Issuer
"City" Development Department
City, State

OBJECTIVE STATEMENT

It is expected that the response to this RFP will serve as the initial project business plan and as a basis for the City's negotiation with one or more development teams. As such, it is in the best interests of all parties to be as clear as possible in all areas for which information has been requested. It is the City's objective to have a high-quality, cost-effective project delivered as soon as possible with as little risk as possible borne by the City. While this seems obvious, the City is committed to the success of this project and recognizes that there may be areas in which it is asked to participate. Further, because House Bill 2282 requires ownership by the City or a nonprofit, municipally sponsored, local government corporation, the City could be brought into a longer-term ownership position under a default scenario. The City's objective is to mitigate this possibility to the greatest extent possible.

The question that follows should be based on research and assumptions developed for and stated in the RFP response. Clarity and brevity in responses is encouraged. The City's intent is to obtain a common response format from all teams so an objective review can be made. As such, the methodology employed in developing requested information should be stated, and the analysis should be clearly presented. The information must be as specific as possible to achieve a clear and precise understanding of what is being presented.

Development of related/supporting entertainment attraction uses is encouraged. Please provide information on these uses. However, to provide for the most objective evaluation possible for the hotel, proposers shall provide separate, specific information for the hotel portion of the project.

REQUESTED INFORMATION

The three categories of information being requested are:

I. Market and Financial Information
   a. Market Demand Analysis
   b. Financial Analysis
   c. Fees and Returns
II. Ownership and Operating Structure; Legal Information
   a. Development Team Structure
   b. Project Ownership Structure
   c. Financing Plan and Structure
   d. Hotel Management Contract
   e. Assurances to the City—Construction and Preopening
   f. Assurances to the City—Operations
   g. Draft Legal Agreements

    h. Site Control and Value

    i. Minority and Women Business Enterprise Program

III. Physical and Cost Analysis Information

    a. Recommended Design Concepts

    b. Urban Design Issues/Project Linkages

    c. Construction Cost Analysis

    d. Time Line for Project Development and Preopening

Specifically, the following information is requested for each category:

I. MARKET AND FINANCIAL INFORMATION

Market demand and financial information should be prepared by an independent entity with appropriate levels of supporting documentation that can be made available to the Selection Advisory Panel upon request.

a. Market Demand Analysis

- Prepare a summary of market demand for the proposed hotel.
- Define expected occupancy and average room rate for the first 10 years of operation.
- Identify expected room nights by major demand category for the first 10 years of operation.

b. Financial Analysis

- Prepare an operating statement for the preopening period and first 10 years of operation
- Prepare a cash flow analysis that reflects the debt/equity structure identified in II. c. below, and the construction costs for III. c. below; the cash flow analysis should identify taxes available to the project via legislation in House Bill 2282.

c. Fees and Returns

- It is the City's intent that equitable fees and investment returns be achieved.
- Identify all expected or potential fees and amounts charged for development services and management services.
- Identify how and which parties will be subordinated (if applicable) relative to fees and distribution of returns.

II. OWNERSHIP AND OPERATING STRUCTURE; LEGAL IDENTIFICATION

a. Development Team Structure

- Specifically identify the key members of the development team and provide a clear organizational chart citing roles and responsibilities.
- Specifically identify which members of the team are Minority and Women Business Enterprises.
- For each major participant, provide a summary of two relevant completed or in-process projects of which this participant was a prime participant. This summary should cite role played and current status of project and provide a reference for the project. At a minimum, the following members shall be profiled:
Developer
General contractor
Architectural firm
Hotel management company(s)
Hotel chain(s)
All specialty subconsultants expected to earn $1,000,000 or more in project fees
- If multiple participants are included in the development venture, each venture partner shall provide requested information.
- Identify how roles and responsibilities may change in the preconstruction/development phase, construction, and first 10 years of operation.

b. Project Ownership Structure

- Via a chart and brief commentary, clearly illustrate how the project ownership structure is contemplated.
- Indicate legal form of ownership, development, and operating entities.
- Indicate intended use of a nonprofit, municipally sponsored, local government corporation to be formed as per House Bill 2282.
- Identify how site is to be conveyed to City or nonprofit, municipally sponsored, local government corporation.

c. Financing Plan and Structure

- Via a chart and brief commentary, specifically identify debt and equity composition and parties providing equity and debt.
- Letters of interest or commitment shall be provided along with term sheets, signed by agents authorized to provide such commitment.
- Discuss subordinations.

d. Hotel Management Contract

- It is the preference of the City that the hotel management company have a stake in the hotel's success. This could be accomplished via equity participation as well as base fees, top- and bottom-line incentives, and subordinated fees.
- Provide a draft management contract to be entered, including term sheet.
- Identify project manager to be assigned by the hotel company and provide resume.
- If more than one management company/chain is being presented, and a final choice is to be made at a later date, parallel information shall be developed for each company.

e. Assurances to the City—Construction and Preopening

- The City expects that certain performance guarantees and bonds will be posted, ensuring project completion as contemplated.
- Identify what assurance system has been devised for the construction and pre-opening period.
- Provide a brief case study outlining how the assurance system would operate.
- Provide documentation outlining commitment for bonding and performance guarantees, signed by agents authorized to provide such commitment.

f. Assurances to the City—Operations

- It is expected that the early years of the project's debt will create the greatest burden on the hotel. Cite how that risk has been mitigated.
- Present two brief cash flow scenarios and case studies illustrating the "expected" scenario and "less-than-expected" scenario.
- Specifically identify which parties would infuse additional equity support.

g. Draft Legal Agreements

- Provide draft legal agreements with the nonprofit, municipally sponsored, local government corporation and your team's role, for use in negotiation with the City.

h. Site Control and Value

- Identify a specific site or sites that will be used for the hotel.
- Identify nature of ownership.
- If site is not owned, demonstrate how site will be obtained; provide documentation.

i. Minority and Women Business Enterprise Program

- Provide proposed program for ensuring the full and fair opportunity for Minority and Women Business Enterprises to participate in all aspects of the project's pre-construction/development phase, construction, and operation.

III. PHYSICAL AND COST ANALYSIS INFORMATION

The intent of this portion of the request is to assist the City in understanding the physical and cost aspects of the team's proposal. It is recognized that significant variation will occur subsequent to this proposal based on negotiations and team refinement.

a. Recommended Design Concepts

- Provide conceptual design information and a site plan for the proposed hotel.
- Provide program of spaces for the proposed property:
  - Guest rooms
  - Meeting rooms
  - Ballrooms
  - Public areas
  - Back of house
  - Support retail
  - Parking
  - Connections to adjacent land uses
  - Other
- Provide breakdown of room mix by category.

   The developer shall provide narrative and descriptions of the project. The proposal shall contain sufficient quantity and detail in drawings and/or other illustrations to explain the proposer's architectural and urban design intent. All drawings shall be delineated or mounted on 30" by 40" illustration boards with proposer's and architect's names appearing only on the back. Only one set of boards is required with the submittal.

b. Urban Design Issues/Project Linkages

- Briefly describe how the proposed hotel will be integrated into the urban campus.
- Describe what role the hotel will play in adjacent land uses, especially the convention center and other adjacent land uses.

c. Construction Cost Analysis

Provide a cost analysis outlining the following information:

- Cost category—budgeted amount
- Preliminary development
- Architectural/Engineering/Consultants
- Interior design
- Professional fees
- Construction
- Furniture, fixtures, and equipment
- Project management
- Project coordination
- Preopening expenses
- Working capital
- Contingency
- Before financing costs
- Capalized interest
- Estimated finance
- Transaction costs
- Total project costs

d. Project Development Time Line

- Provide a Gantt chart with milestones for the preconstruction/development phase, construction, and preopening period.

SUBMITTAL INSTRUCTIONS

Short-listed teams shall prepare one original and 12 copies (excepting large-scale drawings) of proposals in response to this request in 8½" by 11" format. Proposals must be organized following the outline provided in the Information Requested section of this RFP and must include at least the requested information. The City reserves the right to request additional information during the review of responses.

Responses must be submitted no later than 5:00 P.M. on Friday, February 18, 19XX. The response must be bound and sealed when submitted. The response must be delivered to:

"City" Downtown Management Corporation
9999 Smith Ave., Suite 9
City, State, Zip

The envelopes or boxes must state "RFP Response—Convention Center Headquarters Hotel Due 5:00 P.M., February 18, 19XX."

Responses should be accompanied by submittal fee of $15,000 made payable to the City of "X" Civic Center Department. This submittal fee, plus the $10,000 fee from Phase I RFQ solicitation, will be refunded in its entirety to those proposers who are not selected to enter negotiations in Phase III.

Questions concerning the RFP should be directed to Mr. Jones at (999) 999-9999. Questions or clarifications relating to definitions or interpretations of this RFP or about operations of the Convention Center must be submitted in writing on or before 5:00 P.M., December 15, 19XX, to Mr. Jones, "City" Downtown Management Corporation, 9999 Smith Ave., Suite 9, City, State, Zip.

Responses to questions and RFP addenda received in writing prior to December 15 will be made in writing and distributed to the short-listed teams by December 23, 19XX. Oral explanations or instructions shall not be considered binding on the City. Respondents will be notified in writing of any change in the specifications contained in the RFP.

Neither the City, the "City" Downtown Management Corporation, Central "City," Inc., nor any of their officers, agents, or employees shall be responsible for the accuracy of any information provided to any proposer as part of this procurement. All proposers are encouraged to independently verify the accuracy of any information provided. The use of any of this information in the preparation of a response to this request is at the sole risk of the proposer.

CONDITIONS AND LIMITATIONS

This RFP does not represent a commitment or offer by the City to enter into a lease or other agreement with proposer or to pay any costs incurred in the preparation of a proposal responsive to this request. The proposals and any information made a part of the proposals will become part of the City's official files without any obligation on the City's part to return them to the individual proposers. This RFP and the selected firm proposal may, by reference, become a part of any formal agreement between the proposer and the City resulting from this solicitation.

The proposer shall not offer any gratuities, favors, or anything of monetary value to any official or employee of the City, "City" Downtown Management Corporation, or Central "City," Inc., for the purpose of influencing consideration of a proposal.

The "City" Fair Campaign Ordinance makes it unlawful for a contractor to offer any contribution to a candidate for city elective office (including elected officers and officers-elect) during a certain period of time prior to and following the award of the contract by the City Council. The term *contractor* includes proprietors or proprietorships, all partners of partnerships, and all officers, directors, and holders of 10 percent or more of the outstanding shares of corporations. A statement disclosing the names and business addresses of each of those persons will be required to be submitted with each bid or proposal for a City Contract (Exhibit B.2). See Chapter 18 of the Code of Ordinances, City, State, for further information.

The proposer shall not collude in any manner or engage in any practices with any other proposer(s), which may restrict or eliminate competition or otherwise restrain trade. Violation of this instruction will cause the proposer's proposal to be rejected by the City. The prohibition is not intended to preclude joint ventures or subcontracts.

All proposals submitted must be the original work product of the proposer. The copying, paraphrasing, or otherwise using of substantial portions of the work product of another proposer is not permitted. Failure to adhere to this instruction will cause the proposal to be rejected.

The City has sole discretion and reserves the right to reject any and all proposals received in response to this RFP and to cancel the RFP at any time prior to entering into a formal development agreement.

The City reserves the right to waive any irregularities in any or all proposals or any part thereof. Failure to furnish all information requested may disqualify a proposer. The City reserves the right to request clarification of proposal data without changing the terms of the proposal.

The proposer must furnish a Certificate of Authority, signed by the chief executive officer or managing partner of the company, with its proposal. The Certificate should list the specific officers who are authorized to execute agreements on behalf of the company.

The proposal shall be signed by a person or persons authorized to legally bind the proposer and shall contain a statement that the proposal shall remain firm for a period of 180 days from the date of receipt of the proposal by the City.

If selected, the proposer must furnish evidence that the team is in good standing and authorized to transact business in the State prior to awarding of the contract.

Agreements with the selected proposer will require that the selected proposer provide workers' compensation insurance, commercial general liability, and automobile liability insurance, and the City and/or municipally sponsored local government corporation will be included as an additional insured.

Development agreements with the selected proposer will require indemnification of the City and/or the municipally sponsored local government corporation by the selected proposer in form and substance satisfactory to the City Attorney.

Agreements will require a performance and payment bond commensurate with the contract of the selected proposer's contractor. Such bonds will be in a form and with a surety acceptable to the City. In addition, the City may require other forms of assurance from the selected proposer of successful completion of development.

Pursuant to Chapter 15, Article VI, of the City Code of Ordinances, the successful proposer will be required by the development agreement to complete and to return to the City an Affidavit on Nonviolation of Restrictions on Certain Business Transactions Related to South Africa.

MINORITY AND WOMEN BUSINESS ENTERPRISE REQUIREMENTS

It is the policy of the City of "X" to stimulate the growth of local Minority and Women Business Enterprises (Disadvantaged Business Enterprise), to encourage the full participation of Minority and Women Business Enterprises in its procurement activity, and to afford them a full and fair opportunity to compete for all City contracts.

1. The successful proposer must ensure that Minority and Women Business Enterprises, as defined in the Minority and Women Business Enterprise Ordinance No.84-1309 passed August 22, 1984, have a full and fair opportunity to participate. In this regard, the successful proposer shall take all necessary and reasonable steps to meet the Minority/Women/Disadvantaged Business Enterprise (M/W/DBE) goal for this contract.

2. The successful proposer and any subcontractor shall not discriminate on the basis of race, color, national origin, or sex in the performance of this contract.

3. The successful proposer will be required to provide documentation of having met the M/WBE goals or good faith efforts if the M/WBE goals have not been met. Evidence of good faith efforts is outlined in Section E, "Contract Responsibilities of the Bidder Requirements for Minority and Women Business Enterprise Program," available from the Director of the Affirmative Action Division of the mayor's office.

4. The successful proposer's performance in meeting the M/WBE participation goals during the capital improvements portions of the development agreement will be monitored by the Affirmative Action Contract Compliance Division of the mayor's office.

The percentage goal for M/W/DBE is 15 percent. When the successful proposer chooses an operator, provision shall be made for adequate participation by M/W/DBE.

PROPOSER'S FINANCIAL DATA

Financial Statement

Proposer, owner, corporation of proposer, and any person or business entity guaranteeing the performance of the proposer, as well as the construction management firm or contractor and hotel management company, must attach a complete report, prepared in accordance with good accounting practices, reflecting current financial condition. The report must include a balance sheet and annual income statement. The person or entity covered by the statement must be prepared to substantiate all information shown.

Financial information shall be treated as confidential, except in any litigation or arbitration proceedings between proposer and the City. The City may furnish this information to another government agency requesting the information.

The following is required from each firm reporting financial information:

- *Surety Information.* Has any surety or bonding company ever been required to perform upon your default?   Yes   No
  If yes, attach a statement naming the surety or bonding company, date, amount of bond, and the circumstances surrounding said default and performance.
- *Bankruptcy Information.* Have you ever declared bankruptcy?   Yes   No
  If yes, state date, court of jurisdiction, amount of liabilities, and amount of assets.
- *Pending litigation.* Provide information regarding pending litigation, liens, or claims involving any participant for whom financial data is presented in the proposal.

Exhibit B.1   Declaration

Name, Title
City, State
Submittal Date

The undersigned, as proposer, declares that the only persons interested in this proposal are those named herein, that no other person has any interest in this proposal or in the agreement of development to which this proposal pertains; that this proposal is made without connection or arrangement with any other person; and that this proposal is in every respect fair, in good faith, and without collusion or fraud.

The proposer further declares that he has complied in every respect with all of the instructions for proposers, that he has read all addenda, if any, and that he has satisfied himself fully relative to all matters and conditions with respect to the project to which the proposal pertains.

The proposer agrees, if this proposal is accepted, to execute appropriate agreements for the purpose of establishing a formal contractual relationship between the proposer and the City of "X" and/or a nonprofit, municipally sponsored, local government corporation for the performance of all requirements to which the proposal pertains.

The proposer states that this proposal is based on the proposal documents and addenda, if any.

Name of Firm/Individual/Corporation

Signature

Title

Exhibit B.2   Contractor Submission List—"City's" Fair Campaign Ordinance

This list is submitted under the provisions of Section 18-36b of the Code of Ordinances, City, State, in connection with the attached proposal, submission of _____ ("the firm"), whose business mailing address is _____.
The firm is organized as a (check one as applicable): _____ sole proprietorship whose proprietor is _____
(include the business mailing address of the proprietor or note "same" if it is the same as above) (include the business mailing address of each person or note "same" if it is the same as above) _____, a corporation, each of whose officers, each of whose directors, and each of whose holders of 10 percent or more of the outstanding shares of stock are: _____
(include the business mailing address of each person or note "same" if it is the same as above). I certify that I am duly authorized to submit this list on behalf of the firm, that I am associated with the firm in the capacity noted below, and that I have personal knowledge of the accuracy of the information provided herein.

Preparer _____

Printed name _____

Title _____

Note: This list constitutes a government record, as defined by §37.01 of the State Penal Code. Submission of a false government record is punishable as provided in §37.10 of the State's Penal Code. Attach additional pages if needed to supply the required names and addresses.

Request for Qualifications for the Master Developer for the Finance, Design, and Development of the University X and the University Community

Date: _____

PREFACE

Over the past several years, the University X system has accomplished great strides toward developing the new University campus. But now we need the expertise of a comprehensive development team to complete the predevelopment process and begin construction on several fronts, including the campus, the required public infrastructure, and support commercial development. It is very important for developers to realize that the University is under enormous pressure to start construction in the latter part of 20XX and begin classes in the fall of 20XX. Equally important, the University is dedicated to working closely with the City and County and other important public partners throughout the predevelopment and development processes.

Sealed responses containing qualifications for the finance, design, and development of the new University X campus and University Community will be received by University X, 1170 Any Avenue, Suite I, City, State, Zip, prior to 5:00 P.M. PST on January 17, 20XX.

The developer request for qualifications (RFQ) document may be obtained from Mr./Ms. _____, title _____, University X.

All respondents will be required to comply with _____.

University X reserves the right to reject any or all responses to this RFQ, to advertise for new RFQ responses, or to accept any RFQ response deemed to be in the best interest of the University.

A response to this RFQ should not be construed as a contract nor indicate a commitment of any kind. The RFQ does not commit the University to pay for costs incurred in preparing a submittal in response to this RFQ or for any costs incurred prior to the execution of a final contract.

December 13, 19XX

Mr. Issuer
Chancellor, University X

Contents

Overview of the University Community

The Vision for University X
Purpose of the Request for Qualifications
Accomplishments to Date
Project Location

The University Community Concept Plan

Open Space Concept
Land Use Concept
Circulation Concept
University Campus

Project Setting and Support Systems

Project Setting
Infrastructure
Environmental Findings

Master Developer Responsibilities

Master Planning
Design
Entitlements/Development Approvals
Financing Infrastructure and Development Costs
Construction
Facility Maintenance and Operation

Development Schedule

Submission Requirements and Schedule

Submission Requirements
Submission Schedule
Evaluation Criteria for Developer Proposals
Developer Selection Process

Limitations and General Conditions

Minority and Women Business Enterprise Requirements

OVERVIEW OF THE UNIVERSITY COMMUNITY

The Vision for University X

A dynamic new University Community will evolve on the lands north and east of Lake X, just outside of State. The heart of the Community will be University X. The campus will serve as the hub of a network of educational services, research activities, and technological innovation reaching out to the community and the state. The Community will be a crossroads for people of all ages, economic backgrounds, cultures, and nationalities. It will be a marketplace of ideas, culture, business, and technological advancement and will serve as the stage for community activity and celebration. The Community will offer choices in housing, business, recreation, social activity, and cultural pursuits. The design of the Community will place a high value on livability in balance with stewardship of important natural resources of the site.

Purpose of the Request for Qualifications

University X is seeking a qualified master developer who will comprehensively manage the complex development process of the X acres that comprise the University Community property. The master developer will work closely with University X, local government agencies, and its consultants to create a project that will achieve the goals of the City in creating a "University Community" as defined within this request for qualifications (RFQ).

It is the intent of University X to select a master developer who is sensitive to the land use desires of the University and the community. The developer needs to assemble a team that can design, finance, develop, and construct a first-class educational campus that will be acceptable to the surrounding community as well as the various regulatory agencies. At the same time, University X is interested in creating a true public/private partnership with the master developer to structure creative approaches to ensure the maximum return to University X on its land holdings while simultaneously minimizing financial and development risk.

University X will select a master developer on the basis of the submission requirements and evaluation criteria contained in the Submission Requirements and Schedule section. University X will then enter into an Exclusive Right to Negotiate for some agreed-upon term.

Accomplishments to Date

Expected to open in 20XX as the University of X's, University X will be the first American research university built in the twenty-first century. The campus will incorporate digital technology to create an educational network serving students and communities throughout the area. Students are already enrolled in courses in the community at sites such as the Center in City. University X will have an integral role in improving the educational attainment of community students and in fostering the economic development of State.

The main campus, with its sweeping vistas of the X Mountains, will be part of a vibrant X-acre planned community. A University Community Concept Report has been developed that serves as the foundation for detailed planning and development of the new Community and as the framework for development and conservation. It is based on forecasts of growth and development within the context of likely demographic and market conditions in the region. University X will draw upon the vitality and rich history of the community to fulfill State's historic commitment to excellence in teaching, research, and public service.

Several actions over the last four years have demonstrated the commitment of the University X Board of Regents, City, County, and their partners to the development of the University Community and University X. In May 19XX, the regents of University X selected a site near Lake X for the development of the campus of the University X. In December 19XX, the campus was designated as the University X, University X.

In October 19XX, the County Board of Supervisors amended the County General Plan to acknowledge the site for the future campus and to identify a Specific Urban Development Plan (SUPD) boundary for the University Community as the planning area for development adjacent to the campus. The lands within this boundary were designated "University Community Urban Reserve," reflecting the County's commitment to plan this area comprehensively in cooperation with the University, landowners, and other public agencies.

In April 19XX, the City of State completed a comprehensive update of its General Plan. Through this update, the City included the University Community SUPD within its sphere of influence and agreed to cooperate with the County in planning the University Community.

In February 19XX, the County Board of Supervisors approved a guidance package for University Community planning that clarified the relationship and roles of the various participants and outlined the subsequent planning steps. The first step in the process was a concept planning phase to provide an overall vision and framework for development of the University Community.

The University Community Concept Planning process was initiated in April 19XX and completed in March 19XX. The University Community Concept Report forms the basis for two subsequent planning documents, which will be completed by the concept planning participants and managed by the master developer:

- The University Community Plan, which is being produced by the County of State as an amendment to the County General Plan and which will be approved by the County Board of Supervisors
- The University X Long-Range Development Plan, which is being prepared by the University X and will be approved by the Board of Regents

In addition, the University Community Concept Report provides the framework for ongoing collaborative planning between the City and County of State, University X, and the Trusts.

Project Location

The proposed development site is located in County in the heart of the Community. The Community is composed of X counties: County, County A, and County B. The population of the region is 10 percent of State's population. By the year 20XX, Area will have over 6 million persons, according to population projections by State's Department of Finance. Land is plentiful and inexpensive, and there is a deep pool of qualified people in the labor market.

The County is one of the area's major employers, with a workforce serving a diverse ethnic population. The total area of County is approximately X square miles.

UNIVERSITY COMMUNITY CONCEPT PLAN

The University Community concept planning process began in April 19XX as a collaborative effort to formulate a development concept for the 11,200-acre new Community that will include University X, University X. The University Community includes approximately X acres owned by Trust 2, Y acres owned by Trust 2, 200 acres owned by the County, and Z acres that will be donated by the Trust for the University campus.

The property owners, the University, and local government agencies that will be involved with development of the University Community have jointly undertaken the concept planning process. These include University X, the County, Trust 1, Trust 2, City of State, and the State Irrigation District. This core team retained planning associates to facilitate and provide technical support for the planning process.

As part of the concept planning process, several development scenarios were generated. Based on an evaluation of economic feasibility, consistency with the Vision Statement, relationship to the existing community and region, environmental stewardship, and community character and quality, three concepts form the foundation for the development of the University Community.

1. *Open space concept*—depicts how open space may be used to protect the site's important natural resources and shape development.
2. *Land use concept*—depicts the pattern and relationship among the land uses to be developed.
3. *Circulation concept*—depicts the backbone network of circulation modes and networks that may be developed to support the land use pattern and link the University with the surrounding areas.

Open Space Concept

The University Community will integrate state-of-the-art concepts of natural resources management and environmental preservation, open space planning and design, and University X academic programs to create a community that represents an exemplary balance of urban development and open spaces, and of economic development and natural resources conservation.

Open spaces will be used to provide on-site amenities and recreational opportunities, maintain view sheds, and protect significant natural resources. A network of linked open spaces, including developed parks, natural greenways, open lands, and natural preserves, will provide amenities to the community and will connect the campus and town center with residential neighborhoods and the surrounding region.

Natural and developed opens spaces will be used to shape the character of developed uses. Development will be oriented to emphasize long-distance views to the X Mountains, Lake X, and other natural features.

A strategy will be developed to preserve and enhance important natural resource habitats in the University Community. The area around Lake X will be protected and enhanced as a major regional recreation resource.

Land Use Concept

The University Community land use concept provides for the concentration of development around a high-intensity activity center consisting of the core campus and town center. This center will blend a mixed-use and pedestrian-oriented town center (retail, office, housing, entertainment, culture, and recreation) with campus uses, and shared uses will be developed around common public areas and public transit facilities. On the periphery, the town center may transition into concentrations of employment-generating uses and/or housing.

A network of residential villages will be developed around the core area, each distinctly identified by a common neighborhood center and through its architectural and landscape design. An areawide greenway system will be designed to connect the villages and activity centers and to provide access to surrounding open spaces. Developed uses will be balanced into a variety of open lands including parks, passive recreational areas, open spaces, and natural preserves, encouraging an outdoor lifestyle.

Projected Land Use and Build-Out

Residential		
Housing (total)	1,500 acres	11,800 units
Single-family		6,660 units
Multifamily		5,200 units
Parks	150 acres	
Schools	175 acres	
Commercial/Industrial		
Retail	75 acres	450,000 square feet
Office	150 acres	1,400,000 square feet
Industrial	150 acres	1,250,000 square feet
University Campus		
Core campus	200 acres	
Open space/research	1,800 acres	
Total	**5,000 acres**	

Circulation Concept

The circulation concept provides for the development of multimodal corridors that will provide access to the City, State, surrounding areas, and the regional circulation network. Primary access to the University Community will occur from (1) the proposed Campus Parkway from the south, (2) Dirt Road from the southwest, and (3) Main Street from the northwest in the long term for network continuity.

An internal network of circulation corridors will be developed off of the entry corridor, providing access to and interconnecting the Community's neighborhood and centers and the campus. The major arterial corridors will be an appropriate right-of-way to accommodate an evolving mix of circulation modes including automobile, bus and rail transit, bicycles, and pedestrian. A transit mall will be established near the interface between the town center and campus core to emphasize pedestrian and transit use.

Pedestrian, bicycle, and other trails will be developed along drainage corridors and in greenways connecting the residential villages, community centers, and campus.

University Campus

The dynamic new University Community will evolve on the lands north and east of Lake X, just outside of State. The heart of the University Community will be University X, the campus of the University X.

The University X campus will encompass 2,000 acres, with the campus core developed on approximately 200 acres. The campus will be a high-density activity area that will include the majority of academic programs, student services, and other support activities. Some housing, recreation, and commercial activities may also be located within or near the core to facilitate connection to the town center proposed as part of the University Community, and the opportunity for share use of public facilities.

The balance of the campus area will contain a variety of functions, as well as open space for habitat preservation and instruction and research purposes. Areas outside the core will be used for specialized research, housing, athletic and recreation, utility, and corporation yard facilities. Some land may be set aside for potential revenue-generating uses such as a research and development facility, as well as for expansion areas for academic programs.

A cohesive network of walkways, bicycle paths, and open spaces will link the campus to the surrounding community and will connect the developed areas of the campus. This will occur both at the intersection of the campus core and the town center, as well as along the remaining campus boundaries. A common center for transit services will serve the campus core and town center.

PROJECT SETTING AND SUPPORT SYSTEMS

Project Setting

Development of the University Community, to include University X, will be influenced by the site's natural characteristics; by the demand for growth and development, based on existing trends within the region, adjusted for the University's presence; and by decisions regarding how infrastructure and services will be provided to support development of the site.

The University Community area represents a transition between the flat agricultural lands of the Community and the rising mountains. Its rolling topography provides an opportunity to shape patterns of development into distinct districts and neighborhoods, in contrast to the uniform sprawl that characterizes many residential subdivisions and commercial developments across the State. Within the site, slopes frame distinct topographic bowls and ridges that provide a special character and identity.

Higher elevations on the site offer spectacular long-distance views of the X Mountains, agricultural lands, and the City, and shorter-distance views of such local amenities as Lake X, County Regional Park, and the State Hills Golf Course. The varied topography offers opportunities to stage a progression of views from enclosed bowls to corridors that visually open into wide panoramas.

The site's setting near the X foothills, the center of State's story, provides a history of places, buildings, mine tailings, and memories that can serve as the foundation for the University Community's identity, character, and physical development. The mountains, including National Park, provide an easily accessible recreational amenity that will be highly desirable to the University Community residents, the campus, and visitors.

Infrastructure

Because the University Community site is totally undeveloped, completely new infrastructure systems will be required. While this is a substantial undertaking, it offers opportunities to develop state-of-the-art systems and techniques and advance practices of environmental stewardship. The determination of infrastructure service providers and design of facilities will be accomplished during subsequent planning phases.

For the purposes of concept planning, preliminary infrastructure analyses and plans were prepared in order to better understand the costs of development in the University Community. Conservative assumptions were made in terms of infrastructure and public services costs, because these costs are key factors in the determination of financial feasibility. Some assumptions about the provision of infrastructure and services may not necessarily represent the ultimate approach. Subsequent planning tasks will identify the final array of infrastructure solutions.

Environmental Findings

The rolling grasslands, canals, and stock ponds of the University Community site are home to a variety of habitats that present both opportunities and challenges for campus and community development. The site is dominated by rolling grasslands and wetlands, including complexes of vernal pools.

The natural habitats and species present on the site create a variety of opportunities for open space planning, recreation, and education within the University Community. Large, contiguous blocks of habitat, if preserved, can give physical form and structure to the community and its neighborhoods. Undeveloped natural habitats in the community can also be used for recreational purposes, including hiking and equestrian trails, nature centers, and the like. Similarly, undeveloped natural open spaces present educational opportunities, including research, educational trails and walkways, seasonal swales and drainages, and seasonal and year-round creeks. The site, especially the wetlands, is known to be home to state and federally listed endangered species. The grasslands and wetlands on the site are part of a larger grassland/wetland ecosystem that stretches for many miles to the east, north, and southeast.

The development of University X will require an Environmental Impact Report (EIR) and Section 404 permits issued by the Army Corp of Engineers.

MASTER DEVELOPER RESPONSIBILITIES

This section describes a general overview of the anticipated responsibilities of the master developer. Following selection of the master developer, these responsibilities will be more specifically defined and detailed in the development agreement that is negotiated between University X and the master developer. The selected master developer must (at a minimum) provide the following services.

Master Planning

The County is currently preparing the University Community Plan, a master plan for the new community that will develop on the property around the University X campus. The University Community Plan will be incorporated into the County General Plan and will establish the patterns and guidelines for future development of the University Community. In conjunction with the County Plan, University X is developing the Long-Range Development Plan. This plan, in conjunction with the University Community Plan, will be tested, refined, and modified based on the University Community Concept Report, a collaborative planning effort between the County, University X, and the Trusts. University X has retained several firms to assist in facilitation of the process and provide technical support for the planning process.

Working closely with the City, County, and University X and its team of consultants, the master developer will be responsible for designing and implementing a master plan that achieves the intent of the University Community. This master plan must be governed by the influences of the site's natural characteristics, as well as the demand for growth and development based on existing trends within the region as adjusted by the University's presence. In addition, the master plan will define a vision of the future, incorporating thoughts on planning for urban development, environmental stewardship, and how the infrastructure and services will be provided to support the development of the site and contiguous development.

Design

Based on the approved master plan, the master developer will be responsible for developing an overall "architectural theme" for the University Community that establishes the general design parameters on which the designs for each individual facility will be based. The master developer will present several design schemes to University X to solicit their input and subsequent approval. The architectural theme will take into account the vision of University X, as well as draw from the history of the region and its agricultural and foothills setting.

The master developer will be responsible for developing schematic, design development, and construction documents (collectively, the "Documents") for each individual facility. University X will review and approve the Documents to ensure the facility design meets the architectural and functional objectives of each College/

Department of the University that will be the end user of the facility. The master developer will also be responsible for providing all applicable geotechnical, testing, inspection, and other engineering studies for each facility built.

Entitlements/Development Approvals

The master developer will be responsible for procuring all necessary land use entitlements, permits, and regulatory approvals for development of the property. This includes any required environmental documentation, reports and approvals, building permits, and so on. University X and the City and County will assist the master developer in these efforts.

Financing Infrastructure and Development Costs

University X has estimated that the development costs for backbone infrastructure systems and public facilities to be approximately $300 million at the time of build-out. This excludes costs for "in-tract" roads and other improvements traditionally borne by developers. The cost estimate included backbone water, wastewater, storm drainage, and transportation facilities; parks, police, fire facilities, and schools; and environmental mitigation fees. The $300 million investment in infrastructure and public service facilities will support development of a total estimated real estate value build-out of $2 billion in private development. Real estate values at build-out are estimated (in current dollars):

Residential	$1,600,000,000
Retail	$100,000,000
Office	$175,000,000
Business park	$125,000,000
Total	$2,000,000,000

To date, the state legislature has already approved and budgeted approximately $25 million in discretionary funds and another $55 million in the form of a bond measure to finance the project. In addition, the federal government has appropriated approximately $22 million for the campus parkway and other roadway improvements. The $25 million investment by the State includes a continuing annual appropriation of approximately $10 million for campus planning and academic program development. University X has determined that the $10 million annual appropriation will not be sufficient in fiscal year 20XX–20XX because of the costs in hiring the required faculty.

The master developer will be responsible for developing alternative public/private financing structures and obtaining the financing to optimize the use of the aforementioned state and federal funding. This includes the financing engineering of both tax-exempt and taxable financing for facilities to be occupied by University X, as well as facilities developed for lease by private-sector users who are located on the campus property to further support the University's mission and student needs. The master developer will be responsible for financing the entire cost of the proposed development or credit enhancing public financing of the project. This includes all predevelopment costs such as infrastructure; public communications; entitlements; environmental, traffic, soil, or other studies; design and construction costs; and off- and on-site work, including all utilities.

University X will consider a long-term ground lease of selected sites to the master developer. This will reduce up-front capital investment by the master developer. The minimum term for a ground lease has not been determined and will depend on the nature of the development. University X has not yet decided to provide a long-term ground lease. However, University X expects to receive minimum annual ground lease rent and/or a percentage rent, as negotiated between University X and the master developer. University X is interested in maximizing the value of its property holdings and expects to measure this value in terms of the annual returns to University X from the public/private financing and ownership structure proposed by the master developer.

Construction

The master developer will be responsible for the construction of all necessary off-site and selected on-site improvements, including, but not limited to, all infrastructure (utilities, roads, etc.); the buildings' cores and shells; tenant improvements; fixed furniture, fixtures, and equipment; and landscaping. The master developer will be required to comply with all applicable state and federal regulations concerning prevailing wage and other labor-related issues. The master developer will also be responsible for packaging selected land parcels for development by third-party developers. In addition, the master developer will be responsible for negotiating all development agreements with third-party developers.

Facility Maintenance and Operation

University X is considering having the master developer provide the entire requisite ongoing maintenance and operation of the buildings developed on the University campus. Should University X decide not to provide these services with employees of the University, the master developer will need to be prepared to provide these services, which include, but are not limited to, maintenance of the roofs and buildings' shells, heating/air conditioning systems, elevators, plumbing, electrical and other building systems, janitorial, security, carpet and paint, water, landscaping, and trash disposal.

DEVELOPMENT SCHEDULE

In conjunction with the University X team of consultants, the following general schedule has been prepared for the development of the University Community. This schedule will continue to evolve and be refined as the planning and entitlement process continues. University X is committed to maintaining this schedule and the occupancy by University operations in the first buildings in the last half of calendar 20XX and the enrollment of the first students in the fall of 20XX.

Year   *Milestone Activity*

20XX   Completed long-range development plan and associated environmental documents to be presented to Regents in late fall. University X retains master developer in first quarter. Master planning process continues and is finalized.

20XX   Campus site development and construction activities commence in the summer.

20XX   Campus operations move into the first buildings during the last half of the year.

20XX   First students enroll in classes on campus in the fall.

The master developer will be responsible for developing detailed schedules of the numerous planning, design, financing, construction, and operations activities. The master developer will be responsible for the coordination of all agencies, consultants, architects, engineers, contractors, property management, in executing and maintaining the aforementioned schedule. It is imperative that this schedule be maintained and achieved. University X, County, State, and all other applicable agencies are committed to work closely with and support the master developer in achieving this schedule.

SUBMISSION REQUIREMENTS AND SCHEDULE

Submission Requirements

University X intends to select a master developer based on a review and evaluation of the information submitted in response to this RFQ and subsequent negotiations. As such, University X is not seeking a detailed development program and financial plan. Rather, University X seeks information concerning the respondent firms' accomplishments, capabilities, and experience. Each Statement of Qualifications should be organized in the following order/sections. Respondents should label and "tab" each one of the sections for easy and consistent reference:

Title page.   The title page should show the respondent's name, RFQ title, and date of submittal.

Letter of introduction.   Within one page, the respondent should include the name, address, and statement of whether the respondent is an individual, partnership, corporation, joint venture, special-purpose entity, or other entity. The letter should also provide the name of the person(s) authorized to make representations for the respondent and his or her phone number. The person authorized to represent the proposal must sign the letter.

History of key team members.   Identify the legal entity that will serve as the principal in the proposed development, and provide a brief history of that entity and the parent company, if applicable.

Project team.   Provide in-depth resumes on the key individuals who will be responsible for managing the finance and development process. Also, describe the level of commitment for each member of the development team.

Relevant project experience.   Provide project descriptions that include scope, building use(s), cost, and geographic location of each project. University X officials are most interested in public/private developments completed in the past five years. Identify finance and development partners for each project. Also, describe the role the developer performed in the development partnership. Emphasis should be placed on complex public/private development projects commensurate with the scope and nature of University X projects.

Demonstrate the developer's creativity in structuring public/private partnerships. University X officials are focused on the track record of the developer to structure public/private partnerships, which reduce the public partner's capital investment and risk. Developers are also encouraged to describe examples of creative deal structuring for public/private partnerships achieved in the past five years.

Financing relationships and sources.   Indicate the source(s) of both debt and equity financing for each project, and a detailed description of the firm's commitment and capability in providing the capital to competitively and successfully finance the University X project. Indicate the respondent's experience and relationship (if any) to the firm providing the financing. If the respondent is not providing any or all of the financing, the financing entity is to provide a letter indicating their interest, capability, and preliminary commitment to providing both tax-exempt and taxable capital required to successfully finance the project.

Project management expertise.   Provide a summary of the respondent's experience in managing large, complex projects that required interaction with a broad range of interested parties from both the public and private sectors. For the project summary, include a listing of all team members, their role, and the contractual relationship among the parties.

Project approach.   Briefly describe the developer's approach to managing the finance, design, development, and construction of the University Community, including how the developer will interact with the University and other public partners and participants.

References.   Provide financial and development references (name, title, entity, telephone number, and contractual relationship to respondent) that can be contacted at this time with respect to current and past project development experience, including key public officials involved in the respective project(s).

Deposits.   There will be two deposits associated with a response to this development opportunity, as summarized below:

1. *RFQ Deposit:* A $1,000 nonrefundable deposit associated with the submission to this RFQ.
2. *Development Agreement Deposit:* A $250,000 nonrefundable deposit submitted by the selected master developer. The nonrefundable deposit will ensure the master developer's participation, negotiation, and execution of a master development agreement between University X and the selected master developer.

The respondent should prepare the RFQ deposit check, payable to: _____.

Submission Schedule

The following is the schedule for this developer RFQ process:

December 13, 19XX	Issue RFQ
January 5, 20XX	Preproposal conference

January 17, 20XX	RFQ statements due
January 27, 20XX	Board of Regents approves selection of master developer

University X is committed to retaining a master developer in order to achieve the aforementioned project development schedule. In addition, University X understands the amount of time and expense for firms to respond to the RFQ and has specifically designed the RFQ process to minimize these submittal costs while simultaneously ensuring that the University will be able to select the most qualified master developer.

Evaluation Criteria for Developer Proposals

The following criteria, listed in order of importance, will be used to evaluate developer proposals.

1. In the past three years, demonstrated ability to access and obtain private equity and debt, as well as public bond financing for major university facilities, public infrastructure, and commercial developments completed using the public/private finance and development approach
2. Demonstrated ability to structure public/private partnerships, which reduce the public partner's capital investment and risk
3. Experience working with public entities to structure public/private finance plans for major mixed-use developments, infrastructure, and university projects in the past five years
4. Experience implementing major public/private mixed-use, infrastructure, and university development projects in the past five years
5. The extent of public/private finance and development experience of the specific individuals assigned by the developer to the proposed project team
6. The level of creativity demonstrated by the developer for public/private projects completed in the past three years (examples are limited to five projects)
7. Demonstrated experience and financial strength to complete a project of this size on budget and on schedule
8. The developer's proposed project approach
9. The level of comprehensiveness of the developer's proposal for University X
10. References for the developer, architect, and construction company

The evaluation of the developer submittals in response to the RFQ does not constitute any form of commitment by the University. It is anticipated that each submittal will be evaluated based on the information submitted plus any other independent information developed by the University. The University reserves the right to request clarification or additional information from a respondent if necessary.

Developer Selection Process

The University is facing a very demanding schedule in order to begin construction by 20XX. Therefore, University officials have designed a two-step process to select and negotiate a master development agreement.

Step one.   University officials will appoint a selection committee including individuals from the University, the City and County, and other experts in the fields of real estate and finance to review and score all developer submittals in accordance with the evaluation criteria. The selection committee will then select the three highest-ranking teams.

Step two.   University officials will then identify a three-member University X negotiation team and a lead negotiator for the public partner entity. This negotiating team will then enter into an Exclusive Right to Negotiate (ERN) with the developer ranked number one of the three top-ranked developer candidates. The term of the ERN will be 180 days. If the University X negotiation team cannot structure a mutually agreeable financial and master development transaction in that period of time, the negotiation team has the ability to terminate or extend negotiations with number-one–ranked developer. If the team terminates the ERN, they proceed with negotiations with the developer ranked number two among the three top-ranked developer teams, or the University X team can cancel the process.

   This two-step RFQ/negotiate process eliminates the lengthy RFP process and the interview process.

LIMITATIONS AND GENERAL CONDITIONS

The RFQ does not represent a commitment or offer by University X to enter into an agreement with a proposer or to pay any costs incurred in the preparation of a response to this request. The responses and any information made a part of the responses will not be returned to proposers. This RFQ and the selected firm's response to the RFQ may, by reference, become a part of any formal agreement between the proposer and University X resulting from this solicitation.

   The proposer shall not offer any gratuities, favors, or anything of monetary value to any official or employee of University X for the purpose of influencing consideration of a response to this RFQ.

   The proposer shall not collude in any manner or engage in any practices with any other proposer(s) that may restrict or eliminate competition or otherwise restrain trade. Violation of this instruction will cause the proposer's submittal to be rejected by University X. The prohibition is not intended to preclude joint ventures or subcontracts.

All responses submitted must be the original work product of the producer. The copying, paraphrasing, or otherwise using of substantial portions of the work product of another proposer is not permitted. Failure to adhere to this instruction will cause the response to be rejected.

University X has the sole discretion and reserves the right to reject any and all responses received with respect to this RFQ and to cancel the RFQ at any time prior to entering into formal agreement.

University X reserves the right to request clarification of RFQ data without changing the terms of the RFQ.

MINORITY AND WOMEN BUSINESS ENTERPRISE REQUIREMENTS

Text should reflect local MBE/WBE policies.

Request for Proposals— The James F. Oyster School Public/Private Development Partnerships

"City" Public Schools
415 Any Street
City, State, Zip
The James F. Oyster School Public/Private Development Partnership

For further information, please contact:
Authorized representative of
"City" Public Schools
Mr. Issuer
The Education Company
1401 Any Street
City, State, Zip
(999) 999-9999

THE DEVELOPMENT PARTNERSHIP

Proposed Development

The "City" Public Schools (CPS) and government of State will make the 1.67-acre school site available for matter-of-right development via a long-term land lease or subdivision and fee simple sale. The district government will also dedicate the property taxes from the private development of the site toward school construction as payment in lieu of taxes (PILOT). In exchange, a private developer shall finance, design, and construct or modernize the school on the site in accordance with CPS specifications.

Context

The elementary school is a nationally recognized dual-language public school program. The school community initiated this public/private joint venture development in an effort to modernize or replace its 71-year-old facility and enhance its educational program. Community involvement is a cornerstone of the project, as is the use of private-sector expertise for solving problems associated with antiquated schools and lack of capital funds.

The formulation of the project is supported by grants from the Jones Foundation and the Smith Foundation. The project is viewed as a pilot program and model for real estate development, which can provide State with other sources of funds and expertise needed to modernize its educational facilities.

Partnership Objectives

- To generate the funding necessary for school replacement and/or improvements
- To use, to the greatest extent feasible, private-sector practices to facilitate efficient, high-quality construction
- To add to the City's economic base through creative development strategies
- To encourage private capital investment for projects that provide incentive and reasonable expectations of return for developer partners

PROJECT INFORMATION

Location of Development

The site is located in the northwest section of City in the Smith Memorial Park neighborhood. The address is commonly known as 999 Main Street, City, State, Zip.

The site is bordered by a seven-story apartment building to the north, Elm Street to the south, an extended-stay hotel/residence to the east, and 26th Street to the west. Hotels and residences, as well as banks, restaurants, and shops, are all in close proximity to the site.

The neighborhood is served by Metrorail and Metrobus. The property is approximately two blocks from the Smith Memorial Park-Zoo Metrorail Station (the Red Line) on X Avenue.

Metes and Bounds (Site Survey)

The area of the entire site (school and private development) is approximately 72,714 square feet or 1.67 acres. The general dimensions of the irregular, rectangular-shaped site are 452 feet in width and 175 feet in depth.

Zoning Information

The site is zoned R-5-D. The R-5-D designation permits matter-of-right general residential uses of high-density development, including single-family dwellings, flats, apartments to a maximum height of 90 feet, a maximum floor area ratio (FAR) of 3.5 for all structures, and a maximum lot occupancy of 75 percent. Accordingly, it is estimated that the maximum allowable building area for the property is 254,500 gross square feet of FAR space (essentially above the adjacent grade), including school use.

The allowable maximum height for this property is 90 feet. The elevation of the upper level of the site is approximately 150 feet above mean sea level, and the lower level is an elevation of 127 feet. The upper level is an area equal to two-thirds of the entire site surface. Therefore, it is our opinion that the maximum elevation for any building on this property is 240 feet.

The portion of school development that is above grade is expected to be counted toward the total FAR. A new school requires approximately 47,000 gross program square footage. Assuming that all of the school FAR is above grade, the available FAR for residential development would be approximately 207,500 square feet.

The CPS believes the foregoing statements as to zoning, permitted uses, and development potential to be accurate in all material respects. However, the CPS makes no representations or warranties regarding same and strongly encourages all prospective offerors to perform their own due diligence review of the zoning regulations, permitted uses, and development potential prior to submission of proposals.

Description of Existing School on the Site

The original building of the James F. Elementary School was constructed in 1926. It incorporates 26,591 gross square feet and provides 16,701 square feet of net program space in the original building. The footprint area of the school is 10,864 square feet. An additional total of 2,000 square feet is enclosed in three temporary classrooms. The school is not in a historic district and has not been deemed historic by the district.

Description of Proposed School Modernization

The Board of Education previously approved educational specifications for a new or modernized school with an enrollment capacity of approximately 350 students. The educational specifications delineate the architectural program requirements. They were revised by the CPS in cooperation with the School Restructuring Team in June 19XX.

The revised educational specifications provide for 32,495 square feet of interior net program space. Basic requirements are for 14 grade-level classrooms; one self-contained special education classroom and support spaces; three special-purpose resource classrooms for music and computer instruction; multipurpose, media/library, and physical education spaces; and administrative and building support areas. There are also required outdoor program areas for athletics, play, and environmental study, as well as for parking, which is anticipated to be underground. The complete educational specifications are available in hard copy on request from The Education Company or on the Internet at (www.edu-infra.com).

Scope of Services for School Design and Construction

The CPS has prepared a Scope of Services for School Design and Construction ("Scope of Services") to describe the process of designing and constructing the project. An important function of the Scope of Services is to define the roles and responsibilities of each party, including the CPS, the developer, and the local school community. The Scope of Services is available in hard copy from The Education Company and from the Web site on the Internet (www.edu-infra.com). Offerors should notify the CPS in writing of any recommended changes to the Scope of Services with submission of their proposal.

CPS Interim School Construction Standards

The CPS has prepared Interim School Construction Standards ("Standards") to clarify expectations about construction materials and methods. These are not intended to supersede the developer's architectural team's creativity or professional responsibility for the project, but rather to (1) assist offerors in assessing the cost of constructing the school portion of the project, and (2) set a benchmark against which the developer's design and construction specifications will be evaluated. The Standards are available in hard copy on request from The Education Company or through the school Web site at (www.edu-infra.com).

Local School and Community Support

The school community looks forward to an exemplary design and high-quality construction of a new or modernized school. The quality and quantity of outdoor space available for school and public use is of interest to the school community.

The school will be relocated during construction of the new school. The duration of the construction period and anticipated completion date are important factors in the project.

The Smith Memorial Park Community Association executive committee voted to support matter-of-right development of the site in order to modernize or replace the school. The school is the only public facility in Smith Memorial Park, and residents are interested in enhancing the school in their neighborhood and increasing access for recreation, community meetings, and adult education.

The Smith Memorial Park Community supports and encourages high-quality design and construction of both the school and the residential portion of the development. Adequate parking to accommodate both new apartment residents and school activities, and improved traffic patterns associated with student pick-up and drop-off and for the newly created residential development are of interest to the Smith Memorial Park Community.

Availability of Financing

The developer is responsible for obtaining financing for the entire development, including the school and residential portions of the project. Due to the unique nature of this project and challenges that developers may face in financing the school portion, some preliminary financing alternatives have been explored.

The Housing Finance Agency has undertaken a preliminary review of this project and determined that "City" Housing Finance Agency (HFA) has the authority to issue tax-exempt bonds for this development, including ancillary educational, recreational, community, and civic facilities. Tax-exempt bonds will make available lower-cost financing for this project. The processing time for a bond issuance, provided all major business issues are resolved, is approximately three to six months.

Developers who wish to obtain more information on bond financing should contact:

Mr. Jones, Director
State's Housing Finance Agency
1275 Any Street

City, State, Zip
Phone (000) 000-0000
Fax (000) 000-0000

Payment in Lieu of Taxes (PILOT)

The property taxes on the private development of the site have been dedicated to re-paying debt associated with the construction of the school. This revenue, in combination with the value of the land lease or purchase price, will be used to finance improvements at the school.

SUBMISSION REQUIREMENTS

Proposal Cover Letter

The respondent must provide the following on letterhead of the offeror, signed by a legally authorized representative:

- A general description of the development as proposed by offeror
- A clear identification of the offeror, form of organization, and its principals
- A contact person, address, phone number, and fax number

Evidence of Developer's Financial Capacity to Perform

The respondent shall submit information in such form and content as to permit the CPS to assess the capability and resources of the respondent to implement the proposed project. At the minimum, information should include:

- The nature and share of each participant's investment and financial interest in the project
- A statement describing the intended sources of financing for the project (equity and debt)
- Anticipated lending source name, contact, address, and phone number (subject to change)
- Current audited or CPA-prepared financial statements to include any outstanding liens or tax liabilities imposed by or owed to State respectively

Experience and Qualifications of the Developer

The respondent shall submit information in such form and content as to permit the CPS to assess the capability and resources of the respondent to implement the proposed project. At the minimum, information should include:

- A resume of prior experience of the respondent, specifically including projects similar in size and scope to that as proposed
- Illustrative material and addresses of said projects
- Names, addresses, and telephone numbers of references familiar with previous projects

Proposed Project Architect

The respondent shall submit information in such form and content as to permit the CPS to assess the capability and resources of the respondent to implement the proposed project. At the minimum, information should include:

- A resume of prior experience of the respondent, specifically including projects similar in size and scope to that proposed
- Illustrative maps and addresses of said projects
- Names, addresses, and telephone numbers of references familiar with previous projects

For previous school project experience, include building name and address, date completed, local Board of Education contact, scope of project, description of design concept or features, construction cost, and percentage of change orders.

Description of Proposed Development for School and Nonschool Facilities

Developers are encouraged to be as creative as possible. The CPS is willing to consider a new school or a complete modernization of and addition to the existing school as a separate structure, or as part of a combined-occupancy structure. The school portion must retain a clear identity, access to daylight and views, and inviting outdoor play areas.

Offerors should provide a written description of the proposed management administrative structure of the development project for both school and residential development.

- *Residential:* A written statement describing the type of residential development and its proposed physical composition, including proposed square footage, number of units and unit mix, area per unit, and description of amenities. A chart showing the floor area, building coverage, building height, FAR, and number of parking spaces must be included.
- *School:* A detailed written description of the school improvements adhering to the educational specifications must be included with your proposal. A chart showing the floor area, building coverage, building height, FAR, number of school dedicated parking spaces, and amount of exterior space dedicated to school must be included.

Required Architectural Submittals

Submit conceptual architectural drawings of the proposed development, which adequately present the quality and character of the proposed development. At a minimum, this should include:

1. A site plan (1" = 20'-0" minimum scale) identifying the school and nonschool buildings and use of outdoor spaces

2. Bubble diagrams (preliminary space plans) for each floor level showing the following areas at a *minimum:*
    - Early childhood area
    - Classrooms
    - Administration
    - Media
    - Multipurpose area
    - Building services
3. Principal elevations at California Street and 29th Street
4. Building section through school, showing relationship to site
5. Site sections along two axes
6. A sketch, rendering, axonometric drawing, and/or model of the proposed development showing massing

Development Schedule

The CPS wishes to operate in the new or modernized facility beginning no later than December 19XX. The CPS is receptive to occupancy earlier than December 19XX subject to the mutual agreement of the parties. Factors to be considered for early occupancy include the school calendar, temporary school space arrangements, and equipment and book delivery.

The CPS will work with the Department of Consumer and Regulatory Affairs to obtain expedited reviews, approvals, and inspections in an effort to maintain the approved project schedule. It is our intention that the developer shall not be eligible to receive a certificate of occupancy for the residential portion of the development until such time as beneficial occupancy of the schools for the CPS has been achieved. This shall be a condition of the developer agreement.

The respondent shall provide a detailed development schedule for completion of school and residential portions of the development.

Summary of Development Costs and Benefits to the CPS

The developer should provide design and construction cost estimates for both the school and residential development per the attached forms. The Financial Proposal Summary of Benefits to the CPS should be completed in its entirety.

PROPOSAL EVALUATION CRITERIA

Evaluation Factors

The following criteria will be used as the general basis for review of the proposals and selection of a developer. Respondents should be certain that the response to this request for proposal (RFP) is complete and contains all required information. Incomplete proposals may be considered nonresponsive and may or may not be reviewed at the CPS' discretion.

Development Program and Project Concept

The CPS will review the proposed development concept and program for consistency with the general guidelines and goals provided in this RFP, the goals and provisions of the R-5-D zone, and the general objectives and policies of the Comprehensive Plan for the State. Special attention will be paid to the likelihood that the project concept and program will accommodate the needs of the school, as described in the Educational Specifications. The CPS will also review the proposed organization and management plan for the development.

Developer Experience and Capability to Perform

The developer's financial resources and the developer's ability to obtain the necessary financing for the project are essential elements of the project. Proposals that include commitments and/or letters of interest from lenders will be given extra consideration.

The respondent's collective capability and experience in the development and construction of high-quality projects of a similar scale, with established budgets and schedules, are critical elements of the RFP response. The experience and creativity of the architect or architects in school and residential design will be considered. Previous development or architectural experience in the City, while not required, is considered desirable.

Development Schedule

Schedules that assure timely delivery of the school are mandatory. Well-conceived schedules with appropriate tasks and milestones for both the CPS and the developer should be submitted.

Financial Proposal/Benefits to CPS

The financial proposal and benefits to CPS will be evaluated and compared.

DEVELOPER SELECTION

Interviews of Top-Ranked Proposals

Once all proposals are evaluated, a review panel established by the CPS will conduct interviews with the three top-ranked proposals. Interviews will be scheduled individually at the CPS Education Building, 999 Any Street, 10th Floor, Conference Room. Subsequent to interviews, the review panel will select the winning proposal and one alternate. The winning proposal will be presented to the chief executive officer of the State Public Schools, the Emergency Transitional Education Board of Trustees, and the Financial Responsibility and Management Assistance Authority for approval.

CPS's Right to Negotiate

The CPS reserves the right to negotiate with any and all offerors on a nonexclusive basis throughout the bid process up to the time at which a developer has been selected and a letter of intent has been executed with the winning developer. Thereafter, the CPS shall enter into exclusive negotiations with the developer to negotiate and execute a developer agreement acceptable to all parties.

Contract Execution/Negotiation

Upon selection, the successful developer and the CPS will negotiate in good faith and execute and deliver a development agreement, land lease, and any other such documents and agreements as may be determined necessary by the parties. Failure to execute said agreements within the time period allowed shall, at the reasonable discretion of the CPS, be grounds for termination of developer's exclusive right to negotiate without liability or expense to the CPS.

Performance Bond

A performance bond will be required and incorporated by reference into the developer agreement.

STATEMENT OF LIMITATIONS AND GENERAL CONDITIONS

No Obligation to Proceed

The RFP is an invitation to solicit development proposals for the school site. The CPS may or may not proceed with the project discussed herein at its sole and absolute discretion.

Property of Material Submitted

The CPS reserves the right to retain all materials, documents, data, communications, and information submitted or prepared in response to this RFP.

Accuracy of Information Disclaimer

Information that has been presented in any medium as part of this RFP and many supplemental materials, which may in the future be provided, is for the convenience of the respondents only. It is not warranted by CPS, and respondents shall verify and rely only on their own surveys, observations, investigations, studies, descriptions, and conclusions in connection with the decision to submit a response to the RFP and in the preparation and submittal of any such response.

Site Conditions Disclaimer

The CPS makes no representations regarding the existing buildings, soil, or other surface or subsurface conditions, including any environmental conditions or utilities that may be located on the site. A Phase I Environmental Survey was completed and is available for inspection. The respondent shall make its own conclusions concerning such conditions that may affect the methods or costs of construction.

Compensation for Predevelopment Fees of the City School Fund

The City School Fund has provided the CPS with private-sector expertise in finance, real estate, architecture, and construction management. The City School Fund has also interfaced with the local community and district agencies to ensure an efficient, expeditious process for the developer. Once the developer is selected, and at the time of execution of the developer agreement, the developer shall be required to reimburse the City School Fund, on behalf of the CPS, the sum of $200,000. Such compensation shall be based on actual invoices for any services performed by the City School Fund.

Address for Submission and Deadline

All responses to this RFP shall be delivered to the following address no later than 3:00 P.M. on January 30, 19XX.

State Public Schools
School Procurement Branch
Room 800
999 Any Street
City, State, Zip

Any response to this RFP received after 3:00 P.M. on January 30, 19XX, may or may not be considered at the CPS's sole and absolute discretion.

Prebid Conference

A prebid conference will be held on December 10, 19XX, to discuss the project in more detail. Any person interested in the project may attend. The conference will be held at 10:00 A.M. at 999 Any Street, City, State, Zip.

Requests for Information and School Site Inspections

All interested parties and their consultants are invited to inspect the site. To set an appointment or for further information, please contact:

Mr. Principal
The Education Company
1401 Any Street, N.W., Suite 210
City, State, Zip

SUPPLEMENTAL MATERIALS

Hard copy available on the Internet at The Education Company (www.edu-infra.com) includes:

- Request for proposal
- The educational specifications
- The Scope of Services for School Design and Construction
- CPS Interim School Construction Standards
- Phase I Environmental Survey
- Market study
- Feasibility study

All supplemental materials are available upon request in hard copy from The Education Company. A nominal reproduction charge of $50 will be assessed by The Education Company for hard copy supplemental materials.

Glossary

Acre   Measure of land area equal to approximately 43,560 square feet (4,840 square yards).

Basis Point   Yields on municipal securities are usually quoted in increments of basis points. One basis point is equal to 1/100 of 1 percent.

Bond   An interest-bearing promise to pay a specified sum of money—the principal amount—due on a specific date.

Bundling Projects   There are instances in which, in order to implement a group of projects, some of which are not financially feasible, a public partner may want to package the projects that are weaker financially with those projects that are financially feasible.

Capital Markets   Markets for trading of debt and equity securities.

Cash-on-Cash Return   The rate of return on an equity investment measured by the cash returned to the investor, exclusive of income tax savings.

Cash Flow   Cash flow is cash receipts minus cash disbursements from a given operation or asset for a given period of time.

Catalytic Projects   In order to jump-start the redevelopment of a specific area, government entities will often identify a project that they believe, if successful, will cause the private development community to proceed with commercial projects they would not have without the implementation of the initial catalytic project.

Certificates of Participation (COPs)   A method of long-term public financing of public facilities through a lease. Capital is raised from investors by the sale of certificates of participation in the lease of the building to the public partner. The certificates are secured by the public partner's lease rental payments. When the certificates of participation are paid off, title to the public facility is transferred to the public partner.

Credit Enhancement   Credit enhancements are financial arrangements intended to reduce the risks associated with nonrecourse project financing. They can improve credit ratings, reduce interest costs, and improve access to the capital markets.

Debt Service   The payments required for interest on and repayment of principal amount of debt.

Due Diligence   The investigation undertaken to make sure that a proposed project is financially and economically sound so that the principal and interest will be paid on time.

Enhanced-Use Lease (EUL)   An EUL is an asset management program in the Department of Veterans Affairs (VA) that can include a variety of different leasing arrangements (e.g., lease/develop/operate, build/develop/operate). EULs enable the VA to long-term lease VA-controlled property to a private partner or other public entities for non-VA uses in return for receiving fair consideration that enhances the VA's mission or programs.

Equity   The difference between fair market value of the property and the amount still owed on its mortgage. Equity is also known as the cash investment often required to obtain conventional financing. The equity portion of project financing typically ranges from 10 to 40 percent of the total development budget for a project.

Exclusive Right to Negotiate (ERN)   Once a developer has been selected through one of the alternative developer solicitation methods, the public and private partners may enter into an exclusive negotiation agreement. This agreement defines a period of time during which the public partner will negotiate exclusively with the developer for the purpose of concluding a binding agreement for the lease and development of a certain property.

Fee Simple   A fee simple is an absolute and unqualified estate providing the owner with all incidence of ownership, including the unconditional power of disposition.

General Obligation Bonds   A bond secured by the pledge of the issuer's full faith, credit, and taxing power.

Gross Square Feet (GSF)   The total square footage of a building, including the walls.

Ground Lease   A lease for the use and occupancy of land only, usually for a long period of time, ranging from 30 to 99 years. It is also called a land lease.

Highest and Best Use   The most advantageous and profitable land and building use to which the property is adaptable, considering the present and future condition of the local development market and uses authorized by applicable zoning and planning.

Interest Rate   The percentage rate at which the bond bears interest. Interest is generally payable semiannually.

Internal Rate of Return (IRR)   The rate of interest that discounts the total expected cash flows from an investment to a present value that is exactly equal to the amount of the original equity investment.

Investment Risk   Probability that an investment's actual yield will be less than its expected yield.

Issuer   A state, political subdivision, agency, or authority that borrows money through the sale of bonds or notes.

Lease   A lease is a written agreement between the property owner and a tenant that stipulates the conditions under which the tenant may possess the real estate for a specified period of time and amount of rent.

Lease Revenue Bonds   A bond secured by a lease agreement and rental payments from a public agency (lessee) to another (lessor). Lease payments are typically made from revenue sources including general fund, enterprise fund, or user fees. The lessor and issuer of the bonds may be a city, county, nonprofit corporation, redevelopment agency, joint powers authority, parking authority, etc. The title reverts to lessee after bonds are retired.

Master Developer   A single developer of a large site usually composed of many parcels, which is responsible over an extended period of time for bringing about the comprehensive, integrated development of the site.

Monetize Government-Owned Assets   This is simply another term for converting an underutilized government-owned real estate asset into a source of nontax income.

Municipal Bond   A bond issued by a state or local government entity.

Noncapital Investment   In lieu of capital investment, the public partner can provide investments, which do not require issuing debt or cash outlays. Examples of noncapital investments include providing land at no cost, issuing additional development rights, and reducing the number of parking stalls required for the project.

Nonrecourse Financing   In nonrecourse financing, the sponsor has no direct legal obligation to repay the debt used to finance the project. Instead, the lender relies on the cash flow generated by the project to cover the debt service payments, since they have no recourse to the assets of the project sponsor.

Nontax Income   The two ways that public partners can benefit from the implementation of a public/private development project are nontax income and tax revenue. Forms of nontax income include land lease payments, participation rent payments, holding rent payments, etc. Public partners can also realize substantial tax revenue from the property tax, sales tax, and other applicable taxes on the leasehold improvements.

Predevelopment Activities   Predevelopment activities are the hundreds, sometimes thousands, of tasks that must be performed in order to begin construction of a project.

Pro Forma (Cash Flow Analysis)   Financial projections including an income statement for a real estate project that shows capital costs, operating income and expenses, and return on investment over a single year or for five or ten years or longer.

Ramp-Up Years   These are the early years of a project prior to stabilized income is achieved. During the first five years, the cash flow is often not sufficient to generate a net cash flow, or worse.

Glossary

Referendum The fight of the electorate to vote on a legislative action of the community, including the adoption or amendment of a redevelopment plan.

Rentable Area The space in a building that is available to lease, exclusive of space that is not leased, such as elevator shafts and so forth.

Return on Cost (ROC) An important calculation used by developers to assess the financial feasibility of a project. The calculation is the projected net operating income (NOI) divided by the total development budget for the project.

Sales Tax A tax imposed on every retailer for the privilege of selling tangible personal property at retail. The rate of the tax is based on a percentage of the gross retail sales.

Sensitivity Analysis A method of financial analysis that measures the impact on the project's return to changes in the underlying assumptions.

Subordinate To make subject or junior to.

Tax Increment Financing Bonds that are secured and repaid by increased property tax revenues, associated with an increase in assessed valuation over the frozen base. Also known as tax allocation bonds (TABs) in California.

Tax-Exempt Bonds Municipal bonds, the interest of which is exempt from federal income, state income, or state and local personal property taxes.

Tax Increment Property tax revenues allocated to the redevelopment agency, which are generated by the increases in assessed value in the project area after the establishment of the redevelopment project area.

Total Development Budget A total development budget includes all of the hard and soft costs required to finance, design, develop, and construct a building. Hard costs include the costs associated with actually constructing the project, site development, and land costs. Soft costs include costs such as consulting fees, investment-banking fees, interest during construction, etc.

Transient Occupancy Tax (Hotel Tax) A form of excise tax designed to raise revenue that is imposed on temporary occupants of property rather than on actual property owners.

Underwriter A dealer firm that purchases municipal bonds from the issuer and then resells them to the public. The underwriter assumes the risk of ownership until bonds are sold.

Usable Area The area of a building that the tenant actually occupies.

Index